IRVING R. MELBO

Dean of the School of Education (1953-1973).

The Melbo Years

A History of the School of Education of the University of Southern California 1953-1973

BY MARY C. LANE, Ed.D.

UNIVERSITY OF SOUTHERN CALIFORNIA PRESS

Los Angeles ☙ *California*

Library of Congress Number 74-12808
ISBN 0-88474-017-X

ACKNOWLEDGEMENTS

Acknowledgement is made to Dr. Irving R. Melbo, who, in the spring of 1973, commissioned the author to prepare a history of the School of Education for the period 1953 through 1973, the years in which Dr. Melbo served as Dean of the School of Education. Dean Melbo generously placed at the disposition of the author the files of the Office of the Dean, School of Education, and through his guidance, inspiration, and extensive comments on the manuscript greatly assisted in its composition.

Particular acknowledgement is made to the Board of Directors of EDUCARE, the support group of the School of Education, University of Southern California. Through EDUCARE's financial support the printing of the manuscript was made possible. To Dr. Verna B. Dauterive, president of EDUCARE 1974-1975, grateful acknowledgement is made for her loyal support and encouragement of the project.

The final preparation of the manuscript for printing and the many details incident to its publication were supervised by Mr. Clarence N. Anderson, University Editor, University of Southern California. The assistance of the University Editor and of Miss Patta Steele, Editorial Intern to the University Editor, are gratefully acknowledged. Recognition also is made to Art Smith, graphics designer, Los Angeles, and to George Francuch, artist, for their contributions.

iii

The author wishes to accept, of course, responsibility for errors or misinterpretations of historical material, should such be found.

MARY C. LANE, Ed. D.

School of Education
University of Southern California
June 1974

iv

TABLE OF CONTENTS

V

vi

vii

viii

ix

TOMMY TROJAN

The life-size statue of a Trojan warrior, which stands on the USC campus, symbolizes the University's strength, determination, and courage.

Overview: 1953

A New Dean Is Named

He retired at his own request—popular Dean of Education, Osman R. Hull. Fred Fagg accepts with regret, thanks him for most outstanding service and reassigns him as professor of school administration until his retirement.

Thus, in January 1953, did the University of Southern California's *Alumni Review* announce the impending loss of Osman R. Hull as dean of the School of Education.[1] The brief announcement also signaled the end of one era and the beginning of another in the history of the School of Education.

As early as November 1952, Hull had requested, for reasons of health, that he be relieved of his responsibilities as dean and return to full-time teaching as of September 1953. In accepting the resignation, the University's President, Fred D. Fagg, Jr., requested the School of Education's Central Committee, in conference with C. C. Trillingham, superintendent, Los Angeles County Schools,

---

1. *Alumni Review,* 34(4), p. 1.

to confer with him on the appointment of Hull's successor. The committee's recommendation, accepted and confirmed by the University administration, was to name as dean, effective with the academic year 1953–54, Irving Robert Melbo, professor of educational administration in the School of Education.

The choice was not unexpected. Since his appointment to the faculty in 1939, Melbo had played a prominent role in activities of the School and the University. Born in Gully, Minnesota, June 20, 1908, the son of Hans H. and Hilda J. (née Bergdahl) Melbo, he had come to the School of Education with an unusually broad experience in education at all levels and a distinguished academic background.

Even before his graduation from New Mexico Western College in 1930, he had served as teacher and principal in the Minnesota public schools. At college he worked as research assistant to the president, and remained three years after graduation as instructor in social science and supervisor of student teachers, earning meanwhile in 1932, his Master of Arts degree.

Leaving New Mexico in 1933, Melbo entered the University of California at Berkeley, where in 1934, he earned his Doctor of Education degree, and then entered the California system of public education as staff member of the Division of Textbooks and Publications of the State Department of Education. In 1935, he became director of the department of research and curriculum, Oakland Public Schools. In 1936, he was one of two persons in the nation to be appointed to a postdoctoral fellowship in the Advanced School of Education at Teachers College, Columbia University. In 1938, he was appointed deputy superintendent and director of curriculum, Alameda County Schools, Oakland, California. It was from there that, in 1939, he was invited to join the faculty of the University of Southern California's School of Education.

From the start Melbo was recognized by his colleagues as a man of progressive, creative ideas as well as administrative acumen. Shortly after his arrival, Hull, then a professor of educational administration, selected Melbo as teammate for the school sur-

2

veys Hull had been conducting for a number of years in southern California. Following Hull's appointment as dean in 1946, responsibility for the surveys devolved on Melbo. By 1953, he had directed 22 such surveys and in other ways had proved himself a leader among the faculty.

In no sense a rebel, Melbo had on numerous occasions evinced his support of increased faculty representation in the decision-making process within the School of Education. In intra-University relations he showed himself a stalwart champion of the autonomy of the School of Education. Typical of the precision with which he voiced his convictions was an incident related in later years by Hull. A question had arisen whether University College or the School of Education was to control education classes offered on campus in the late afternoon and evening. Melbo was convinced, and openly stated, that the curriculum of a professional school could not be directed by the clock. At a hearing before President Fagg, it was Melbo who voiced the decisive argument. According to Hull:[2]

> Melbo came through with a masterpiece. He said, "Gentlemen, when it comes to professional training which is the responsibility of the professional schools, University College is a college without a curriculum, it grants no degrees, it grants no certificates, it has no permanent faculty. I think it's quite obvious where responsibility should lie."

"That's about all he said," continued Hull, "but they had no answer to that."

During the years of World War II, Melbo served as a lieutenant in the United States Naval Reserve. He was attached to the Training Division of the Bureau of Naval Personnel of the Department of the Navy. From that headquarters, he was assigned to work in numerous naval establishments, both in the American-Atlantic and European-Mediterranean Theaters of Operation.

Melbo's broad interests, which extended into the fields of history, social science, and natural history, were evidenced by his

---

2. Levitt (1970), p. 413.

publications. Among his works, a number published as textbooks, were *Social Psychology of Education* (1937), *Our America* (1937 and 1948), *Our Country's National Parks,* a two-volume work (1941, 1950, 1961, 1964, 1973), and *The World about Us* (1949). *Our America* was widely used in the public schools of the United States, and was translated into German for use in the schools within the American Zone of Germany in the postwar period. The two-volume set on the national parks was the outgrowth of a hobby interest. Acknowledged standard works on this subject, they were widely reviewed and quoted frequently.[3]

Melbo's literary interests also extended to editorial experience. In his student days he was editor-in-chief of New Mexico Western's *The Mustang,* the student newspaper. In later years he served as editor for a number of professional yearbooks, and was on the editorial board of several professional magazines.

Small wonder that Melbo's rising star was recognized, first by appointment to the School's Administrative Committee in 1945, next by election in 1947 and reelection in 1949, to the University's Academic Senate, and finally by appointment in 1953, as dean.

Facilities

Over the years, as veteran professors acquired a national reputation and younger men like Melbo, Nelson, and Cannon joined the faculty, the School of Education's stature in the professional world of education greatly increased. Facilities, however, remained far from prepossessing. Administrative offices and a few classrooms were located in the south wing of the third floor of the George Finley Bovard Administration Building, to which they had

---

3. In 1964, Melbo was awarded by the Freedom Foundations at Valley Forge the Freedom Leadership Award, in part for "academic brilliance in the training of teachers and school administrators," in part for his "consistent leadership in building understanding of the American Credo; for his writings about our great leaders and patriots emphasizing their character traits and for his inspiring books about our National Parks and historic shrines."

4

been moved in 1921 from Old College.[4] In honor of Thomas Blanchard Stowell, chairman of the Department of Education (1909–18) and first dean of the School of Education (1918–19), the south wing of Bovard Administration Building was named the Thomas Blanchard Stowell Hall of Education, paralleling the north wing, named the James Harmon Hoose Hall of Philosophy.[5]

Education classes were held throughout the campus. Among

---

4. Old College was the name given to one of the earliest structures erected on the campus of the University of Southern California. Its cornerstone, which is still preserved in the foundation wall of Founders Hall, was laid September 20, 1884. Designed as a three-story brick structure, with two wings added in 1905, the building occupied the site where Founders Hall is now situated. Old College was razed in 1948 to make way for Founders Hall, the cornerstone of which was laid October 5, 1949. For photographs of Old College in 1885, 1908, and 1940, see Servin and Wilson (1969), following page 28. George Finley Bovard, president of the University of Southern California (1903–1921), was the younger brother of the University's first president, Marion McKinley Bovard (president 1880–1891), and was one of the three first graduates of the University, graduating in 1884.

5. The names of Hoose and Stowell are inextricably interwoven in the early history of the University of Southern California. Lifelong friends and colleagues, their careers were as parallel as the building structures which memorialized their names.

James Harmon Hoose was born January 24, 1835, in Cobleskill, New York. He took his A.B. (1861) and A.M. (1863) at Genesee College (later renamed Syracuse University) and his Ph.D. (1873) at Syracuse, He was organizer and first head (1867–1891) of Cortland State Normal School, New York. In 1891, he left New York State for California, where he settled in Pasadena as a fruit farmer. In 1896, he became professor of pedagogy and philosophy at the University of Southern California and remained until 1911, as a distinguished professor of philosophy and chairman of the Graduate Council of the University. In 1913, the University of Southern California conferred upon him the degree of Doctor of Laws. He died August 31, 1915, at age 80.

Thomas Blanchard Stowell was born in upstate New York in 1846. He took his A.B. (1865) and A.M. (1868) at Genesee College and his Ph.D. (1881) at Syracuse University. From 1865 to 1870 he was principal of various secondary schools: the Academy at Addison, New York (1865–66), Union School at Morrisville, New York (1866–67), and Morris High School, Leavenworth, Kansas (1868–69), as well as professor of mathematics at Genesee Wesleyan Seminary (1867–68). In 1869, he began 20 years as head of the Department of Natural Science at Cortland State Normal School, Cortland, New York, where Hoose was president. In 1889, he became head of the State Normal and Training School at Potsdam, New York, retiring in 1909. In that year, St. Lawrence University conferred upon him

5

the buildings used in 1953 were Founders Hall, Bridge Hall, and Doheny Library on University Avenue; the Annex on 35th Place Walk, N Building on 36th Street, and Harris Plaza on 37th Place. Other facilities included the Education Library, housed in rooms on the north side of Doheny Library; a demonstration school at the 32nd Street Elementary School; and, in cooperation with the University's Psychology Department, a Psychological Service Center, with clinical training and reading at 915 West 37th Place, and speech and hearing facilities at 930 West 37th Street.

The adverse effect of the inadequate facilities on the professional program of the School was recognized. In 1956, the report of an Accreditation Committee stated:[6]

While the classrooms are not especially crowded, the members of the school and their classes are quite widely scattered. Office and classroom space are not planned to promote frequent staff and student contacts. There is little opportunity for privacy for counseling of students. Noise in the offices is distracting. This tends to discourage proper counseling and encourages the faculty to stay at home except for their classes.

Elaborating on this theme in 1973, Raymond C. Perry, professor of education and member of the faculty since 1945, remarked:[7]

Private offices for faculty were unknown in those days. Two

---

the degree of Doctor of Laws. In the same year, he began his duties as head of the Department of Education of the University of Southern California. Under his guidance, the department rose to true graduate status and in 1918, was recognized as a separate School of Education. In 1911, Stowell succeeded Hoose as chairman of the Graduate Council of the University, and in 1912 was named first dean of the University's Summer Session. A slowly advancing disease of which he was conscious forced him to submit his retirement in 1919. On August 3, 1919, he and his beloved wife, Mary Blakeslee Stowell, celebrated their golden wedding anniversary; and on June 21, 1921, from a room apart he was present at the dedication of the Thomas Blanchard Stowell Hall of Education. He died in 1927. In a personal tribute to him in 1921, Dean Ezra A. Healy of the Maclay College of Theology said: "As a teacher of teachers it has been his privilege to multiply a thousand fold the influence of one good man." (*Alumni Magazine*, 3 (December 1921), p. 10). In his honor the Stowell Research Library was established as a special collection of the Education Library.

6. *Agenda*, May 7, 1956.
7. Personal interview, February 1973.

or more regular faculty occupied partitioned spaces (partitions were about six feet high) and expected other part-time faculty members to use their desks as required. Faculty members were advised to leave only items in or on their desks that they would be willing to lose. When new faculty were interviewed, they were advised that they should expect to maintain regular offices in their own homes and use the campus space only for required office hours. One of Dean Melbo's first announced policies was to work toward private office space for each faculty member. Few in 1953 thought he had any possibility of achieving his goal.

Administration

The administration of the School of Education in 1953 was under the general direction at the University level of Educational Vice-President, Albert S. Raubenheimer.[8] Within the School proper, in addition to Dean Melbo, were Dean Emeritus Lester Burton Rogers[9] and Assistant Dean Elmer E. Wagner, who was also

8. Raubenheimer was born in South Africa, where he received his under-graduate training at the University of the Cape of Good Hope and his M.A. at the University of Cape Town. In America, he studied at Columbia University and in 1923, received his Ph.D. in Educational Psychology at Stanford University under the guidance of Lewis M. Terman. In that year he was appointed to the faculty of the USC School of Education. For the next 37 years he served the University as professor; dean of the College of Letters, Arts, and Sciences; director of the Educational Program; and from 1946 to 1960 as Vice-President, Academic Affairs. In 1949, he served as chairman of the Governor's Committee on Mental Health, and later as chairman of the Governor's Committee on Penal Institutions. A man of steadfast devotion to duty, sterling integrity, and firm but considerate adminis-tration, he was twice a member of an interim administrative committee when the University was without a president. In 1960, the University conferred upon him the honorary degree of Doctor of Science and named him Professor Emeritus of the School of Education.

9. Lester Burton Rogers (1875–1959) was Dean of the School of Education from 1919 to 1945. A graduate of Moore's Hill College in Indiana, he earned his M.A. degree at Columbia University in 1909 and his Ph.D. degree at Teachers College, Columbia University in 1915. He came to the University of Southern California in 1919 on leave of absence from the faculty of Lawrence College, Appleton, Wisconsin, and remained to serve as dean of the School of Education

7

associate professor of education in guidance and counseling. Administrative assistants were Syra Gold, credential secretary; Mabel A. Schulte, head, Education Library; and Edith Weir, director, Bureau of Teacher Placement.

Faculty

In 1953, the faculty numbered 68, of whom 52 were members of the faculty of the School of Education only, and 16 held dual appointments with their respective disciplines.

The tenured faculty of the School of Education was one of long standing. The one professor emeritus was Merritt Moore Thompson, who had been appointed in 1921 and retired in 1952.[10] Full professors numbered 10. They were, with the date of

for a quarter of a century. Forceful and authoritarian, Rogers was responsible for the professional growth of the School of Education and its recognition by the University as an autonomous School of the University on the same status as the School of Law and the School of Medicine. It was Rogers, also, who led the School through the difficult years of World War II, when both faculty and student body were greatly depleted. Of him one who served under him for many years and who did not always agree with his decisions, nevertheless said in retrospect: "Dean Rogers was a man in a million. He was canny, very canny. . . . He knew what motivated people. He knew how to build up an organization and keep himself in the background. . . . He was tough in a good sense; he wasn't knocked over. . . . He didn't mind if people didn't like him particularly if he got a good job done. That's what he was after. . . . Rogers had a great vision of teaching as a service to the community and . . . lived by that ideal and passed it on to our young people." (From personal interview with Frederick J. Weersing, quoted by Levitt 1970, pp. 436–437.)

10. Distinguished scholar and beloved teacher, Thompson was born September 17, 1884, in Hurffville, New Jersey. In later years he enjoyed reminding USC alumni that his birth had occurred just three days before the cornerstone of Old College was laid (Thompson 1958, pp. 2–3). A 1905 graduate of the New Jersey State Normal School at Trenton, he had earned his A.B. at the University of Denver in 1909. From 1911 to 1914, and from 1919 to 1921, he was director of the Methodist Episcopal Mission Schools in Peru, South America. Coming to the University of Southern California in the Department of Spanish in 1921, he had been drawn by Rogers into the field of education and from 1921 to 1928 he served as principal of the University High School. The University High School was discontinued in September, 1928, when the Los Angeles Board of Education gave USC students the right to practice teach in the public schools. Thompson then became director of student training, and in 1936 the head of the history and

8

appointment: Osman R. Hull (1924), Claude C. Crawford (1926), D. Welty Lefever (1926), Frederick J. Weersing (1927), Fay Greene Adams (Fay Adams Teigs) (1929), Louis P. Thorpe (1937), Theodore Hsi-En Chen (1938), Irving R. Melbo (1939), D. Lloyd Nelson (1947), and Wendell E. Cannon (1948). Associate professors numbered eight: Elmer E. Wagner (1941), Raymond C. Perry (1945), Edward H. LaFranchi (1946), C. Edward Meyers (1947), James D. Finn (1949), Myron S. Olson (1950), Robert L. Brackenbury (1952), and Emery Stoops (1953); and two assistant professors: Earl F. Carnes (1949) and Robert A. Naslund (1950). Among the 22 lecturers were several whose names would be linked in various capacities with the School of Education in coming years: Charles C. Carpenter, Lionel De Silva, Robert O. Hall, Schuyler C. Joyner, and William B. Michael.

The 16 members holding dual appointments included: Professor Albert C. Fries and associate professor J. Frances Henderson in education and office administration; assistant professors Michael F. Andrews and Mildred Henard (Taylor) in education and fine arts; Frances L. Spain, professor of library science; professors Charles C. Hirt, Raymond Kendall, and Max T. Krone, associate professor Ralph E. Rush, and assistant professor Janice Bryan Hawkinson in music and education; and in physical education and health, professors Elwood C. Davis, John W. Fredericks, William R. La Porte, and associate professors John M. Cooper, Aileene J. Lockhart, and Lenore C. Smith.

Standing Committees

For some years the faculty of the School of Education had had a strong voice in the governance of the School through a system of Standing Committees. This system, which was to play a role of continuing importance in the history of the School, had been

philosophy department, a position he held with great success until his retirement in 1952. He died November 27, 1970. Prior to his death, he had completed a draft of a chronicle of the School of Education up to 1959, the typewritten copy of which is on file in the Office of the Dean of the School of Education.

inaugurated in 1945, amid circumstances surrounding the retirement of Dean Rogers. Prior to 1945, as Thompson observed, "There had been no order or systematization of committees or committee work. Each one had been appointed and continued as long as seemed required."[11] During the late 1930s and early 1940s, however, the faculty, particularly some of its younger members, had grown restive with the administration and with their lack of representation in decisions affecting their profession and welfare, especially salaries. Rogers' retirement presented the opportunity they had long sought for a more active voice in governance. Said Levitt:[12]

> Dean Rogers' precipitant retirement, the University's disinclination to rush into appointment of a new dean, the climate of democracy abroad in the University, and the faculty's apparent desire to pre-empt administrative prerogatives, all combined to enable the faculty of the School of Education to seize the day. Their strategy—if strategy it was—was to establish standing committees which would assume many of the decision-making processes that had previously resided with the dean and, subject to the approval of the entire faculty, thereby to administer the School of Education.

An important feature of the standing committee system was the formation of an Administrative Committee to which all committees reported. This powerful committee, composed of Lefever, Melbo, and Hull, with Hull as chairman, administered the School of Education for the academic year 1945–46. In 1946, at the insistence of both Hull and Melbo and as circumstances made imperative, the University at last appointed a new dean. The choice fell upon Hull. With his appointment, the Administrative Committee was disbanded. Its influence, however, was carried forward in the newly formed Committee on Curriculum, Schedule and Personnel or, as it was more familiarly known, the Central Committee. (It had been the Central Committee, it will be recalled, that in 1952,

11. Thompson, n.d., p. 66.
12. Levitt (1970), p. 437.

had been requested by President Fagg to consult with him on the appointment of a successor to Hull.)

Standing committees as of 1953 were: Basic Sequence; Comprehensive Examinations; Curriculum, Schedule and Personnel; Curriculum Laboratory; Doctoral Program; Master's Degree; Research and Publication; and Student Organizations.

Departments

Departmentalization came slowly to the School of Education, partly because of University opposition and partly because of Rogers' strong antipathy for specialization among the faculty. Said one long-time member:[13]

> De-departmentalization had been a major policy of Dean Rogers. He had argued that any professor of education should be competent to teach all the courses in the School of Education. Merritt Thompson once noted that he had taught 66 different courses at SC. Whenever Rogers came to feel that a professor had staked out an area for himself, he saw to it that the next semester that professor would get entirely new courses. This "divide and conquer" technique kept Rogers in a more secure position (as far as he was concerned). While this may have made him look like an autocrat, it was only through these dictatorial procedures that Rogers could fight the other divisions of the University.

Nevertheless, categorization increased, as veteran professors drifted toward specialization to meet curricular needs or to satisfy their own proclivities and as new members were added to the faculty because they possessed specialized knowledge and skills. In 1943, largely as a result of faculty pressure, the loose interlocking instructional responsibilities were transformed into "instructional groups," each with its own chairman and a measure of curricular authority. After Rogers' retirement, the Administrative Committee recommended and gained ready faculty approval for the organization of the School into departments. To protect against dynastic ambitions, each chairman served on a rotating basis of two or three years; to preserve faculty participation in the

---

13. Personal interview, February 1973.

11

selection process, chairmen were appointed by the Central Committee and the dean on the nomination of the department. University opposition to departmentalization also weakened in the wake of the growing reputation of the School and its professors:[14]

> Public school specialists were gravitating toward USC because of the names of Melbo, Nelson, and LaFranchi in administration; Lefever and Thorpe in psychology ... Wagner in guidance; Naslund in elementary and Finn in audio-visual, to mention just a few.
>
> The professors were building national reputations in their own right as scholars and innovators and on the strength of their doctoral graduates' and their other students' becoming leaders in public education and professors in colleges of education and, thereby and by word of mouth, spreading the reputation of the School of Education for excellence in the several specializations.... Equal prestige accrued to the Department of Teacher Training as USC's graduating teachers proved their mettle in the classrooms throughout the nation, but especially in southern California, and the name of Dr. Cannon increased in reputation and drawing power.

Departments and chairmen for the academic year 1953–54 were: Administration and Supervision (Nelson), Audio-visual Education (Finn), Business Education (Fries), Elementary Education (Naslund), Fine Arts (no chairman), Guidance (Meyers), History and Philosophy (Brackenbury), Industrial Arts (no chairman), Music Education (Rush), Physical Education and Health (La Porte), Psychology (Meyers), Secondary and Higher Education (Olson), and Teacher Training (Cannon).

The Department of Teacher Training was in charge of preservice preparation of classroom teachers, including student teaching, curriculum and methods work closely related to the student teaching experience, and the undergraduate basic sequence of professional courses prerequisite to student teaching. Other departments offered elective and collateral courses for preservice teachers, certain courses which graduates might take in lieu of

12

---

14. Levitt (1970), pp. 474–475.

portions of the basic sequence, inservice workshops and seminars, and courses leading to the various credentials, degrees, certificates, and diplomas appropriate to the departmental fields. All departments except Teacher Training offered practicum and project seminars leading to the degrees of Master of Science in Education and Master of Education. Most offered sufficient work for a declared major or supplementary field for the degrees of Doctor of Philosophy in Education or Doctor of Education.

Credentials

Since 1911, when the University of Southern California had first been given the right to grant the high school teachers' certificate,[15] the School of Education had made steady progress both in number and types of credentials it was authorized to recommend.[16] Responsibility for keeping informed on State requirements, for assisting students in their applications, and for maintaining credential records was that of the credential secretary, Syra Gold.[17]

---

15. Roy W. Cloud, State Executive Secretary of the California Teachers Association, 1927–1947, provides an important historical comment. "For many years," says Cloud (1952, p. 134), "the University of California and later Stanford University had the exclusive right to confer the high-school certificate upon graduates who had completed certain required courses during their college years. At a meeting of the State Board of Education held at Sacramento on February 10, 1911, the University of Southern California was granted the right to give similar courses to the students of that institution, and upon their successful completion to confer the high-school certificate. This was hailed as a forward step in bringing the University at Los Angeles into line with northern California institutions."

16. By 1953, the credentials the School of Education was authorized to recommend were: Kindergarten-primary; general elementary; general secondary; junior college; special secondary in art, business education, music education, and physical education; librarianship; elementary school supervision; secondary school supervision; special subject supervision; general supervision; elementary school administration; secondary school administration; and general administration. (See Appendix A for statistics.)

17. In 1924, Katie L. Humrichouse, secretary to Dean Rogers, was assigned responsibility also for credentials. She continued to perform this task in addition to her secretarial duties until 1930, when the School of Education established the position of credential secretary. (Miss Humrichouse continued as Dean Rogers' secretary and performed the duties of secretary to the faculty until her death,

13

Degrees

The degree of Bachelor of Science in Education (B.S. in Ed.) was established in 1932, when President von KleinSmid[18] discontinued the Bachelor of Arts with a major in education, and placed all undergraduate education majors within the jurisdiction of the School of Education. In 1953, students were admitted to the School of Education for the B.S. in Ed. degree only after meeting the requirements for admission to the University and completing two full years of acceptable college work.[19] Requirements for award of the degree included prescribed numbers of academic units, maintenance of acceptable scholarship average, and completion of the Professional Aptitude Test (PAT).[20]

The Master of Science in Education (M.S. in Ed.) degree had

August 27, 1951.) The position of credential secretary was held successively by Gertrude Jennings (1930–35), Anna Watt (1935–36), Gwendolyn Miller (1936–38), Marva Harrison (1938–42), Lucile Winter (1942–47), Helen Frahm (1947–52), Syra Gold (1952–55), and Helen Frahm (1955 on). The title of the position was changed to credential technician in 1953, and to credential supervisor in 1965.

18. Rufus Bernhard von KleinSmid (1875–1964), President of the University of Southern California, 1921–1946; Chancellor, 1946–1964.

19. For a number of years after the degree of B.S. in Ed. was established, students were admitted to the School of Education at the beginning of their college work. Years later, partly in response to a move to increase the professional image of the School of Education and partly out of the recognition that commitment to a teaching career was too much to ask of most young people embarking on their college career, admission to the School of Education was restricted solely to upper division and graduate students. The lower division work might be done at the University of Southern California or at other colleges or universities. Among the 60 required units of lower division work were certain general requirements. These requirements, with the number of units specified, were: Art or Music Appreciation (2), English (6), Foreign Languages (12), General Studies (6), Literature (4), Physical Education (6), and Sciences (11). *Bulletin,* 1954–56.

20. In the last two years of the curriculum for the B.S. in Ed., the student specialized in three fields of study: Education, major, and minor. Requirements were 24 units in education courses, of which 12 must be completed in residence; and 24 units for a credential major, 12 of which must be upper division. The student was also required to take the PAT during the first semester of upper division work. A scholarship average of 2.00 (C) was required in all units attempted at the University of Southern California, in all courses in the School of Education, and in all upper division courses in the credential major.

14

been established in 1933, to replace the former Master of Arts in Education offered under the jurisdiction of The Graduate School. Designed to develop qualities and techniques requisite to leadership in professional service, its requirements included specific courses in the area of education and completion of a thesis or project.[21]

The Master of Education (M.Ed.) degree, first announced in 1939, was designed for high school, junior college, and college teachers who desired to combine work in education with advanced training in a subject field, and for educational specialists who desired a high degree of training within a specific area of education. A heavy program assured that the degree was one of substance and that it provided professional study beyond that required for the M.S. in Ed. degree.[22]

The Doctor of Philosophy (Ph.D.) degree was first offered at the University of Southern California in 1924. The first degree, significantly in education, was conferred on D. Welty Lefever in 1927. Lefever, who served for forty years (1926–1966) on the faculty of the School of Education, brought it great distinction both in scholarship and teaching. As Levitt aptly remarks, "If the University had been allowed to choose the scholar who would

21. Prerequisites for the degree of M.S. in Ed. were a bachelor's degree from an accredited college or university and 12 undergraduate semester units in Education, with at least one course in either the undergraduate or graduate program in each of the four fields of history or philosophy of education, educational psychology, educational measurement and evaluation, and organization and administration of public education. Admission to candidacy was by recommendation of the student's advisor on the basis of acceptable scores on the Graduate Survey Examination, a grade point ratio of 1.75 in all previous graduate work attempted, and a satisfactory personal and professional record. A minimum of 28 units was required: 10 in graduate (500) courses in Education; two of practicum; 12 of electives; and four of thesis or project. Not more than eight units earned in other institutions were to be counted toward the total number of 28 required units.

22. Normally, two academic years of full-time graduate study or the equivalent were required for the unit requirement of 52 semester units of graduate study, of which 24 must be done in residence. The candidate was required to meet all the requirements for the M.S. in Ed. degree, including thesis or project, after which he was permitted to proceed to the second half of the program, under one of the program's objectives.

15

earn its first doctorate, it could not have chosen one who would bring it greater credit than would Dr. Lefever."[23] The Doctor of Education (Ed.D.) degree was first offered by the University in 1928, and was conferred for the first time in 1931 upon two recipients: George Henry Bell and Verne Ralph Ross. Although essentially the same amount and quality of graduate work and research were required for the two degrees, the Ed.D. was designed especially for the preparation of highly specialized and competent professionals in education, particularly for various aspects of leadership in its practice. The Ph.D. in Education degree tended to provide more emphasis upon theoretical preparation designed for some types of college or university teaching and for certain kinds of research.[24] Dissertation subjects and research design reflected the difference in emphasis. The Ph.D. in Education was established and remained under the jurisdiction of The Graduate School, whereas the Ed.D. was under the jurisdiction of the School of Education.[25]

Development of Programs

Two programs in the School of Education merit special attention because of their importance and durability. These are the pro-

---

23. Levitt (1970), p. 216.

24. In terms of specific requirements, essential differences as of 1953, were: in number of graduate units required (for the Ph.D. in Education, 60 units of graduate work; for the Ed.D., 76, including at least 52 in education); for the Ph.D., a reading knowledge of German and French. Procedures involved in the programs for the two degrees remained in general the same.

25. As of 1953, the University of Southern California had granted 350 doctoral degrees in the field of education, of which 256 were Ed.D.'s. In line with the national trend, the doctoral program in education at the University had shifted in the postwar era from an emphasis on the better preparation of teachers to one of specialization, particularly in the field of educational administration. Surveys of doctoral graduates of the School of Education, (Calvert, 1947; Walker, 1953; Levitt 1970, pp. 314–315), indicate that the area served by the School of Education of the University of Southern California remained fairly provincial. Three-fourths of the doctoral graduates remained in California and the majority in southern California, specifically Los Angeles County. (See Appendix B for statistics on the doctoral program of the School of Education, 1927 through 1973.)

16

grams which were instituted in the early years of the School and which have continued throughout later years to attract young men and women who have become prominent teachers and administrators, particularly in the State of California.

The creator of the program for the preparation of elementary teachers was Dr. Fay G. Adams, now professor emeritus, School of Education. Year after year this program attracted the finest young women to the University of Southern California. Year after year it produced a superior group of beginning elementary teachers who were at a premium in the placement market. They were much sought after by the personnel directors and superintendents of the metropolitan area school systems.

The basic design of the program was so sound that it continues virtually without change for a quarter of a century, and it still continues with but slight modification. The professional preparation was child-pupil oriented. It provided preparation and experience at two levels, primary and upper grade, so that a student completing the sequence could teach effectively in any classroom within the elementary school. For the most part, the experiential aspects of the program were organized around the 32nd Street School. There Dr. Adams organized the demonstrations, the observations, and the activities into which the students were programmed. In addition, this school was the center for the practice-teaching experience, although the pressure of numbers required that some student teaching be done at the nearby schools. However, it was widely recognized that the excellence of the 32nd Street faculty was such that student teaching at that school was a choice assignment and even a professional privilege.

Over the years, and particularly during the long tenure of an outstanding principal, Mrs. Sophia Lounsbery, with whom Dr. Adams maintained a close and effective working relationship, the reputation of the school enabled it to attract many of the most skilful teachers in the Los Angeles school system. The 32nd Street School was widely known as *the* training school, and an assignment to it as a training teacher was a stepping stone to a subse-

17

quent appointment as an elementary school principal. More than one hundred of the best elementary school principals in Los Angeles were "alumnae" of 32nd Street during the 1940s and 1950s. Still other principals came from the training teacher experience at Sixth Avenue School, Menlo Avenue, Windsor Hills, and Baldwin Hills, all of which were highly important links in the chain of select training schools working with Dr. Adams and the University of Southern California program.

Dr. Adams also developed the concept of having carefully selected personnel from the Los Angeles schools assigned to the University for purposes of supervising the student teachers in the various training schools and to assist the principals and teaching faculty in such schools. The position was officially established by the Board of Education as "Coordinator," and it exists at this time as an established relationship between the School of Education and the cooperating schools and principals. The plan has been mutually beneficial and productive for both the School of Education and the school system. Other teacher training institutions in the area and elsewhere in the country soon began to make similar arrangements. Observed Dean Melbo on several occasions, "The real significance of the plan was that it truly made the school system and the University partners in the teacher training enterprise."

The other program which merits special attention is the preparation of administrators and supervisors for the public school system. This program, which continues to be one of the strongest in the School of Education, had a long background of acknowledged strength and superiority. During the 1930s the work of Dr. Osman R. Hull and Dr. Willard Ford had established a pattern of field-oriented course work and research. Professors Hull and Ford were also personally active in the conduct of field studies and educational surveys for school districts, including one of the Los Angeles city school district. With the resignation of Professor Ford to become the chief deputy superintendent of schools in Los Angeles and later superintendent of the Glendale (California) public schools, Dr. Hull was assisted primarily by

18

lecturers drawn from the field and, in the area of supervision, by Professor William H. Burton, whose books and other contributions to this area of specialization brought him national renown.

When Professor Burton left in 1939 to accept an appointment in the Harvard School of Education, his position on the faculty of the School of Education was filled by Dr. Melbo. Thus the new "team" in educational administration at the School of Education became Hull and Melbo. They were assisted by part-time lecturers from the local area school systems. From 1939 to 1941, Professors Hull and Melbo began the work of course revision in the area of educational administration. For each course they published a syllabus which gave direction to student learning and which allocated a nonoverlapping content to the basic sequence of courses preparatory for the award of the State of California administration credentials. For many years, until the increasing importance of the state colleges in this area, the School of Education was by far the leading institution among institutions recommending award of the administrative credential. It has never lost that preeminence.

It was also in the years before the Second World War that Dr. Melbo introduced the "Case Study—Simulated Experience" approach in his courses on elementary school administration and supervision. This was a development which added substantially to the reputation of the School of Education's administration courses as current, realistic, and practical. It was an approach that was given renewed emphasis and pertinence following World War II, when the flood of war veterans took advantage of the G.I. Bill to return to their studies. These students brought with them into the university classrooms a personal life philosophy strongly oriented toward pragmatism. Their advent and their philosophical orientation brought renewed emphasis to the Hull-Melbo approach to the preparation of future school administrators. In turn, their approach was adopted to a considerable extent by the part-time lecturers and by the visiting professors of educational administration during the summer sessions.

19

During the postwar years two significant faculty appointments were made in the field of educational administration. One was that of Edward H. LaFranchi, then superintendent of the St. Helena, California, School District and an alumnus of the University of California at Berkeley, where he had been a classmate of Dean Melbo. Dr. LaFranchi, who retired from the School of Education in August 1973, chose to develop the areas of secondary school administration and school housing as his fields of specialization. He achieved eminence in both areas. The other full-time appointment of the postwar years went to Dr. D. Lloyd Nelson, then assistant superintendent for business services for the Los Angeles County school system. Dr. Nelson's doctorate had been awarded by the University of Southern California, where his faculty adviser and chairman had been Dean Melbo. During his many years at the School of Education, Dr. Nelson elected to develop as his specialties the areas of school finance, school business administration, and school law. He soon became widely recognized as the nation's preeminent leader in the field of school finance and business administration and a formidable figure in the state of California.

Through the medium of the educational surveys directed by Dr. Melbo, with the outstanding assistance of Nelson and LaFranchi, and through the timely research and dissertations which they directed, as well as their active personal participation in local, state, and national professional activities, the trio of Melbo-Nelson-LaFranchi enhanced the reputation of the University of Southern California for excellence in the world of educational administration. In addition to good teaching, a genuine concern for each student, and a strong commitment to practical research, these professors systematized and expanded the professional curriculum and programs of the Department of Educational Administration and Supervision. They built the first program in the country to train specialists in the administration of school business affairs, and later the first program in the administration of school district personnel. Both programs were far ahead of their times. The trio of Melbo-Nelson-LaFranchi also pioneered in the

20

scientific study of administrative leadership skills, organization of school districts, and school-community relations, all currently vital concerns. They developed operational standards and evaluative criteria for the guidance of practicing school administrators in almost every important facet of administrative practice.

One of the most successful aspects of the Department of Administration and Supervision has been its active role, in cooperation with the School of Education's Educational Placement Office, in helping to place their students in good administrative positions in local, county, and state school systems and organizations, not only in terms of initial placement but also in subsequent promotions. The concept of a continuing career interest in their graduates became a part of the new evolving professionalism in educational administration. Perhaps no other American school administrator has prepared and sponsored so many students who have subsequently achieved eminence as educational administrators as has Dean Melbo. His former students have held positions as superintendents of schools in United States cities from San Francisco to New York, and hundreds are located in important administrative assignments in public school systems, colleges, and universities all over the world. His students are also credited with research that has led to the solution of many administrative and fiscal crises in the schools of California, and under his guidance have developed administrative procedures for the school systems and school-board relations which have made California an educational model for many states in the Union. Influential also have been the dissertations written under the direction of the department's faculty, which have been particularly recognized for their "tightness" of design, the hardness of their findings, and the utility of their conclusions, all of which have given the School of Education of the University of Southern California a signal reputation for the practicality and effectiveness of its preparation of professional school administrators. The preeminence of the School of Education in the field of educational administration, thus begun and developed, has been continued over the years by the work of De Silva, Ferris, Muelder, Murdy, and Stallings, all

21

proponents of the same concern for their students and the professionalization of the field of educational administration.

Societies

Increasingly important during the School of Education's history, and particularly so during Melbo's administration, was the support of the various educational societies connected with it: Phi Delta Kappa, Pi Lambda Theta (replaced after 1968 by the Honorary Association of Women in Education), the Society of Delta Epsilon, the Education Alumni Association, the Education Council, the California Student Teachers Association, and others to rise under Melbo's aegis: EDUCARE, Education Graduate Organization (EGO), and International Educators Association.

Phi Delta Kappa, professional educational fraternity, was installed on the campus of the University of Southern California in 1922. The USC chapter, designated Alpha Epsilon, loomed large in enhancing the University's national and international prestige. Four members of the Alpha Epsilon chapter served during the period 1946–1973 as national and international presidents. They were Osman R. Hull (1946–1948), Emery Stoops (1953–1955),[26] John C. Whinnery (1958–1960),[27] and Ted Gordon (1972–1974). In addition to monthly meetings, devoted to educational topics, the Alpha Epsilon (later designated the USC Chapter) regularly contributed to educational activities of the School of Education. Its monthly meetings, at which educational topics were presented by authorities; its annual sponsorship of Future Teachers Conferences, which were attended by thousands of young men and women; and its monetary support of the Education Library, educational publications, and student loans made it one of the

26. It was during Stoops' incumbency that, with the addition of a Phi Delta Kappa chapter in Ottawa, Canada, the society became international in scope.

27. John Carroll Whinnery (A.B., University of California, Los Angeles (1931), M.A., Occidental College (1937), and Ed.D., University of Southern California (1954)), was Superintendent of Montebello city schools from 1946 to 1966. From 1954 to 1965, he was lecturer and adjunct professor in the School of Education, and in 1965 he held the Delta Epsilon Lectureship.

22

most important of the societies associated with the School of Education. By 1970, it was the largest chapter in the entire Phi Delta Kappa organization and its Fiftieth Anniversary was recognized by joint resolutions of the California Assembly. Its Fiftieth Anniversary publication noted proudly:[28]

> These have been, not fifty years, but fifty single years, each marked with the toil of the men of USC, building a legacy steeped in accomplishment and pride in fulfilling the chosen life task of the members through the guiding principles of Phi Delta Kappa.

Pi Lambda Theta, the women's counterpart of Phi Delta Kappa, established a chapter at the University in 1924. Its purpose was to honor outstanding women engaged in education and to involve them with others in an organization dedicated to high scholastic achievement and continuing professional attainment. At first largely an off-campus group, in 1942 an on-campus society was formed. An early member of Pi Lambda Theta who achieved great distinction was Ethel Percy Andrus, founder and first president of the National Retired Teachers Association and the American Association of Retired Persons. In her honor the present Ethel Percy Andrus Gerontology Center was established and named at the University of Southern California. Dr. Andrus (M.A. in Education (1928) and Ph.D. (1930), University of Southern California) was made a member of Pi Lambda Theta in 1928. Each year Pi Lambda Theta presented an award of a gift of books to a woman in the School of Education whose scholarship, personality, and other evidence of promise were most nearly identified with the ideals of the association.

The Society of Delta Epsilon was organized May 14, 1947, as an outgrowth of the Doctoral Club.[29] The purposes of Delta Epsilon were to advance the interests of public education, foster professional growth among members, acquaint members with recent findings in education, and advance the welfare of the

---

28. Alpha Epsilon Chapter, Phi Delta Kappa (1972).
29. A local group, organized in 1937, to recognize those who had taken their doctoral degrees in education at USC (Levitt 1970, p. 227).

23

School of Education. In succeeding years, the Delta Epsilon Society was to play an important role with the founding of the Delta Epsilon Lectureships.

At the strong urging by Melbo to the Central Committee, the Education Alumni Association was established March 12, 1947. Its purposes were to promote the interests of the University of Southern California; to further the recruiting, selection, and training of teachers; and to work with the General Alumni Association in its projects. In addition to annual homecomings, the Education Alumni Association sponsored an annual spring conference on an educational topic. Again, at Melbo's suggestion, the association inaugurated an annual Honors Convocation of the School of Education. Participating groups named, within general policy criteria established by the association, their own recipients of awards. "If we do not recognize the achievements of our students, who will?" argued Melbo to the faculty. "Our alumni need to feel that they belong to a specific professional school, not just a university."

The Education Council was the representative and executive group of the students of the School of Education, the constitution of which was approved in 1947. The council consisted of officers elected annually by the students. It was represented in the University's Student Senate, and member of the council acted as liaison between the students and the Education Alumni Association.

University Council on Teacher Education

While the University appropriately delegated to its professional School of Education the leadership role in teacher education, it nevertheless recognized that teacher preparation demanded the concern and collaboration of all facets of the total institution. As a result, the University Council on Teacher Education was established in 1943. This was the first such all-University council in the nation. It was widely observed, imitated, and adopted by other institutions throughout the country. Council members, appointed each spring for the next academic year by the president of the University, were suggested by the chairman of the preceding year, whose nominations were generally endorsed by an all-University

24

Faculty Senate. As a president's committee, the council reported to him through the Vice-President, Academic Affairs.

As of 1953, the council membership consisted of the dean of the School of Education as chairman, the director of Teacher Education as executive officer, the University's Registrar, five professors of education, and one professor each from the University departments of history, English, Spanish, economics, music, physical education, art, business, mathematics, and physics. An academic member was traditionally elected recording secretary.

The council's four chief functions were: (1) to develop patterns of preservice teacher education which met the legal credential (certificate) specifications and which carried out the philosophy of the institution to the extent possible within the limits of time and other circumstances; (2) to set standards for admission to, continuance in, and completion of directed teaching and for the University's endorsement as a credentialed teacher; (3) to encourage University-wide concern for, and participation in, teacher education, both preservice and inservice; and (4) to advise the University Curriculum Committee as to whether proposed courses relating to teaching were or were not needed and, if needed, in which department they might most appropriately be offered.

The first of these functions resulted in specified "credential majors and minors," which represented minimal standards for continuance as credential candidates. The second was implemented through a subcommittee on personnel and credentials, which interviewed all candidates not clearly included or excluded on the basis of council policies, or who wished to appeal a staff decision. The other functions were advisory, but there was little question but that sponsorship of the council encouraged the various departments to consider requests or suggestions more readily than if they were to come from the student himself or a single department.

Over the years, the council contributed, measurably and realistically, to the mutual support and common endeavor of professional and academic wings of the University and to the overall effectiveness of the University's program of teacher education.

25

CAMPUS, UNIVERSITY OF SOUTHERN CALIFORNIA

University Avenue, showing Bovard Administration Building.

CHAPTER 2

Start of a New Era: 1953–1959

It is the business of the future to be dangerous. The great danger is that we will make the wrong choice. The great opportunity is that we will make the right one. This is the time for us to make big plans, to aim high in hopes, remembering that a noble plan once recorded will never die.

I.R.M. TEACHERS FOR METROPOLIS, 1962

Philosophy and Goals

What, it might be asked at the start of the new era, were the essential ingredients of the man named dean in 1953? How did he perceive his task? What was his philosophy? What were his goals?

Of Melbo's personal qualities, first was his ability to conceptualize a problem and place it in proper perspective. His was an almost uncanny power to analyze data on economic, political, and social conditions and to envision modes of education responsive to changing conditions. He had a genius for formulating programs that met the new demands and for organizing resources to execute them. Finally, there was his ability to pick the right man for the right job, and then give him full rein to accomplish the task, using

27

his own creative energies. A keen and experienced analyst of administrative problems and processes, Melbo had long been advising superintendents that their personal success was really measured by the success of the members of their organization. "A prime function of a leader," he was wont to say, "is to release the intelligence of his associates so that they can do the things they know how to do better than anyone else."

His own task, as he perceived it, encompassed twelve major functions. Set forth in a document issued to the faculty in October 1953, they blueprinted his conception of his role:[1]

1. To provide general direction for the School of Education;
2. To serve as executive officer for the faculty;
3. To prepare and administer the budget;
4. To organize and administer the selection and assignment of all faculty personnel;
5. To develop and coordinate relations with all other divisions of the University;
6. To coordinate the program of public and professional relations;
7. To represent the School of Education in governmental, organizational, and institutional relationships;
8. To develop and administer instructional and operational policies;
9. To administer supplementary funds;
10. To coordinate the activities of attached offices, services, or divisions;
11. To assign, in coordination with the assistant dean, faculty advisers and appoint committees on studies for doctoral candidates; and
12. To direct the preparation of an annual report, or periodic reports, on work and needs of the School of Education.

The philosophy which was to mark the new dean's administration was a mixture of the old and the new. From its earliest

1. *Agenda,* October 5, 1953.

beginnings, the philosophy of the School of Education at the University of Southern California had been best characterized, perhaps, as pragmatic eclecticism modified by personal idealism. From that philosophy had arisen the School's long-standing commitment to the ideal of service as a primary goal; its involvement, with all that term implies of interest, concern, accessibility, helpfulness, and the scholarly application of theory and science to pressing societal needs; and its concern for the education of the "whole person."

While these ideals remained basic, there is little question that Melbo injected into the School and its activities a new note of *Realpolitik,* of political sophistication and operational realism. It is noteworthy that, while still a professor of educational administration, it was he who had, as chairman of the Committee on Curriculum and Schedule, prepared the wartime services report to the faculty prior to his own departure for military duty. Similarly, his return in November 1944, signaled in a very real sense the beginning of the postwar era, and within two weeks of his return he was named by Dean Rogers chairman of a newly formed committee on postwar planning. Certain it was that from his energizing influence sprang the aggressive expansion of the School of Education during the 1953–59 period into new and significant areas of wider service.

As administrator, Melbo focused on improving the existing structure of governance and procedures. As leader, he directed his creative genius to the exploration of new fields, to experimentation with new approaches to educational problems, and to the sagacious acquisition of financial support to meet expanding needs. The melding of the newer philosophy with the old and Melbo's personal synthesis of the administrator-leader dichotomy found expression in the objectives he set for the School:[2]

1. To prepare well-qualified persons for general and specialized service in public school systems, colleges and universities, and other educational organizations throughout the United States and the world;

---

2. *Bulletin:* 1970–72; 1972–74.

2. To plan, design, conduct, and stimulate research of both theoretical and applied nature which is of present and future significance to the entire field of education;

3. To provide expert field service to the educational community and to assist public and private school organizations to resolve current problems, to plan effectively for future developments, and to evaluate objectively the results of educational efforts; and

4. As the inescapable responsibility of a mature professional school, to serve as a critic of the profession and, through the intelligent exercise of this role, to assist the educational endeavor in its drive for continued improvement.

Administration

In 1956, the California State Board of Education's Accreditation Committee commended the School of Education of the University of Southern California on its internal organization. "The Dean," read the report, "has worked hard and effectively in setting a good internal organization."[3] From the very start, the thrust of Melbo's administrative acumen had been directed toward the building of an effective, streamlined internal organization for the School of Education. His approach to that goal included: strengthening the position of the assistant dean, regularization of faculty participation in the decision-making process, reorganization of the standing committees, a continuing reassessment of the departmental structure in relation to contemporary needs, and a determination to maintain and extend the unique autonomy of the School of Education as a professional school in the University organization.

The position of the assistant dean was strengthened by the promulgation of the functions of the assistant dean and by the firm support of the dean in their execution. Major functions of the

30

3. *Agenda,* May 7, 1956.

assistant dean were delineated as the organization and administration of the program of advisement and counseling service for students, registration activities, graduate degree examinations, and schedule of classes; assignment of all clerical and secretarial personnel; establishment and maintenance of adequate records systems for all degrees and credential objectives; and, in coordination with the dean, assignment of faculty advisers and appointment of committees on studies for doctoral candidates. The usefulness of the firm delineation of functions was borne out in succeeding years, not only by the improved operations within the School of Education, but also by the betterment of relations with other divisions of the University.

Realistically assessing the increased burden which would now fall upon the assistant dean, particularly with the increased enrollments, Melbo upgraded in 1953 the position of credential secretary to credential technician, and established in November 1953, the position of graduate degree technician, with responsibility for personal records of all graduate students working toward advanced degrees in the School of Education. Rita Rose, the first appointee, was succeeded by Eve Kerr, and in November 1959, by Ruth Farrar.

Well aware from his own experience of the importance and value of faculty participation in the decision-making process, Melbo sought from the first to increase the faculty's knowledge of matters pertaining to the School's activities and to provide the basis for informed decisions on the part of the faculty. The method he selected was the issue, prior to each faculty meeting, of a complete agenda. Beginning in October 1953, and continuing thereafter without interruption, each faculty member was provided, several days before a scheduled faculty meeting, with an agenda containing both informational and action items, supported by pertinent background information and documents. All items were classified as to general functions, faculty-staff personnel matters, instructional program, student personnel, professional-public relations, fiscal matters, university coordination, or other

31

appropriate subdivision. Melbo's assessment of the value of these agenda was expressed in the first issue:[4]

> It is contemplated that an agenda of the type presented herewith will be developed for each faculty meeting as a means of transmitting complete information on matters of concern to the School of Education. Departments, committees, and individuals are invited to submit informational or action items for inclusion on the agenda. If a file is maintained, each faculty member will have a cumulative and comprehensive record of all matters coming before the faculty.

Procedural rules adopted at the first meeting of the faculty in 1953 served to channel faculty participation. It was agreed that regular meetings would be held monthly during the academic year in accordance with a schedule to be adopted by the faculty at the first meeting of each academic year, and that special meetings were to be called by the dean upon prior written notice of three or more days. It was also agreed that at any meeting, regular or special, the faculty would take action only on those items which were a part of the agenda for that meeting, except when there was a two-thirds consent of faculty present to act on an item not on the agenda.[5]

The School's standing committees were reorganized in 1954, and their number reduced to six: Curriculum, Schedule and Personnel (Central Committee); Doctoral Program; Master's Program; Bachelor's Program; Research and Publications; and Student Organizations.[6] The Central Committee retained its preeminence as a committee on committees, which recommended to the faculty a framework of standing committees and nominated the necessary personnel; assisted the dean in the preliminary structuring of policy changes for presentation to the faculty; recommended to the faculty approval or disapproval of proposed curriculum changes; served as an advisory committee to the dean and faculty; and represented the faculty in the consideration of problems pertaining to the School of Education which would not be

---

4. *Agenda,* October 5, 1953.
5. *Minutes,* October 5, 1953.
6. *Minutes,* December 6, 1954.

START OF A NEW ERA: 1953–1959

appropriate for discussion at a general faculty meeting. The various degree committees reviewed problems pertaining to their respective fields, initiated changes in policy for faculty approval, and recommended candidates for admission or completion of the degree. The Research and Publications Committee recommended policy governing publications sponsored by the School of Education and reported to the faculty on research being conducted by the faculty. The Committee on Student Organizations, which was discontinued in the academic year 1958–59, recommended appropriate changes in policy on student organizations within the jurisdiction of the School of Education. Committee chairmen rotated on the basis of one to three years in office.

Departments underwent few structural changes. In March 1955, a continuing dearth of enrollments in the Department of Industrial Arts caused the dean to request Crawford to make a thorough review of the department. Crawford's report noted that enrollments were chiefly in courses for elementary teachers. Prospects for improvement in enrollment appeared slight, partly because the state colleges were offering much competition in the field and partly because the School of Education lacked equipment, facilities, and personnel to carry out an effective program of industrial arts.[7] In view of this discouraging report and the limited financial resources available, the decision was made to discontinue the department with the academic year 1956–57. The course in handicraft for the elementary teacher, which had proved popular, was transferred to the Department of Teacher Training.

Two unsuccessful attempts were made on the part of faculty members to gain faculty approval for changes in their departments. In October 1953, Brackenbury recommended that the name of the Department of History and Philosophy of Education be changed to "Education—Social and Philosophical Aspects," and that a number of changes be approved in the courses given by the department bringing the content closer to the proposed title. Al-

---

7. "Industrial Arts Education at U.S.C." (A Committee Report by C. C. Crawford, April 18, 1955). *Agenda,* May 9, 1955.

33

though the faculty approved most of the course changes, the name of the department was retained. Only in 1956 did this occur, when the name of the department became "Education—Social and Philosophical Foundations."

The proposed merger of the Departments of Psychology and Guidance also met with faculty disapproval. The proposal, jointly made by these departments, set forth the arguments for and against the merger.[8] The two departments, it was pointed out, had had for many years a common chairman and had performed as one in matters of programming and selecting instructors. No sharp distinction of subject matter was involved and combining the departments would offer the most wholesome background for the doctorate in education by providing a broad orientation in educational disciplines of the sort it was difficult to acquire outside the academic atmosphere. On the other hand, it was also pointed out, the merger would open the risk of loss of identity by one or the other as a specialized field. It would also prohibit a doctoral candidate from taking one as a supplementary when the other was a major, thus possibly reducing specialized preparation. The arguments against the merger apparently seeming the stronger in the faculty's opinion, the proposal was not approved by the faculty at its meeting in December 1953, and the departments remained separate. The vast increase in the field of counseling which developed during the 1950s and 1960s, as well as the greatly increased specialization in the field of educational psychology, proved the wisdom of the faculty's decision.

Faculty

By 1959, the faculty of the School of Education, including those holding dual appointments, had increased to 90. Of these, 67 were members of the faculty of the School of Education only, a number approximately equal to that of the entire faculty in 1953. Also

8. *Agenda,* December 7, 1953.

reflecting the growth of the School were a substantial increase in the number of full professors, addition of new members, and the creation of the adjunct rank. Growth and promotion continued to be the pattern of the Melbo Years. As of 1973, the dean had either appointed or promoted every member of the faculty of the School of Education. "If we don't have a good faculty," he told alumni groups, "it's my own fault!"

During the 1953–59 period, three professors joined Thompson as *emeriti:* Weersing in 1954,[9] Crawford in 1956,[10] and Hull in 1958.

Of the 18 professors who were members of the faculty of the School of Education only in 1959, eight had been promoted from within during the 1953–59 period: Brackenbury, Finn, Meyers, Michael, Olson, Perry, Stoops, and Wagner. Additions in rank of professor were Carl Hancey, Dean of the University College; Herman J. Sheffield; and Earl V. Pullias. Of the seven associate

---

9. Frederick J. Weersing was born October 13, 1889. A graduate of the University of Minnesota and Teachers College of Columbia University, he taught for a number of years at Fukien Christian University, Foochow, China, and the University of Kansas, before coming to the University of Southern California in 1927, where for many years he headed the department of secondary education. A teacher of great merit, Dr. Weersing in later years stated that if a unifying philosophy must be found for the School of Education, it should derive from the conviction of the professors of the School that teaching was a 'calling.' This conception he related to the University's Methodist heritage. "Keep in mind," he counseled, "that USC in 1928 was more than half staffed by children of the Methodist church. . . . and that atmosphere pervaded the whole institution. They were excellent people. They were people with vision—people who sacrificed a great deal to make the service they were making to the University and the student body and to the state and the country." (Interview, reported by Levitt 1970, p. 491.)

10. Claude C. Crawford was born November 16, 1897, at Hillsboro, Texas. A graduate of East Texas Normal College, he received his B.A. and M.A. at the University of Texas, 1918 and 1919; did graduate work at the Carnegie Institute of Technology, 1921–23; and received his Ph.D. at the University of Chicago in 1924. Prior to his appointment to the faculty of the School of Education in 1926, he was teacher and principal in Texas and professor of secondary education at the University of Idaho (1923–26). Consulting activities during World War II with wartime defense production, civil defense, and later consultantships with federal, state, and local agencies which placed great demands upon his time compelled him to seek retirement in 1956.

35

professors, two (Carnes and Naslund) had been promoted from within; five were new appointments: Leonard Calvert (1954), Charles M. Brown (1955), Newton S. Metfessel (1956), Donald E. Wilson (1956), and Wallace R. Muelder (1958). Newly appointed assistant professors were William Georgiades (1956) and David W. Martin (1958).

Appointments made to meet an expanded program were Edgar L. Lowell, as of 1958 associate professor of Education as well as administrator, John Tracy Clinic; Victor Garwood, associate professor of speech; Robert Baker, head counselor, Veterans Counseling Center (1954), succeeded in 1956 by John T. Palmer and in 1958 by Loren Gray; and, in connection with teacher training projects; Keith Oakes, Earl M. Grotke, and Donald E. Wilson (1954), Leslie Nason (1957) and Paul V. Robinson (1958).

Faculty members who held dual appointments with their respective disciplines numbered 23, of whom 12 were in the physical education department. Other disciplines represented included business communications, fine arts, librarianship, music, and speech.

Inauguration of the adjunct rank was an important change in the faculty structure of the School of Education. The proposal, initiated by Melbo in December 1959, won faculty approval January 11, 1960. Eligibility was determined on the basis of prior service, normally three years, in a teaching capacity with the School of Education. Rank (professor, associate professor, assistant professor) was determined on the basis of academic and professional qualifications equivalent to those for a regular faculty appointment in comparable rank, and entitled the holder to certain faculty privileges.[11]

11. Appointments were made by nomination by the department in which the person was teaching, confirmation by the faculty, and appointment by the dean. The appointment was for an indefinite period, depending upon and concurrent with continuing service with the School of Education in accordance with the general policies which applied to the regular faculty. Persons holding an adjunct professorial rank were entitled to all concomitant faculty privileges, except those involving tenure in position, membership in the University's retirement system,

Commenting on the initiation of the adjunct rank, Melbo said:[12]

The faculty included a substantial number of part-time persons with great clinical experience in their respective fields of specialization. I was confident that this concept and relationship could be made to apply equally well to the school of education as it did to a school of medicine or, indeed, to a school of law. I had also observed that some of the very best teaching in our program was provided by men and women whom we brought in from the field as part-time members of the faculty. They had an unmatched expertise and frequently a reputation of such magnitude that it would have been impossible to match them with full-time personnel in terms of the University's salary structure. Moreover, I had found that these people really enjoyed helping those in the profession who were about to come after them and stand beside them, and that the act of teaching helped them to synthesize their own experiences and to sharpen their own concepts about their respective fields of specialization. It therefore became a matter of some mutual advantage to recruit and retain for our own exclusive use a substantial number of highly able men and women.

By developing the concept of the adjunct rank and the policies associated with it, we obtained the exclusive use of these very competent, highly specialized individuals and they in turn were proud to be identified with a school of education that recognized their achievements and their great worth as teachers, advisors, and researchers. To be located in a great metropolitan area was a tremendous opportunity to add to the strength of its faculty by the device of the adjunct professorship. The relationship is mutually advantageous to the regular full-time faculty member as well as to the adjunct. Each learns from the other and each obtains a broader appreciation of the professional nature of his particular field of specialization.

This is one of several processes by which the School of

and similar relationships. Membership on graduate study committees and participation in departmental and general faculty meetings, as well as on standing and special faculty committees, were permitted.

12. Tape recording, April 1973.

Education attempted to integrate itself effectively with the professional field which it was designed to serve. In turn, the professional field, as represented by adjunct professors and lecturers, came to look upon the USC School of Education as the one professional school which was vitally concerned with their problems and their successes as well as with the total field of education. Even more, the presence of the adjunct professor injected an element of contemporary concern and an up-to-dateness with regard to the prospects and patterns of development in all educational endeavors. It tended to make current the teaching program and the learning of those who were entering the profession. It bridged the gap between theory and clinical practice. It simply is not possible to give enough credit to the tremendous contributions of the adjunct faculty in the development of the School of Education and in the effective preparation of truly competent professionals from the ranks of our students.

Those holding adjunct rank as of 1960 were: Professors Charles C. Carpenter, Lionel De Silva, Jefferson L. Garner, Harry W. Smallenburg, Jane Warters, and John C. Whinnery; associate professor Robert Gerletti; and assistant professors Marcella R. Bonsall, Frank Hodgson, Samuel J. Rowe, and Sophia T. Salvin.

Lecturers as of 1959–60 numbered 17, and instructor-coordinators six. Among the newly appointed lecturers were some whose names would continue to be associated with the School of Education for many years; notably Chester E. Gilpin and Jessie Graham.

Delta Epsilon Lectureships

In 1954, began the enduring and professionally rewarding relationship between the School of Education and the Society of Delta Epsilon in the form of the Delta Epsilon Lectureships. Modeled on the contributive services plan in operation in some of the great universities of the United States in their schools of medicine and law, the plan was personally drafted by Melbo and approved

38

by the faculty, with considerable expression of doubt that it would work, on February 8, 1954.[13]

The purposes of the lectureships were to serve the interests of those who teach and those who seek advancement in the field of education; to provide students with the opportunity to benefit from the experience of prominent graduates of the University of Southern California's School of Education and to inspire students to greater achievement in the field of Education; to assist the School of Education to increase and broaden its offerings by making available the services of prominent leaders in the field of Education; and to publicize Delta Epsilon and its aims. Said Melbo in 1973:[14]

> I have always been convinced that no man succeeds by himself alone, and that everyone in the profession owes some responsibility to help those who will come after them in the professional field. My thought in establishing the Delta Epsilon Lectureship was first to give recognition to those of our graduates who had achieved distinction, and this was important in a field and at a time when little recognition or credit was ever given to those who had done well. My second thought was that the Delta Epsilon Lectureship (limited to one a year as a matter of distinction, even though we could have had one each term easily after the program got underway) ... would be a means of providing people in the profession with an opportunity to contribute significantly to those who were in the training program, and at the same time serve the interests of personal philanthropy on the part of those who made a contribution. It was also, of course, a professional recognition of their competence and achievement. This recognition by the School from which they had graduated became a significant factor, perhaps even greater than that of an honorary degree, for those who were so recognized and chosen by their peers to be the Delta Epsilon Lecturer on the basis of their contributions to the field of their specialized interest.

The first Delta Epsilon Lecturer was Harry M. Howell, who

---

13. "The Society of Delta Epsilon Lectureship." *Agenda,* February 8, 1954.
14. Tape recording, April 1973.

had completed his doctorate in 1950 under Melbo's chairmanship, and who in 1954, was associate superintendent, Los Angeles city schools.[15] From the first, the lecturship plan was an outstanding success and afforded both the School of Education and the Society of Delta Epsilon a mutually rewarding experience. Appendix C contains a list of Delta Epsilon Lecturers through 1973. A similar listing is engraved on the bronze plaque at the entrance to Waite Phillips Hall.

Accreditation

In January 1955, the dean announced to the faculty that committees representing the California State Board of Education and the Western College Association would visit the University in the coming months to determine reaccreditation for current credential programs and initial accreditation for any new programs. He assigned Cannon responsibility for organizing and preparing the report to be made on behalf of the University for teaching credentials.[16]

The Accreditation Committee, chaired by J. Paul Leonard of San Francisco State College, visited the campus February 13–15,

---

15. Harry Morganroth Howell (USC '24, M.S. in Ed. '37, Ed.D. '50) was born in Shamokin, Pennsylvania. He began his service with the Los Angeles school system as a teacher with the Harding High School (later University High) in 1934. In 1933, he entered the Los Angeles city school system as acting director of efficiency, budget bureau. From 1934 to 1935 he was assistant director of the budget; from 1938 to 1949 assistant superintendent, budget division; and from 1949 until his untimely death, September 7, 1955, associate superintendent, budget, and acting superintendent. Howell's doctoral dissertation on the equalization of assessment practices in California as they affect the program of education was the basis of California legislation in school finance. Struggling with an incurable illness during the last year of his life, he had just completed at the time of his death a four-volume survey of the salary structure of certificated employees of the Los Angeles school system, ranked as the most comprehensive study produced on that subject in Los Angeles. Of him Melbo said, "Harry Howell had a very real significance nationwide in achieving equity in school support as affected by State and local assessment practices. He was unique in California education." (Quoted from *Alumni Review,* 37:1:30.)

16. University of Southern California, School of Education (1956).

40

1956. On the basis of its recommendation, the State Board of Education reaccredited the School of Education for five years, until June 30, 1961, for credentials in all areas for which reaccreditation was sought, and for three years, until June 30, 1959, for credentials for which original accreditation was sought: pupil personnel services and the credential to teach exceptional children.[17]

The Accreditation Committee particularly commended the dean for the development of good internal organization of the School of Education and the dean and his staff for the excellence of intra-University relationships:[18]

> The Dean has worked hard and effectively in setting a good internal organization and the relations between the School of Education and the rest of the University are good. Part of this results from the work of the Council on Teacher Education. . . . Commendation is also due the liberal arts faculty for their interest, support and participation in the credential program.

Constructive criticism included the observation that an attempt should be made to better physical facilities (the major problem which gave the Dean much concern), reduce staff loads and class size, and improve the coordination of the program leading to the credential to teach exceptional children.

To the last problem much effort was given during the next two years. As a result, when the Visitation Committee, headed by Wesley P. Smith of the California State Department of Education, visited the campus December 2–3, 1958, much improvement in that program was noted. The committee recommended, and the State Department of Education approved, reaccreditation to June

---

17. The term "exceptional child" is used to refer to three general classes of children: (1) those who stand at the extremes of some trait which all display to a greater or lesser degree (e.g., the mentally gifted and the mentally retarded); (2) those who exhibit some outstanding peculiarity in which the majority do not share at all or, at most, only to a minimal degree (e.g., the physically handicapped); and (3) those who show very unusual combinations of mental or psychological traits. The year 1957 marks the first year in which credentials were issued on the recommendation of the School of Education for the teaching of the deaf and hard of hearing. This capability was a direct result of the cooperative arrangements made in 1954 between the University and the John Tracy Clinic.

18. *Agenda,* May 7, 1956; and *Agenda,* June 4, 1956.

41

30, 1961, the term for which all other credential programs of the School were last accredited. It also noted in particular the exceptionally high level of training in the specialization of teaching the deaf or hard of hearing in special classes, and in speech correction and lip reading in remedial classes.[19]

The process of accreditation, never taken lightly by the School of Education, was greatly assisted during the 1950s and early 1960s by Dean Melbo's guidance and direction. As a member for ten years, 1953 through 1963, of the Committee for the Accreditation of Teacher Education of the California State Board of Education, including two years (1961–1963) as chairman, the dean was thoroughly familiar with the many requirements. His comprehensive information on a variety of matters was extremely valuable to the School with respect to these requirements and the ways in which the School could best approach meeting them.

Credentials

The addition of the two new credentials authorized in 1956 brought to 16 the number which the University of Southern California was authorized to recommend in the field of teaching. In cumulative totals for the period 1949–59, the University of Southern California retained its lead over other institutions in California, although increasingly the state colleges rivaled or surpassed it in yearly totals. In the number of administration and supervision credentials, the University of Southern California continued to maintain a wide lead. In the 1957–59 period, it recommended 89 more persons than its nearest competitor, Los Angeles State College, and 148 more than the total number recommended by the University of California, Berkeley and the University of California, Los Angeles.

Much of the credit for the outstanding success of the University of Southern California in the credentialing process was due

---

19. Letter, J. Burton Vasche to President Norman H. Topping, dated June 5, 1959, inclosing a copy of the evaluation (*Agenda,* June 5, 1959).

from 1955 on to the credential technician (after 1965, credential supervisor), Helen Frahm. Mrs. Frahm, who had previously served as credential secretary (1947–52), entered upon her work in 1955 with a firm grasp of the complexities involved. Her detailed knowledge and unfailing helpfulness to all who sought her assistance made her a valued member of the staff and an influential person on credentialing matters throughout the state. On many occasions, Dean Melbo said, "Helen Frahm knows more about credentials than anybody in California. When they don't know what to do about a credential matter up in Sacramento, they get Helen Frahm on the telephone."

Both Mrs. Frahm and Dean Melbo, as well as the rest of the staff of the School of Education, would need all the perspicacity they could muster during the ensuing years. Events which occurred during the late 1950s stirred the troubled waters, nor had the effects subsided by 1973. On December 7, 1954, the president of the California Council on Teacher Education and the superintendent of Public Instruction jointly appointed a 14-member statewide Committee on the Revision of the Credential Structure. This committee presented its recommendations to the superintendent of Public Instruction May 27, 1957. The committee recommended the development of a credential system composed of four credentials: general teaching, vocational teaching, pupil personnel, and administrative-supervision. The most far-sweeping of its proposals pertained to the general teaching credential:

> The general teaching credential would authorize teaching service in the kindergarten through the junior college in all subject fields, and the teaching of exceptional children.... It would encompass five years of collegiate preparation, with the alternative for the candidate at the end of the fourth collegiate year (baccalaureate degree) either to continue a fifth year of preparation or to begin teaching and complete the equivalent of this fifth year of preparation within the ensuing five years. Those electing to teach upon receipt of the bachelor's degree would be issued the general teaching credential on an internship basis subject to renewal requirements until the equivalent of the

43

fifth year was completed, at which time they would be issued a permanent credential for their professional life.

Recommendations for requirements for the other credentials also presented some startling differences from the former requirements:

The vocational teaching credential would be based upon the number of years of experience required for journeymen or technical status in a particular vocation plus a year of professional preparation designed to develop skill and understanding of teaching the trade. Authorization would state that the holder was qualified to teach vocational education in secondary schools.

The pupil personnel credential would include a common core of preparation over the entire area of pupil personnel work, and be based upon successful teaching experience with opportunities for majors in the fields of psychometry, psychology, school social work, and child welfare and attendance. Authorization would be for rendering pupil personnel services.

The administration-supervision credential would be based upon possession of a general or vocational teaching credential or any previously issued general teaching credential. It would require a year of graduate work designed to prepare a teacher to function in the role of a supervisor or administrator of either instructional or noninstructional services. Authorization for service would be general, leaving specific assignments to employing boards of education.

Other recommendations of the statewide committee on credential revision included a change in procedures of securing a credential. Instead of existing procedures which required securing the credential through direct application to the state, a procedure was recommended which would require each applicant to secure a written recommendation from the executive head of an approved teacher education program in the candidate's institution. The credential structure was to be changed to permit each teacher educational institution to employ the type of program it believed would best help individuals to meet credential requirements. Cre-

44

dential requirements, recommended the committee, should be general rather than specific.[20]

The report of the statewide committee was widely distributed throughout California, and members of the profession and others were urged to study the recommendations and send their reactions and recommendations to the Superintendent of Public Instruction, at that time Roy E. Simpson. After careful examination of the report, the faculty of the School of Education unanimously endorsed on March 17, 1958, a statement on the proposals. The faculty report strongly opposed the wholesale scrapping of the legal certification structure, affirmed the faculty's belief in professional preparation, and held that essential elasticity could be achieved in a less dangerous fashion than that proposed.[21] Reactions throughout the state indicated that, although most agreed that the California credential structure needed revision, they also considered the recommendations of the committee on revision too drastic. As of 1959, it was evident that the credential structure of the state of California was under considerable pressure, but no changes were made that year.[22]

Program Expansion

The years 1953 through 1959 saw the first steps toward the vastly expanded program of the 1960s and 1970s. Small and tentative in comparison with the later strides, they were nevertheless significant in setting a pattern for the later developments. So excellent did that pattern appear that in 1959, Thompson assessed the future of the School of Education in terms of the progress made and the pattern set in recent years:[23]

> Let us take just a glimpse into the future through the eyes of Dean Melbo. What does one hope for the future? . . . In a word,

---

20. Simpson (1958).
21. "Statement of the Faculty on Proposed Credential Revisions, School of Education, University of Southern California," dated March 17, 1958.
22. Simpson (1962).
23. Thompson, n.d., p. 118.

45

the hope of the future in the School of Education is to follow the lines now pretty well laid down, but with ever greater effectiveness and satisfaction to those whose creative effort makes them possible in the first place.

The progress and projects upon which Thompson based his "more and better" theory for the future success of the School of Education form the chronicle of the School of Education's development during the first seven years of Melbo's administration. The projects undertaken fell in the areas of teacher education, special education, counseling, international education, and higher education.

USC Southern California Education Project. In the spring of 1953, the Los Angeles Board of Education took under consideration a project proposed by the Ford Foundation's Fund for the Advancement of Education to recruit and train teachers on an emergency basis, with the cooperation of the University of California, Los Angeles, and the University of Southern California. The board's hesitation to enter upon the proposed project paved the way for action on Melbo's part to obtain for the USC School of Education a grant for a similar purpose but an expanded scope to include the school systems of California. In the fall of 1953, therefore, following preliminary negotiations with officers of the Ford Foundation, with whom Melbo was personally acquainted, he recommended to the faculty that it authorize him to submit a proposal to the foundation for a grant to support an experimental accelerated program to prepare selected college graduates for teaching in the public elementary schools of California. With faculty approval of the project, Melbo prepared and submitted to the officers of the Ford Foundation a detailed proposal, which the foundation approved in January 1954, and to which it awarded a grant of $279,000 over a period of four years.[24]

---

24. Servin and Wilson (1969, p. 201) note this grant from the Ford Foundation as an example of the recognition by an outside agency of the academic progress of the University of Southern California. Unfortunately, they fail to mention the recipient of the grant or its purpose.

START OF A NEW ERA: 1953–1959

"Several factors," explained Melbo in 1973, "entered into my decision at the time. One," he continued:[25]

> was the fact of a great shortage of teachers and the need to recruit well-prepared people to enter the field. It was clear that the normal source of students coming through the college and university teacher training curriculum would not satisfy the demand for personnel. It also was time to develop other patterns as well as other sources of recruitment for teacher training. Moreover, it seemed timely and desirable to extend the teacher training program of the School of Education and to open effective working relationships with many school districts in the metropolitan area.
>
> Up to that time most of the teacher training had centered around several schools in the Los Angeles District. The concentration of this training program in a few Los Angeles schools almost seemed to imply a kind of neglect for the smaller but rapidly growing districts in the Los Angeles metropolitan area outside the city. It was time to expand our field relations and our potential market for subsequent placement of those whom we trained cooperatively with school systems other than Los Angeles. This judgment in no way implied a dissatisfaction or unhappiness with the Los Angeles schools. On the contrary, their cooperation with, and support of the School of Education was then, as it is today, a close and magnificent working relationship. It simply was a need to recognize the sources of assistance in the training program and other markets for the teacher product of the University.
>
> It was also clear that no university could limit itself to a single program for training teachers. It was necessary to think in terms of programs—plural—designed for different kinds of student clientele and the preparation of teachers with varying kinds of specializations for service.
>
> Then there were the fiscal considerations. It was always apparent to me that we had a great need for various kinds of student aid, whether it be in the form of a scholarship or a stipend of some kind or some other kind of assistance. The design of a teacher training program which provided some fiscal support for the trainees was also a means of enlarging the stu-

---

25. Tape recording, April 1973.

dent aid capability of the University. At that time, the School of Education had no student aid and the stipends which were received by the trainees in the intern program begun in 1954, were the first massive infusion of student aid funds from external sources.

I also need to state that I was determined to find ways and means of bringing external funding for various programs and projects to the School of Education and not be completely dependent upon the tuition revenue which was generated by the classes in the School of Education. The Ford Foundation, more specifically the Fund for the Advancement of Education, with its expressed interest in improving and helping teacher education offered a wonderful opportunity to bring external funds to the School of Education. On the basis of a rather fortuitous acquaintance with a number of the officers of the foundation, I soon came to realize that Ford needed a university outlet and cooperation in southern California almost as much as the School of Education needed some of Ford's funds. It was a fortunate coincidence that it became possible to achieve the objectives of each party to the agreement as it was subsequently developed.

As has been stated by Dean Melbo, the purposes of the project were to explore the possibilities of recruiting well-qualified, mature persons to meet the critical shortage of teachers and to evaluate an accelerated program of teacher education tailored specifically to the trainees involved. Major features included the recruitment of college graduates who had received their degrees at least two years prior to their proposed employment as teachers; encouragement of superior candidates through offer of scholarships each year to 90 selected candidates; closely knit integration of field experience and theory, particularly of teaching practice and methodology; review of plans with participating school districts; participation by recruits in two summers of course work and practice teaching supervised by University personnel; and evaluation of the program by two University faculty members selected by reason of their experience in research design and procedure.

48   Thus, with the support of the Ford Foundation, and with the

endorsement of the University Council on Teacher Education, state and county departments of education, and the California Teachers Association, the USC School of Education planned and operated from 1954 through 1958 an experimental elementary school teacher recruitment and training program for selected mature college graduates. The program was carried out with the cooperation of nine school districts in southern California.[26] As director of the project Melbo appointed Cannon, and to assist Cannon he brought as visiting professors to the School of Education an able staff drawn from various teacher education institutions: Keith Oakes, Stuart F. McComb, Earl M. Grotke, and Donald E. Wilson. Other members of the project staff were Selma Herr, Evelyn Reeves, and Helen Truher. Oakes, succeeded by McComb, acted as assistant director to Cannon.

Toward the end of the project, Melbo insisted on a comparative evaluation. The evaluative report, written by Lefever and Meyers with Cannon's assistance, was published in 1960.[27] It represented five years of data from the 341 participants, their test records and transcripts, and evaluative reports from their principals and the staff on problems met and degrees of success attained. These data were then compared with similar data regarding 200 "regularly" prepared teachers. It was found that the motivation of the project teachers largely offset the handicap of lesser amounts of student teaching and course work. In the first year, many experienced great difficulty and nearly twice the

26. School districts participating were Alhambra City; Compton City; Lawndale Elementary; Lynwood Unified; Long Beach Unified; Montebello Unified; Norwalk City; Paramount Unified; Redondo Beach City Schools; and Torrance Unified. The program opened with a 10-week summer of course work directed toward the teaching assignment expected in September. The candidate then taught as an intern on a provisional teaching certificate while remaining under the guidance of the University through field observations and evening or Saturday campus classes. An eight-week course during the second summer completed the credential requirement for most of the candidates, providing that the year of teaching had been evaluated as successful. Most of the successful candidates then taught in succeeding years as regularly certificated teachers.

27. Meyers, Cannon, Lefever (1960).

49

"normal" number dropped out. In succeeding years, however, differences between the two groups were rarely of statistical significance.

Specialist-Teacher Program. In 1959, the Ford Foundation's Fund for the Advancement of Education made a second grant to the USC School of Education in the form of $660,000 over a six-year period for an experimental postgraduate program aimed at producing high school teachers who were specialists in their subject fields and who had some new and important kinds of teaching competencies. As director of the project, Melbo named Calvert of the Department of Secondary Education.[28]

In 1973, Dean Melbo provided a valuable historical footnote to the origin of the project:[29]

> In subsequent years, after the first 1954 grant, as the Fund for the Advancement of Education of the Ford Foundation continued its efforts to make an impact on American teacher education, the shortage of teachers tended to become perhaps more acute rather than less acute. There also developed a point of view, both inside and outside the fund, which seemed to imply—and sometimes not too subtly—that professional preparation for teaching was of little or no consequence. The important thing was adequate subject matter preparation and that, perhaps, no more than what was represented by a baccalaureate major. There was inherent a little of the philosophy that teachers were born and not made and all that was necessary was to dump them into the classroom and they would quickly learn to swim. The horrible alternative that they might sink was apparently over-looked!
>
> In any case, the Ford Foundation began to fund a number of programs which seemed to minimize professional preparation and to emphasize the subject matter preparation, but more than anything else a program which would make for a quick

28. Calvert had a record of 25 years as teacher, counselor, and administrator in the public and private schools in the Midwest, Hawaii, and California. His untimely death, December 18, 1964, unfortunately precluded his personal completion of the project which he had admirably directed during the last five years of his life.

29. Tape recording, April 1973.

50

entry into the teaching field. I felt most strongly that this was contrary to the best interests of a professional school of education, and also inconsistent with the facts which were known to almost any knowledgeable observer. I had never seen at the college level, nor at the high school level, a teacher dismissed because his command of the subjects field was inadequate. Rather, he was dismissed because he could not relate effectively to students or, to put it in more simple terminology, he simply was not able to cope with the student demands and interests and to be a good teacher for them.

My thought, then, was that we ought to develop a teacher training program which would focus on the concept of specialization. This would be specialization in two areas: an intense in-depth specialization in the subject field which was the teacher's choice, but also in the teaching of that field which involved the methods and the strategies of learning so that the teacher was, indeed, a competent professional. The concept was that he would be a specialist in the subject matter with more than the normal level of preparation and also a specialist in the teaching of that subject field. The concept further was that such people, not numerous in their presence in any given school, would serve almost as a model for others in the school and would thereby extend their influence.

During this process of planning, Ford announced a time constraint that was very critical to us. So one day I telephoned Dr. Alvin C. Eurich, who was the Vice-President of the Fund for the Advancement of Education, to discuss the matter with him. It happened that I had previously known Dr. Eurich while he was on the faculty at Stanford and I was in the public schools in Oakland. I had also known him during the Second World War, when both of us were officers in the United States Naval Reserve and for a time we were located in the Training Division of the Bureau of Naval Personnel in Washington with adjacent offices. In any case, I explained briefly to Dr. Eurich what I had in mind in terms of a different approach to the preparation of specialist teachers. He said, "Well, send me something, and I think we can be helpful." So I wrote approximately four single-spaced pages of a project proposal and developed a budget involving some $660,000 to supoort the activity over a five-year period, and sent

51

it to Dr. Eurich. Within a few days I had a telephone call from him telling us that the grant would be forthcoming and to get ready to develop the program. This we did, and it was at this point that I asked Dr. Calvert to become the director, a function which he performed most admirably.

The program aimed at the liberal arts graduate who had high scholarship and the desire for a master's degree in an academic subject. Those with previous preparation for, or paid experience in, teaching were not eligible. It was designed specifically to discover: (1) the value of a nonprofessional teaching assisting in the work of a resident classroom teacher; (2) the contribution of a teaching assistantship as an experimental frame of reference for foundation professional courses, for graduate study in the teaching field, for teaching methodology, and for student teaching; (3) the value of extended parallel academic courses, professional theory, and field experiences; (4) the possibilities, in teacher education and in actual teaching, of restructuring instruction in terms of recent technological developments in teaching aids; (5) the developmental possibilities inherent in a sequence of laboratory experiences beginning with a teacher assistantship, moving into student teaching, then into an internship, and finally, in the third year, into regular, fully responsible teaching; and (6) the quality of teacher-scholars who can be attracted to a most rigorous and extended program of preparation for high school teaching.

Since the program was to involve a unique and necessarily close cooperation among elements of the School of Education, the local public schools, and the graduate academic departments of the University, a full year was given over to planning and organizing, with particular attention to the establishment of satisfactory working relationships and procedures among personnel of these disparate segments of the academic world.

The University provided an unused bungalow as headquarters for the project. Remodeling and furnishing to fit the operation was begun in time for the opening of the 1959–60 academic year and the arrival of Catherine Clark, who was to serve as adminis-

52

trative secretary throughout the project's term.[30] Joining the staff in 1959 were John Wilding and Merle B. Marks, both experienced schoolmen and doctoral candidates in the School of Education. Marks, having obtained his doctorate, remained on the staff throughout the experiment and, following Calvert's death in 1964, assumed the role of acting director. In August 1960, Robert Hammond, a graduate student experienced in teacher training at the college level, was added on a full-time basis to replace Wilding who departed for another position having obtained his doctorate.

On October 8, 1959, the Los Angeles City Board of Education took official action "to cooperate with the University in the new program beginning February 1, 1960, and continuing to February 1, 1966." It also announced its intention to consider the placement of district funds in the budget, beginning with the fiscal year 1962–63, to meet the expenses of the teacher-assistant phase of the program, and approved a tentative statement of duties for teacher assistants, a new classification, developed cooperatively by the University and the Los Angeles district's divisions of personnel and secondary education.

In December 1959, an advisory committee was formed to advise, in conjunction with the University Council on Teacher Education, on matters concerning the project. This committee, chaired by Dean Melbo, comprised representatives of the School of Education, the University at large, and the Los Angeles City School District.[31]

---

30. Mrs. Clark was secretary to the president, Pepperdine University from 1942 to 1948. Following conclusion of the project, she became secretary with the Department of Teacher Education, and thereafter senior secretary in the Department of Administration and Supervision. Her competency, devotion to duty, and helpfulness were of an unending quality.

31. Members included, in addition to Dean Melbo: Wendell E. Cannon, director, Teacher Education, School of Education; from the University at large: C. S. Copeland, Chemistry Department; Milton C. Kloetzel, dean of The Graduate School; Bruce R. McElderry, Jr., acting head, Department of English; John K. Steinbaugh, Director of Admissions; and Tracy E. Strevey, dean of the College of Letters, Arts, and Sciences; and from the Los Angeles city schools Ellis A. Jarvis,

53

During the academic year 1959–60, recruitment, characterized by the head of the personnel division of the Los Angeles school system as the most extensive he had ever seen, was carried out and more than 300 applicants were interviewed.[32] In February 1960, five "pioneers" were selected to test the role of instructional assistant at the Susan Miller Dorsey High School, Los Angeles. Evaluation of their performance enabled the staff to plan more effectively for the initiation of the project in the city schools, beginning September 1960.

Directed Teaching Facilities. Since 1940 on a formal basis, and much earlier on an informal, the USC School of Education had arranged with the Los Angeles Board of Education for directed teaching in the city's public schools.[33] During the 1953–59 period,

---

superintendent; William B. Brown, associate superintendent, Division of Personnel; and Robert E. Kelly, associate superintendent, Division of Secondary Education.

32. More than 10,000 brochures were printed; 1,000 announcements for bulletin boards prepared; 11,000 letters to individuals and colleges sent; and many oral presentations made to schools and professional organizations. News coverage was rated excellent. Screening involved receipt of more than 1,000 letters of inquiry and interview of 325 persons. Of these, 100 were encouraged to prepare applications, and 49 were accepted in 1959–60.

33. As early as 1920, Dean Rogers had negotiated agreements with the Los Angeles city schools for the conduct of student teaching in schools at the elementary level. In 1928, these arrangements were extended to the secondary level. Prior to 1928, secondary directed teaching was conducted at University High School, and outgrowth of the former Academy. The Academy had been founded by Professor and Mrs. O. S. Frambes in 1876, and had been adopted by the Southern California Conference of the Methodist Episcopal Church as its own. When the University of Southern California was established in 1880, the Academy was incorporated into the University structure as its preparatory school. Following the granting in 1911 of the right of the University of Southern California to confer the high school teachers' certificate, the Academy's course was expanded, its name change to University High School, and its facilities used for the required student teaching. From 1918 to 1928, the University High School was under the general control of the School of Education and the Dean of the School appointed its principal. It will be recalled that in 1922, Dean Rogers appointed Merrit M. Thompson principal of University High School. As the School of Education grew, the directed teaching facilities of University High School became inadequate. In 1928, therefore, arrangements were made to conduct all directed teaching in designated schools of the city of Los Angeles, a decision supported by Weersing, then

54

under the dean's impetus, the number of participating schools increased from 14 to 57 (18 elementary schools, 19 junior high schools, and 20 high schools) located in the greater metropolitan area.

Teachers of the Deaf. A significant advance in special education was made in January 1954, when the University of Southern California and the John Tracy Clinic combined their resources to offer a program to train teachers of the deaf, especially the deaf of preschool age.[34] Under the arrangements negotiated by Melbo, courses and credits were transferred to the School of Education and the director of the clinic and a number of his staff received dual appointments with the clinic and the School of Education. No budgetary commitments were entailed.

Many advantages accrued from the arrangement, both to the clinic and the School of Education. The School was enriched with access to the clinic's facilities, which included attractive classrooms, well-equipped clinic rooms, audio-visual equipment, and a specialized library. During the University's summer session, the

---

director of Teacher Training; Rogers, dean of the School; and von Klein-Smid, president of the University (Levitt 1970, pp. 203–208). The cooperative teaching education staffing arrangements, first with the city of Los Angeles and later with school districts in the greater metropolitan area, were beneficial to both the University and cooperating districts.

34. The John Tracy Clinic, located at 806 West Adams Boulevard, Los Angeles, not far from the campus of the University of Southern California, was founded in 1942 by Spencer and Louise Tracy, whose son, John, in whose honor the clinic was named, suffered from deafness. In that year, President von Klein-Smid offered Mrs. Tracy and a group of mothers of deaf children the use of a small house on the fringe of the campus, where the clinic is now located. The clinic developed over the years a variety of services in an effort to reach as many parents as possible, including consultations, a demonstration home, classes for parents, nursery school, weekly clinic day, psychological counseling, correspondence course, summer session, and teacher training course. A broad program of continuing research on problems related to the education of young deaf children and their parents was also conducted. All services were provided free of charge, the clinic's operating budget being totally financed by private, voluntary contributions. President of the Board of Directors and director in charge was Mrs. Spencer Tracy; administrator was Dr. Edgar L. Lowell, Ph.D., nationally and internationally recognized authority on the education and problems of the deaf and hard of hearing.

55

clinic provided full-time comprehensive experience for teachers and graduate students who had had training in education of the deaf. The clinic, in turn, benefited through the coordination of the specialized training of the teacher of the deaf with courses in nursery school philosophy, child growth and development, and the adjustment and guidance of parents of the deaf.

The pattern of relationship between the School and the clinic was one which was to be repeated with reference to other programs developed by the School of Education. "I believe," said Melbo in 1973, "all professional preparation programs should have a clinical component—[35]

> where students may experience the realities of the work they are preparing to enter. These clinical components can be obtained by the development of cooperative working agreements between the University and the operating organization or agency. There is clearly a *quid pro quo* for each party to such an arrangement. The agreement with the Tracy Clinic was the first of a series of such joint activities.

The Reading Center. Establishment of a reading center at the University was a major move toward bringing the University of Southern California into step with other leading universities across the country. General policy development was vested in the faculty of the School of Education, with coordination responsibility that of the chairman of the Department of Elementary Education. Direct management of the center was assigned to the director of the Reading Center.

In June 1955, Melbo selected as first director, Charles M. Brown, with responsibility to develop the Reading Center program. By February 1956, a former barracks, Building Q, 3615 South Hoover Street, had been rehabilitated to house the function of the center and in March 1956, Brown moved his office to that location.

Major functions of the center were to provide a situation and facilities to implement instruction in the professional aspects of

35. Personal interview, April 1973.

the teaching of reading, the professional preparation of classroom teachers in that field, and advanced instruction of graduate students who were to become specialists in that area. Reading improvement services were also offered to persons of public school age and to students of the University who desired reading improvement.

During 1956, remedial and corrective work was undertaken, with some work performed by graduate students in educational psychology and guidance. In 1957, part-time instructors were used, and the program was expanded to include high school basic reading and study skills. In that year, also, Brown visited reading centers at other leading universities to observe their program. In his second annual report to Dean Melbo, he modestly but prophetically wrote:[36]

> As the center continues to gain experience, modify its procedures, and grow in professional esteem, its value as an asset to the University and the community should increase.

Veterans Counseling Center. The presence of large numbers of veterans on campus following the end of the Korean conflict in 1953, brought the need for special assistance in guidance and counseling. On the initiative of Wagner and Carnes, a contract was negotiated with the Veterans Administration for the establishment and operation of a veterans counseling center. The center began operations in January 1954, with eligibility limited to those referred by the Veterans Administration. First considered in terms of a two-year operation, the center was continued until 1960, handling approximately 75 veterans each month.

The center was first located at 926 West 35th Street. Later, because of the crowded conditions on campus, relocation became necessary. The center was finally located on Jefferson Boulevard in a former city jail which was rehabilitated for counseling use. The first staff consisted of Robert M. Baker, head counselor, with a staff of four counselors and a psychometrist. In 1956 and 1957, respectively, Baker was succeeded by John T. Palmer and Loren Gray.

---

36. *Agenda,* January 13, 1958.

57

The center, which operated as an activity of the Department of Guidance and with Carnes as faculty supervisor, also provided certain internships and laboratory opportunities for graduate students of that department. The Veterans Counseling Center was thus another of the clinical components which the dean so earnestly sought as a means of upgrading the professional character of the School's teacher training programs.

Counseling Institute. In the summer of 1959, June 29 to August 27, was held what was to be the first of a series of counseling institutes at the University of Southern California under the auspices of the School of Education.[37] Conducted by Carnes, the institute provided advanced counseling instruction and experience to 40 experienced high school counselors.

International Teacher Program. Since the days of President von KleinSmid, the University of Southern California had been heavily involved in international education.[38] In line with this tradition and the growing interest of the United States in international education, the School of Education, from 1955 on, was host annually during the fall semester to some 30 educators and students from various foreign nations for special graduate study in secondary education.[39]

---

37. The institute operated under a $40,000 contract with the Department of Health, Education and Welfare, funded under Title V-B of the National Defense Education Act of 1958 (PL 85–864).

38. President von KleinSmid's inauguration reflected his interest in international affairs. It was attended by 400 delegates to the Pan American Conference then (April, 1922) being held in Los Angeles, and his inaugural address was entitled, "A World View of Education." Honorary degrees were conferred on eight dignitaries from foreign countries. Von KleinSmid was also instrumental in founding the School of Public Administration in 1928 and in the development of a pioneering international relations program in the mid-30s. In 1967, the University created the von KleinSmid Center for International and Public Affairs, and in 1970 erected the building of that name.

39. The program was one facet of the International Teacher Education Program sponsored by the U.S. Office of Education in cooperation with the Department of State. Selection of the University of Southern California to participate in the secondary portion of the program was assisted by the good impression Dr.

As carried out by the Department of Secondary and Higher Education, the program was divided into two phases: university and community. The university phase comprised seminars and informal lectures and a "Fellow by Courtesy" arrangement under which the educators could audit any class in any department of the University. The community phase included conducted visits to schools, industries, and cultural centers, as well as informal visits in homes. The spirit of the program was caught by Dean Melbo's words: "We give of ourselves to others that of others we may gain understanding." In the foreword to the brochure issued at the conclusion of the first program, he wrote:[40]

> For three months this heterogeneous group of world citizenry grew in understanding of America, Americans, and each other and, perhaps, in a broader sense, the world.
>
> Indeed, we who have been privileged to work in this program can think of no more expressive or desirable way of reporting and evaluating than by a thematic presentation of our report via the medium of 'WE—An Experiment in International Understanding.'

A thoughtful reaction from a young German was typical of the educators' reaction:[41]

> As to what I shall take with me to my country there is first of all deep gratitude for the friendliness and the kind forebearance with our shortcomings and peculiarities, the unselfish will to help us and give us as much as possible which was shown in such abundance. The second is more specifically professional: The realization that people here believe more strongly in education than in our country and that they are willing to provide the

Thomas E. Cotner of the U.S. Office of Education received of the University as a possible host to the international educators. "I had invited my friend, Dr. Cotner," said Dean Melbo in 1973, "to visit the campus and the Los Angeles area as my guest. He did, and was impressed with what we could offer. We reached an unofficial but nonetheless effective agreement following an afternoon of ping-pong and swimming at my home." (Tape recording, April 1973) Selected with the University of Southern California for the secondary portion of the program were the University of Oklahoma and the University of Buffalo.

40. University of Southern California, School of Education (1955), p. 5.
41. University of Southern California, School of Education (1955), p. 63.

59

means for it which they are fortunate enough to have to a larger extent than we. I also realized that we should try more earnestly to make all young people in our country share at least part of their experiences, as it is done here under the roof of one common school of all.... I do *not* believe in the same type of education for everybody, but I do believe in the necessity of bringing the different branches of our educational system closer together through common social, recreational, athletic, and cultural activities. This is an ideal which solidified while I was here watching the advantages of this system of general high school education. We cannot imitate or copy or transplant it; what is more, we should not; but striving to avoid its disadvantages, we should try to adopt and adapt its values.

Junior College Project. The rapid growth of community and junior colleges during the 1950s, and the increased number of students attending these institutions, engendered a critical need for instructors in certain areas. To meet the need, the University of Southern California announced in March 1958, the design of a special accelerated program within the School of Education to prepare teachers for the junior college. This program, known as the Junior College Project, was offered to persons qualified or qualifying for the master's degree in fields which cooperating districts declared as areas of critical teacher scarcity. Candidates were provided with the professional preparation needed to qualify for the California general junior college teaching credential while teaching on provisional certificate. Participating districts were East Los Angeles College, El Camino College, Los Angeles Metropolitan College of Business, and Los Angeles City College. Districts which entered the program in 1960 were: Los Angeles Trade Technical College, Los Angeles Valley College, and Los Angeles Harbor College.

Advanced Study Centers. Beginning in 1956, Melbo expanded the range of the School of Education by offering graduate courses in Education through the Community Service Division of University College. These courses were designed specifically for professional educators whose work schedules and distance from campus (from 10 to 200 miles and averaging 60) made it difficult for them

60

to pursue professional course work on campus. "Our concept," reported the dean to alumni groups, "is to take the University to the field. It is also a recruitment program whereby students begin off campus and then come to the campus for courses which enable them to complete a degree or credential objective."

The program, conducted on an experimental basis in Ventura by Nelson and in Riverside by Stoops in 1956, proved so successful that it was expanded in ensuing years to four centers each year. The general plan was to rotate location of the Centers in order to serve the widest number of persons. Locations over the years included such widely scattered places as Anaheim, El Centro, Indio, Little Lake School District, Pomona, Riverside, San Bernardino, Santa Ana, Santa Barbara, Santa Cruz, Torrance, Tulare, Ventura, and Victorville in California and Clark County, Nevada. In the summer of 1956, the first courses offered outside the continental United States were also conducted when Calvert and Larsen offered classes in secondary education in Anchorage, Alaska.

Standards for admission were the same as for graduate courses on campus; and courses were taught solely by regular or adjunct faculty in the rank of assistant professor or higher. The firm adherence to this policy was an important factor in consumer satisfaction and in the phenomenal growth of the off-campus program in the decades ahead both within the United States and overseas. Another factor of great importance of the success of the program was the cooperation of the county superintendent of schools, adjoining school districts, and nearby institutions of higher education.

Graduate Degrees

Master of Science in Education. During the 1953–59, requirements for the degree of Master of Science in Education were gradually streamlined and tightened. Important changes included: raising the required scholastic average in graduate course work; placement of a time limitation on project completion; substitution of

61

the Advanced Test of the Graduate Record Examinations for the Professional Aptitude Test as the required test for admission to candidacy; and reduction in the amount of transfer credits accepted from other schools from eight to four.[42]

M.S. in Ed. degrees granted by the University of Southern California from 1954 through 1960 numbered 3,162 or an average of 450 annually. The project study path to the degree was by far the more popular, accounting for approximately 87 per cent of the degrees granted.[43]

The concern of the School of Education for the welfare of the public school teacher was shown in November 1953, when the faculty unanimously approved credit reinstatement to teachers who were faced with difficulties not of their own making. In that year, the Los Angeles City School District adopted a regulation to require possession of the master's degree in order to advance to a

---

42. In 1954, the required scholastic average in all graduate course work attempted was raised from 1.75 to 2.75 (B−). The time limitation imposed was one year following the end of the semester in which the project studies seminar was taken, with the possibility of one year's extension upon petition. Further extensions were not allowed. The required test for admission to candidacy underwent several changes. In 1954, those who planned to continue beyond the Master's degree to the doctorate were advised to take the GRE instead of the PAT. In 1958, acceptable scores on the Advanced Test of the GRE covering the area of education were required, although those who had completed the PAT, as required for the teaching credential, were not required to take the Advanced Test of the GRE. Limitation on the amount of transfer credit accepted from other schools was placed in effect in 1959. For details see *Bulletins* for 1952–54, 1954–56, 1956–58, and 1958–60.

43. Brown (1961) analyzed selected data pertaining to Master's degrees in Education at the University of Southern California 1947–60. The study revealed that, of the 6,074 degrees granted, 5,281 or 87 per cent were granted on submission of project study; 793 or 13 per cent on submission of thesis. This ratio was in line with the national trend, which indicated that, of the 29,222 master's in Education degrees granted throughout the United States 1959–60, 25,993 or 88 per cent were granted without submission of thesis. Brown's study concluded that the project method was considered a practical approach to current school issues, was most usually limited to a local school plan or district situation, and was most often selected by practicing classroom teachers in the public schools, and to a lesser extent by public school administrators, as the preferred alternate path to the degree.

62

maximum on the salary scale. Teacher groups had protested that many of their members could not meet the proposed effective date because their graduate credits would be outlawed under the prevailing seven-year rule on credit validity. On Melbo's recommendation, the faculty approved a policy under which the seven-year rule pertaining to the outlawing of credits was automatically waived for all candidates for graduate professional degrees in the School of Education[44]

> who were in good standing at the University at the time of their last work and who have been subsequently employed in a professional capacity in the field of education and who are now in good standing as such an employee or who were in good standing at the time of such last employment.

Doctoral Program. The notable increase in the number of doctoral candidates in the field of education, observed during the postwar period, continued during the 1953–60 period at an accelerated rate. From an average of 29 doctoral graduates each year during the eight-year period 1946–53, the number leapt to an average of 50 each year for the period 1953–60. The number of Ed.D.s exceeded the number of Ph.D.s in Education by approximately five to one (251 Ed.D.s and 51 Ph.D.s in Education). The area of educational administration continued to be the most popular field, accounting for 100 Ed.D.'s and 1 Ph.D. in Education, or 41 per cent of all doctoral degrees in the field of education during the 1953–60 period.

Larger numbers of candidates for the doctorate necessitated increased attention to policies on screening and guidance. Major policy changes in the doctoral program, all aimed at tightening requirements, included the addition of a fifth examination in the candidate's major field to the comprehensive examination; inclusion in that examination of questions on elementary statistics; increase of unit requirements in the doctoral year from 20 to 24; and a time limitation for completion of the dissertation after being

---

44. *Minutes,* November 2, 1953.

63

admitted to full candidacy, following the qualifying examination. The time limitation, three calendar years, was applicable to persons who were admitted to candidacy after September 1, 1954. Those admitted before that date continued to have four calendar years before petitioning for time extension.

Procedural changes in the program included in 1957, reduction of the student's committee on studies to three persons; submission of a dissertation proposal to the Office of the Assistant Dean three weeks before the qualifying examination; and augmentation of the committee on studies to five persons for purposes of conducting the oral examination following completion of the dissertation.

Education Library

In 1956, the Visitation Committee on Accreditation had found the Education Library well organized and staffed satisfactorily. Especially commended was the curriculum library, which had been established to replace the former curriculum laboratory. A progress report in January 1955, from the head librarian of the Education Library, Leroy W. Otto, eloquently set forth to Dean Melbo the task which had been involved in setting up the curriculum library:[45]

> The tearing apart of the mass of material that was sent over here from the old Curriculum Laboratory was quite a task in itself. There was a tremendous amount of material to go through. This material has been separated into appropriate groups. There were of course many textbooks. Then there were quite a few Los Angeles city publications. About 200 courses of study were in there. Some L.A. County publications were in it. Some standardized tests were also included. After I saw the wealth of material that came over, I am glad that you encouraged me to take the entire collection instead of burning all but the texts. . . .
>
> Despite all the work that has been done this fall semester,

45. "Progress report on Education Library," *Agenda,* February 14, 1955.

64

much still remains. For instance, all pamphlet material (or most of it) in the collection I sorted and much folder material was set aside to cull through at some later date. This is equivalent to a mere 10 or 12 bushels. So you see there is still a long job ahead.

To insure the currency of the curriculum library, Dean Melbo established in November 1956, a special Curriculum Library Committee, with general responsibility to expedite expansion and development of an appropriate collection of materials. In 1963, he also arranged to have the University of Southern California's School of Education designated as one of the depository sites for state curriculum materials under California's Regional Curriculum Materials Depository system.[46] As a result of these efforts, the Education Library had by 1973, as Dean Melbo noted with justifiable pride, "a truly excellent body of resources in this area of educational activity."

Special Collections. Special collections form an important part of the holdings of the Education Library. The first was that of Dean Emeritus Stowell, presented in 1923, to supply research materials for the School of Education. From that nucleus devel-

---

46. In 1963, after five years of study and deliberations, this system of depositories began operation. An activity of the California State Steering Committee on Publications and Curriculum, the system was organized through the efforts of the Publications and Curriculum Steering Committee of the County Superintendents Association in cooperation with the California Association of School Librarians and the California State Department of Education. The sites for these depositories are located in five county school departments, 14 state colleges, and two universities (University of California at Santa Barbara and the University of Southern California). Collections are kept current and as complete as possible through the contributions of school districts and county school departments which deposit two copies of each new curriculum publication as it is produced. One of the copies is circulated and one kept in a non-circulating reference collection so that a complete collection is always available. Each depository has agreed to make the deposited materials available to any person engaged in curriculum development and study, whether that person in associated with the particular institution or not. Head of the Curriculum Materials Depository at the University of Southern California in 1973 was Janet Harvey, head librarian, Education Library.

oped, through gifts, the Stowell Research Library.[47] Largely as a result of Dean Melbo's special interest, a number of other collections have been added in recent years. Among these are the John A. Sexson Collection, presented by Margaret Sexson in 1954,[48] the Jessie Graham Research Library Fund,[49] the Claude L. Reeves Memorial Instructional Materials Collection,[50] and

---

47. In 1923, Mary Blakeslee Stowell offered the personal library of her husband as a nucleus for a special educational research library. In 1924, a large number of volumes were added through gifts of Juliette Blake Koepfli, Dean Rogers, and others. The bookplate designating these gifts contains a photograph of Dean Stowell and the New Testament inscription (II *Tim.* 2:15) "A workman that needeth not to be ashamed." For an example, see the Education Library's copy of *Twelve Lectures on the History of Pedagogy* by W. N. Hallman.

48. John Amherst Sexson was born November 6, 1881, in Nebraska. He took his professional degrees in Colorado and taught there prior to becoming, in 1924, Superintendent of Schools, Bisbee, Arizona. In 1928, he was appointed Superintendent of Schools, Pasadena, California, an office he held until his retirement in 1948. A figure of great prominence in state and national educational associations, Sexson was president of the California Teachers Association, 1935–39; president of the American Association of School Administrators, 1938–39, the second Californian to be elected to this important post, the first having been Joseph Marr Gwinn, Superintendent of Schools of San Francisco, in 1927; and for many years a member of the National Education Policies Commission, sponsored jointly by the National Education Association and the American Association of School Administrators. Following his retirement, Sexson was for a time lecturer in educational administration with the School of Education. He died April 14, 1952.

49. Jessie Graham was the first woman in business education to receive the doctorate degree in the United States (Ph.D., USC, 1933). She retired in 1956 after many years with the Los Angeles public schools, and following her retirement was lecturer with the School of Education. The fund in her honor was established by the Psi Chapter (USC) of Delta Pi Epsilon, honorary graduate business education fraternity.

50. Claude Lamar Reeves died October 22, 1956, while serving as superintendent, Los Angeles city schools, a position to which he had been appointed in 1954. He was born near Mountain View, Missouri, November 11, 1893; and received his B.A. (1920) and M.A. (1928) from the University of Southern California. He was president of the student body 1919–20. From 1921 to 1949 he served as principal in a number of high schools in the Los Angeles area (Bell High School, 1925; Huntington Park High School, 1938–45; and Los Angeles High School 1945–49). In 1949, he was named assistant superintendent in charge of all high schools; and in 1954 superintendent. Commented the *Los Angeles Times* at the time of his death: "Claude L. Reeves was an excellent executive and had a sure grasp of the difficult problems of his office." (*Los Angeles Times,* October 24, 1956). Beset by

66

the A. Glenwood Walker Memorial Test Collection,[51] the latter two the gift of their colleagues in the Los Angeles schools.

The deep personal interest which Melbo as dean consistently manifested in the Education Library was based on several considerations. First, there was a firm conviction that a strong library was essential to a strong professional school of education. As dean he was committed to do anything he could to increase the holdings of the library and to make its general collection current and up to date, as well as broad in its coverage of the fields represented by the training program. Second, and perhaps even more significant in certain respects, was his grave consideration of securing for the library certain rare collections of books as a cultural and professional addition to the Education Library's resources. Third, was his generous wish to memorialize in some tangible expression those noted educators who had been connected with the School of Education. "I realized," he said in 1973:[52]

> that there were many people in the field who had maintained private libraries of some significance on their own account and that frequently these were neglected, or at least uncared for, after the person who had developed them was no longer personally involved. I had often thought that it might be possible to obtain some of such private library holdings in various professional fields as an additional resource for the School of Education library.
>
> The first opportunity to do this came at the time of the death of Dr. John A. Sexson, who was the long-time superintendent of the Pasadena city schools, a man of national reputation and distinction, and who, after his retirement, had come to our faculty to teach with us parttime in the field of educational administration. I was fortunate enough to have shared a small private office with him in the Bovard Administration Building

---

many difficulties such as teacher salaries, tax ceiling increases, and budget restrictions, his term of office was nevertheless markedly harmonious.

51. A. Glenwood Walker, a graduate student at the School of Education in 1943, was for eight years director of the Los Angeles Office of the Educational Testing Service. In his memory a gift of money was received for the purchase of a file of specimen tests to be selected by the faculty and placed in the Education Library (*Agenda*, March 17, 1958).

52. Tape recording, April 1973.

at the time and thereby to have become quite well acquainted on a personal basis with him. After his passing, I went to talk with his wife, Margaret, with respect to Dr. Sexson's private library and she was most willing to turn over his books and also his files of private writings on various subjects.

In discussing this matter with her, I had suggested that it was appropriate to develop a memorial for her husband and that this collection might well become one aspect of such a memorial. I therefore arranged to have a special bookplate designed with a photograph of Dr. Sexson and wording which indicated that this was a memorial to him and that the book in which the bookplate would subsequently be placed was a gift to the John A. Sexson Memorial Collection from his wife, Margaret. She liked this very much and to this date many of the books in the Education Library have a bookplate commemorating the gift and memorializing Dr. Sexson.

In conference with the Education librarian, it was decided not to house such collections separately for the most part, but rather to use the classification system which was extant in the library and to locate these gift volumes with proper identification in terms of the classification system. They thereby were put on the shelves as they related to the subject field and were available for general circulation rather than limited use.[53]

The concept of the memorial collection was later applied to Mr. Claude L. Reeves, who as superintendent of the Los Angeles city schools was a man with whom I had worked closely on a personal as well as a professional basis. At the time of his passing, I went to see some of the members of his family and his colleagues in the Board of Education. They all were interested in doing something by way of memorial for Mr. Reeves and I suggested that perhaps the most appropriate thing would be a collection of curriculum materials to which the Los Angeles Board of Education could contribute, using the designation "The Claude L. Reeves Memorial Instructional Materials Collection." At the same time, I offered the suggestion to some of Mr. Reeves'

53. This system has been followed with respect to all collections with the exception of such rare book collections as the Donald E. Wilson Old Textbook Collection, according to Janet Harvey, head librarian, Education Library, 1973.

START OF A NEW ERA: 1953–1959

colleagues that they might wish to contribute money to the development of a fund which could later be used to purchase materials to the collection.

This was done with very good results. . . . Later other funds came to supplement the amount originally obtained, and to this date funds have been available and have been used for this purpose.

I decided to continue the concept of expanding the School of Education Library and of enriching its resources by the device of the memorial collection, whenever that was possible. . . . This particular device is a rather inexpensive way of adding substantial resources, sometimes of such significance and magnitude that they could never be obtained directly by a library no matter how much money might have been involved. But perhaps more important, it is necessary for a mature school of education to have various kinds of memorials in existence whether these be scholarships or chairs or buildings or library collections. It is important to recognize and honor those who have made the effort to bring such important collections of learning and instructional materials together. If such persons happen to be alumni of the School of Education, it is all the more reason to provide a recognition of their work and contribution.

Reports of Survey

It will be recalled that, with Hull's appointment as dean of the School of Education in 1946, responsibility for the school surveys Hull had been conducting devolved upon Melbo. In succeeding years, through more than a hundred such surveys, the name of Melbo became recognized as the foremost authority in America in the areas of executive leadership and the organization and structure of school districts. Melbo succeeded to this mantle with the passing of the noted authorities, Strayer and Engelhardt, who are credited with devising school surveys as a means of analyzing the strengths and weaknesses of school districts. In breadth of scope, size of effort, and depth of analysis, however, Melbo's surveys surpassed all which had gone before and remain unrivaled in their

69

field. Widely read and acclaimed for their thoroughness, their factual analysis of educational needs and problems, and their highly practical recommendations, the Melbo reports of survey had a profound effect upon the educational practices and theories of school and district administration.

The surveys fall into two major classifications: general (encompassing all aspects of a school district) and special (concentrating upon one or more aspects such as administration, district organization, future district planning, educational planning and programming, and school housing and plant needs).

Staff for a general survey of average size and complexity numbered about 13, of whom the majority were educational specialists with two or three field assistants drawn from graduate students or assistants in educational administration at the School of Education. Six of the general surveys, however, were assigned a staff of 20 or more members, the largest survey having been that of the Phoenix Union High Schools and Phoenix College System, conducted in Phoenix, Arizona, during July, 1954, for which a staff of 32 was assembled.

Recognizing the need to call upon specialists both from within the University and outside, Melbo drew upon resources encompassing broad competencies. From within the University were drawn specialists in art, business education, chemistry, cinema, English, foreign languages, history, library science, music education, physical education, and the sciences. Most closely associated with Melbo in the surveys were Nelson and LaFranchi of the Department of Administration and Supervision of the School of Education. Each participated in nearly all the surveys, frequently acting as associate director with Melbo. Other members of the faculty who were frequent participants were Cannon, Georgiades, Hull, Muelder, Perry, Stoops, Wagner, and Wilson. Among those whose services were enlisted from outside agencies were Charles C. Carpenter, assistant superintendent, Los Angeles County schools; Donald D. Cunliffe, construction engineer, Los Angeles city schools; and Robert Fisher, personnel director for the Los Angeles Unified School District Personnel Commission.

70

Teams for special surveys ranged in number from three to 15. Notable again for frequent participation were Nelson and LaFranchi. Special surveys tended to reflect the changing needs of the school districts. During the late 1940s and 1950s, school housing and plant needs were the major areas of concentration; during the 1960s, district organization and future district planning were prominent areas of concentration.

Most of the surveys concerned themselves with the public school system, K-12. Several, however, such as the surveys of the Phoenix, Arizona schools (1954), Cerritos Junior College (1959), Citrus Junior College (1965), and Palo Verde (1964), dealt with higher education, as did the two surveys conducted overseas: that of the University of Teheran, Iran (1958), and Soche Hill College, Malawi, Africa (1966). (See Appendix D for a listing of educational surveys conducted with Melbo as director, 1947–1972.)

Teheran University Survey. Under a contract between the University of Southern California and the International Cooperation Administration,[54] and at the original request of the chancellor, University of Teheran, Teheran, Iran, a survey of that institution was undertaken in May 1958, with Melbo as coordinator. The survey team, composed of five distinguished educators in addition to Dean Melbo,[55] represented the highest level of educational judgment and expertise.

The team's report dealt with the organization of the university, its major functions, instructional program, personnel processes, student personnel services, and national service program.

---

54. The International Cooperation Administration (ICA) was the Federal Government's agency for the administration of foreign aid from July 1, 1955 to November 3, 1961. With the passage of the Foreign Assistance Act, November 4, 1961, ICA was succeeded by the Agency for International Development (AID).

55. Members of the survey team were: from the University of Southern California: Tracy E. Strevey, dean of the College of Letters, Arts, and Sciences; George T. Harness, Associate Dean, School of Engineering; Earl V. Pullias, professor of Higher Education; Henry Reining, dean of the School of Public Administration (consultant); and Irving R. Melbo, dean of the School of Education (coordinator); and from the University of California at Davis, Stanley B. Freeborn, provost.

71

The wise restraint of the report with regard to the application of its recommendations was reflected in the report's prefatory remarks:[56]

> The specific procedures can best be worked out by the chancellor and the faculties of the University of Teheran, guided by their wisdom, knowledge of local conditions, and long experience. The survey team has no inclination to project personal opinions into its recommendations or to suggest the adoption of the local procedures of any country. Every attempt has been made to put all recommendations in terms of fundamental principles that are applicable to the development of an excellent university in any modern nation.
>
> In short, these principles must be applied if a society desires the great benefits of a modern, flexible, developing university which serves the needs of a dynamic, developing country. At the same time, the survey team is fully aware that these principles must be applied with wisdom and skill, taking into account the needs, traditions, and customs of Iran. However, the survey team believes it would be a tragedy for the University and for the country, if loyalty to traditions and procedures totally unsuited to a modern nation should serve as an excuse to block the use of methods necessary to the programs and welfare of the University and of the nation.

Professional-Public Relations

The growing reputation of the School of Education and the increasing professionalization of its faculty, as well as the heightened interest of the nation in educational problems, brought about in the 1950s a vastly expanded field for professional-public relations on the part of the faculty and the dean.

Among the faculty, leaders in the area of tests and measurements were Thorpe, Naslund, and Lefever. Under the aegis of Science Research Associates of Chicago, they constructed and published a series of innovative tests designed to measure how

56. University of Southern California (1958).

well students had learned.[57] In 1959, Naslund was on special leave from the University to serve as consultant to that firm in the development of curriculum materials. The extreme, perhaps, in the field of management consultantship was demonstrated by Crawford, whose brisk impact on defense installations, firms, and commercial organizations had been felt since the Second World War. Wrote Crawford in one sales magazine:

> The buzz-write workshop has two values: Participation; Integration. The *buzz* involves participating; the *write* involves everyone contributing to the total pool of sales know-how. But the workshop starts and ends with the write. The buzz comes between.

After 38 years of teaching and 30 years on the faculty of the School of Education, Crawford felt compelled to change his status from professor to management consultant. Said he:[58]

> My leaving SC is not retirement but a change of occupation. I am in business, not just a professor to be called on for free advice, as professors often are.

In recognition of his long service to the University, the title of Professor Emeritus of Education was conferred upon him, the first time this recognition had been accorded to any University faculty member other than those who retired from active service because of age.

As dean, Melbo encouraged professional involvement. At the same time, he warned that such involvement must not impair the primary purpose of the School of Education, which was the instructional program and the student. In 1973, he said:[59]

> Quite early in my tenure as dean, I felt that it was necessary, in developing the reputation of the School of Education, to have members of its faculty participate widely in local, regional, and national activities. To this end, I suggested to each department

---

57. In 1954, a set of tests for the elementary grades was published by Thorpe, Naslund, and Lefever, which incorporated an unusual approach of presentation in story form. This series was followed in 1956, by tests for grades at the junior high school level, and in 1957, by a series at the high school level.

58. *Alumni Review,* 38(2), p. 12.

59. Tape recording, April 1973.

73

and to individual members of such departments that one or more of them identify themselves with the principal professional organization in their respective fields of specialization. I suggested also that they should maintain a continuing membership in such organizations and seek to be active in their work, including, if appropriate, holding offices and participating in the conventions, conferences, or other activities and work of such organizations. To the best of our ability, we would, as a matter of policy, finance the travel of faculty members to participate in such organizational meetings and programs. This policy has been carried forward to this date and, as of the present time, almost every member of the faculty has identified himself with at least one professional organization, for which he is in a sense our representative and to which he is in a sense our active participant and spokesman.

After a time, the development of this policy became so widespread that a problem which I had not anticipated began to develop. The problem was that attendance at various national and regional meetings by many of the faculty, particularly when the meetings were concentrated at various points in the school year, almost left the School of Education deserted for manpower. The problem became how to perform the implied responsibilities of meeting the classes for which a professor was scheduled and, at the same time, participate in the national or regional professional activities. I had always taken the point of view that, when a professor was scheduled for a class and this was printed in the semester bulletin or schedule, there was a personal commitment on his part that he was to be present to work with the students for every meeting of that class. This is still basically my feeling on such matters, and I think it essentially a sound policy. Students frequently are attracted to a class because of the reputation of the professor. If that professor were not the designated instructor, they might not have enrolled. This is particularly true for those professors who have become something of a star in their own right and, as such, attract many students who come not only because of the course but more particularly because they want the experience of having worked with that particular professor. Therefore, absences from class, even for such a worthy purpose as presenting a paper at an important national conference, becomes something of a problem.

74

I do not know that there has been a totally satisfactory solution but I have insisted, with very good cooperation from the faculty, that there be a rearranged schedule of meetings so that a meeting which may be lost one day can be picked up on another, involving the services of the professor. This has been done to a considerable extent, and the students have been very good in cooperating with this arrangement and making themselves available for another time than the regularly scheduled class hours and dates. The other approach, of course, has been to locate a satisfactory substitute who could carry forward the work of the class during the absence of the professor, and this has also been done with rather conscientious concern for the responsibility involved.

What I have emphasized is *not* satisfactory is to leave the class unattended, or simply to cancel the meeting of the class without any proper compensating arrangement for making up the time that thus might be lost, or the procedure of having some student assistant, no matter how good, meet with the class on a rather perfunctory basis.

While I recognize that any or all of these things frequently occur in the university world, I do not think they ought to be common occurrences in any professional school, wherein the personal attention and expertise of the professor are so vital a factor in the life and work of his students. At the same time, it is important to release the professor to make his contribution on a wider basis and to enhance his reputation as a professional person and thereby, of course, the reputation of his school. This is a desirable objective and one which I heartily support and have continued to support over the years by obtaining increasingly more and more funds to provide for such kinds of faculty travel and participation with full coverage of expenses. I believe this policy has enhanced both the reputations of the professors and the reputation of the School of Education and the University of Southern California.

I do recognize that there is something of a dilemma involved in handling the matter, but the necessity for a broad base of professional participation and representation is essential to the work of a dynamic and powerful professional school of education. In one year, for which I recently made a tally, I found that we had expended more than $130,000 for faculty travel and

75

participation at various professional meetings and conferences throughout the country—indeed, throughout the world. This was far in excess of any specific budget provision but, through the availability of certain other funds, it has been possible to provide the means by which almost every professor, at least who had a part in a program, could attend and take part.

Needs and Requirements

As perceived by the dean in 1959, short-range needs of the School of Education included the employment of two additional full-time faculty in the fields of counseling and guidance and of secondary education; provision of suitable office space for faculty personnel; tightening of control of student registration in professional courses; improved advisement of students in all programs; and fellowships and scholarships for full-time graduate students.[60]

The most immediate of the long-range needs was a building, or group of buildings, specifically designed to house the functions of the School of Education. As Dean Melbo indicated to the Vice-President, Academic Affairs, the development of new plants by the state-supported institutions in the region had emphasized the lack of specialized facilities for professional work in Education at the University of Southern California. Continued maintenance of the School of Education's status and leadership position would require the development of superior plant facilities of an advanced design, in addition to the continuance of a unique professional faculty and program.[61]

Fiftieth Anniversary

The academic year 1958–1959 marked two important milestones in the history of the School of Education. One was the fortieth

60. "Statement for Planning Committee, October 1959." Faculty Conference, October 3–4, 1959.
61. Memorandum, Melbo to Raubenheimer, subject: Development of the School of Education, dated December 5, 1958.

76

anniversary of its designation as a separate school of education; the other was the fiftieth anniversary of its founding as a department of education. The school decided to honor the second, and during the year numerous congratulatory messages, resolutions, plaques, and citations were received by the school and the dean from national, state, and local organizations.[62]

Perhaps the most perceptive words of appreciation to the school and its loyal and dedicated faculty and dean were spoken by Professor Emeritus Thompson at the Golden Jubilee Banquet held October 16, 1958. Said Thompson:[63]

> From the humble beginning of a small department in an obscure provincial university, the School of Education has become a powerful and dynamic institution in a great international university whose graduates are filling important positions of leadership not only in the United States of America, but also in distant countries of the world. The true history of the School of Education does not lie in these words, but in the devoted and creative service of the staff members and their influence in the lives of the thousands of students who have passed through the school, and furthermore in the lives of untold numbers of children who have been influenced in their turn by the former students. The contribution has been incalculable and immeasureable.

62. Organizations congratulating the School were the National Association of Public School Business Officials, California Association of School Administrators, California Association of Secondary School Administrators, California Association of Elementary School Administrators, and the Los Angeles County School Trustees Association. To Dean Melbo were addressed a joint resolution of the California Legislature (No. 24, of January 20, 1959); and resolutions of the Board of Supervisors, County of Los Angeles (May 26, 1959); Los Angeles County Board of Education (October 6, 1958); City Council, City of Los Angeles (May 27, 1959), and the National Conference of Christians and Jews (February 25, 1959).

63. Thompson (1958). Thompson's address was the principal address of the evening. The banquet was the annual homecoming banquet of the Education Alumni Association, and was cosponsored by the Society of Delta Epsilon, Pi Lambda Theta, Phi Delta Kappa, the Education Council, and the California Student Teachers Association. Norma B. Gibson, president of the Education Alumni Association arranged the program and presided at the banquet, to which greetings were brought by the then newly elected president of the University, Norman H. Topping.

77

RUFUS B. VON KLEINSMID

President, USC (1921-1946), Chancellor (1946-1964).

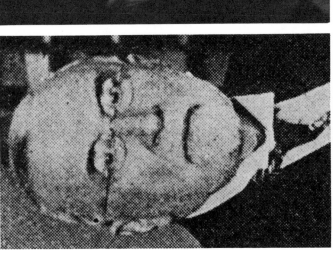

DEANS OF THE SCHOOL OF EDUCATION (1918-1953)

Left to right: Thomas Blanchard Stowell (1846-1927), Dean (1918-1919); Lester Burton Rogers (1875-1959), Dean (1919-1945); Osman Ransom Hull (1890-1968), Dean (1946-1953).

PROFESSORS, SCHOOL OF EDUCATION

Upper left: Frederick J. Weersing (1927-54); **upper right:** Merritt M. Thompson (1921-52); **lower left:** D. Welty Lefever (1926-66); **lower right:** Louis P. Thorpe (1937-65).

FRED D. FAGG, JR.

President, USC (1947-1958).

SELECTION OF A
NEW DEAN (1953)

IRVING R. MELBO
(Photograph 1952)

DEAN HULL AND SELECTION COMMITTEE

Dean Osman R. Hull (seated) meets with faculty committee named by President Fagg in November 1952, to assist in selection of a new dean. **Standing (left to right):** Louis Thorpe; D. Lloyd Nelson, chairman; Elmer E. Wagner, Wendell E. Cannon.

FIFTIETH
ANNIVERSARY
(1958-1959)

Bernard Watson, President, California Elementary School Administrators' Association presents plaque to Dean Melbo. At left is Roy L. Simpson, State Superintendent of Public Instruction. CESAA Annual Conference, San Diego, May 22, 1959.

...elegation from California State Legislature presents the Assembly Concurrent Resolu-
...n (January 20, 1959). Center is President Topping, at left, Dean Melbo.

FIFTIETH ANNIVERSARY, SCHOOL OF EDUCATION (1958-1959)

Presentation of Resolution, Los Angeles County Board of Supervisors, 26 May 1959. **Left to right:** Kenneth Hahn, County

FIFTIETH ANNIVERSARY, SCHOOL OF EDUCATION (1958-1959)

Golden Jubilee Banquet, October 16, 1958. **Left to right:** Dean Melbo; Merritt M. Thompson (speaker); Norma B. Gibson, President, Education Alumni Association; Ellis A. Jarvis, Superintendent, Los Angeles City Schools; Norman Topping, President, USC.

PHILLIPS HAL

WAITE PHILLIPS HALL OF EDUCATIC

CHAPTER 3

Vision and Accomplishment: 1960–1968

What men can visualize, they can also find the will and means to accomplish.

I.R.M. Dedication, Waite Phillips Hall, 1968

The Scene of the '60s

The decade of the 1960s marked for the School of Education, as for the University of Southern California, a period of "meteoric scholastic and physical advancement."[1]

On the national scene, it was the era of the late Presidents John F. Kennedy and Lyndon B. Johnson, whose administrations were dedicated, through massive federal aid, to the spreading of benefits to the masses and to making educational and economic opportunities available to all. Under the guidance of academicians, social philosophers, and social economists, large numbers of Americans came to have a new concern for values which, though always at the heart of the American commitment, had been sub-

---

1. Servin and Wilson (1969), p. 245.

merged to the rush of technological progress. Said John Gardner:[2]

> We found ourselves in a period of unprecedented affluence, and we decided that affluence wasn't enough. We found ourselves in a period of extraordinary technical achievements, and we decided that technical proficiency wasn't enough.
>
> We decided that what we really wanted was a society designed for people:
>> a society in which every young person could fulfill the promise that was in him;
>> a society in which every person, old or young, could live his life with some measure of dignity;
>> a society in which ignorance and disease and want would tyrannize no longer;
>> a society of opportunity and fulfillment.

Ever since the Northwest Ordinances of 1785 and 1787, federal aid to education had been a standing tradition of American culture, and education a public function of national interest. The decade 1958 to 1968, however, brought forth a spate of federal legislation on education unparalleled in the history of not only the United States but of the world. Simply to read the titles of the acts passed in those years is to bring back something of its high hopes.[3]

The years 1964 to 1968 were the years of the Great Society,

---

2. Gardner (1968), p. 12.
3. Important educational legislation included:
   1958: National Defense Education Act (NDEA)
   1961: Area Development Act
   1962: Manpower Development and Training Act (MDTA)
   1963: Health Professions Educational Assistance Act; Higher Education Facilities Act, Vocational Education Act
   1964: Civil Rights Act; Economic Opportunity Act
   1965: Elementary and Secondary Education Act; Higher Education Act; National Foundation on the Arts and Humanities Act; National Vocational Student Loan Insurance Act
   1966: International Education Act, Adult Education Act, Elementary and Secondary Education Amendments
   1967: Education Professions Development Act (EPDA), Public Broadcasting Act
   1968: Elementary and Secondary Education Amendments, Vocational Amendments

80

one of the cornerstones of which was the War on Poverty. Much of the legislation of those years aimed at ameliorating the condition of the disadvantaged, the handicapped, and the mentally retarded; and at devising means for their education and development. Much hope was pinned in the '60s on the use of technology in the form of television, tape, computer, and the teaching machine as teaching-learning devices. The major issue of the times was the crisis of the urban centers, with their large concentrations of the disadvantaged. There, in terms of school enrollment, the minorities had become the majorities. These were the social conditions and the social concepts which profoundly influenced the program of the School of Education.

On the University scene, the School of Education, as a professional school of the University of Southern California, greatly benefited from the new life and vigor imparted by the appointment in 1958, of Norman H. Topping as President of the University. In accepting the presidency, Topping said:[4]

> I fully realize that the community and the university are the important elements in further developing the excellence of the faculty, the quality of the student body, and the total solidarity of the university. Together, with the cooperation of the faculty, and the interest of the alumni, these aims can be realized.

The University's Master Plan, published in 1961 under the title, *The University and the Future,* ushered in an era of enterprise. Excellence became the keyword of the University. Among the goals announced was a building for the School of Education, for many years one of the principal goals of its dean, faculty, and alumni. Other aspects of the Master Plan which affected the School of Education, as well as the University as a whole, were the raising of scholastic standards, curricular reform, reduction of faculty loads, raising of money for research and professional salaries, and increased alumni support.

Not least among the influential factors in the School of Education's advance during the 1960s was its dean, a seasoned admin-

---

4. Topping, Norman H. *Inaugural Address* (1958).

81

THE MELBO YEARS

istrator of courage and foresight, a leader with dynamic and creative ideas, a man not afraid to grasp time by the forelock and bend it to the new demands, as best they could be discerned. In 1962, Melbo challenged his fellow educators to meet the future with high aims and large plans, remembering that there is no turning back to the "good old days":[5]

I am not critical of the past. I am not sure that it is ever appropriate to be critical of the past, because the past is past and it is not very productive to speculate much on what might have been. I think rather it is our concern to be looking ahead, to discern as well as we can the tidal sweep of events which, like the inexorable ebb and flow of the sea, brings changes unseen and unknown even by those who stand on its shores and watch its relentless surge....

The prospect of great change is formidable to many people, and it makes us yearn for the good old days. But there is no turning back. We either lag behind or we move ahead in the operation of our institutions and our programs. The good old days of the past are attractive because they are secure, but they are secure only because they are past. We know what happened, and we know that we survived.

It is the business of the future to be dangerous. The great danger is that we will make the wrong choices. The great opportunity is that we will make the right ones.

This is the time for us to make big plans, to aim high in hopes and work, remembering that a noble plan once recorded will never die.

Organization

The organization of the School of Education continued substantially in the form set during the previous decade. Major facets of governance were the office of the dean, the standing committees, the departments, and the faculty. Changes within these are noted below.

Office of the Dean. In 1962, Wagner, who had served since

5. Melbo, Irving R. *Teachers for Metropolis,* 1962.

82

1951 as assistant dean in addition to his duties as professor of education in the Department of Guidance, returned at his own request to full-time duty with that department.[6] He was succeeded by Wallace R. Muelder, since 1958 a member of the faculty in the Department of Administration and Supervision.[7] By 1966, growth of the student body and the increased number and variety of progams at the School of Education necessitated addition of the position of assistant dean for Graduate Studies and Student Advisement. Edward C. Kelly, since 1963 a member of the faculty in the Department of Secondary Education, was named to that post.[8] In 1968, the positions of assistant dean were upgraded to rank of associate dean in their respective areas.

Other personnel in the office of the dean included, as of 1968, Helen Jones, administrative assistant to the dean, appointed in 1965; Helen Frahm, credential supervisor, appointed in 1955; and Janet Harvey, head librarian, Education Library, appointed in 1966.[9]

Standing Committees. Addition, in 1964, of a library committee

6. Elmer E. Wagner received his B.S. in Ed. (1926) from Southern State Teachers College, South Dakota; his A.M. (1932) from the University of Colorado; and his Ed.D. (1939) from the University of Southern California. From 1926 to 1936, he was high school principal and teacher, Aguilar, Colorado. At the University of Southern California he served as assistant to the dean, School of Education (1939–42) (1945–57) and as professor of education from 1941 to 1973, when he was named professor emeritus.

7. Muelder received his B.S. (1946) at Western Illinois State College, and his M.S. in Ed. (1947) and Ed.D. (1952) at the University of Southern California. Prior to his appointment to the faculty in 1958, he had been chairman, Department of Physics, El Camino College (1947–50); assistant superintendent for Administration, Riverside County Schools, California (1950–55), and superintendent of schools, Palm Springs, California (1955–58).

8. Kelly received his A.A. (1948) at City College of San Francisco; his A.B. (1950) at San Jose State College; his M.A. (1954) at San Francisco State College; and his Ed.D. (1961) at the University of California, Los Angeles. Immediately prior to his appointment to the faculty at the University of Southern California, he had been (1960–63) assistant professor at San Fernando Valley State College.

9. Previous heads of the Education Library (1958–66) were: Lily Hearn (1958–60), Edra C. Bogle (1960–65), Ann Hudson (Acting) (1965), and Joan Silvers (Acting) (1965–66). Mrs. Harvey had had long experience as librarian at various institutions in the Los Angeles area. A graduate of the University of Southern California

83

brought the number of standing committees to six: Curriculum, Organization and Personnel (Central Committee); Doctoral Program; Master's Program; Bachelor's Program; Research and Publication; and Library. In November 1966, two *ad hoc* committees were established: one on governance, the other on retention, tenure, promotion, and salary. As a result of the work of these committees, on which Melbo served *ex officio,* the organization of the School of Education, as of March 1967, was changed in form, although the system of standing committees was retained, and the same committees remained in effect, a few under different nomenclature.[10]

Departments. Until 1962, the School of Education remained organized, as it had been since 1956, into twelve departments: Administration and Supervision, Audio-Visual, Business Education, Elementary Education, Fine Arts, Guidance, Music Education, Physical Education and Health, Psychology, Secondary and Higher Education, Social and Philosophical Foundations of Education, and Teacher Training. In 1962, two changes were made. In March of that year, the Department of Education—Audio-Visual

---

and its School of Library Science, she had served as librarian in Hoover High School, Glendale; the special library of the Los Angeles Transit Lines; the library of the University of Southern California; and from 1956 to 1966, as librarian at Cutler Academy, Los Angeles.

10. Under the 1967 reorganization, faculty participation in the governing process fell within five "schedules," designated Faculty Council; Salary, Promotion, and Tenure Committee; Curriculum Committee; Department Chairmen; and Faculty Committees. The Faculty Council continued the functions of the former Central Committee, with representative, advisory, coordinative, and legislative functions; other committees performed functions as indicated in their titles. Faculty committees, as of 1967, numbered five: Doctoral Program, Master's Program, Bachelor's Program, Research and Publications, and Library. *Ad hoc* committees were appointed as required.

Membership in the Faculty Council and the various committees was predicated for the most part on tenure rank within the faculty and election by faculty members qualified for voting privileges. Chairmen of the various committees were selected by members of the particular committee. One variation was that membership on the Curriculum Committee was determined by lot from among the chairmen of certain curricular areas.

84

was renamed the Department of Instructional Technology.[11] The change in name, together with certain changes in curricular offerings and the establishment of a doctoral program in this area, reflected new concepts of instructional media and the use of mass media in the educational process. Also in 1962, under the stimulus of new social concerns and federal interest in the physically, mentally, and emotionally handicapped, a Department of Exceptional Children was established.

The year, 1964, however, brought a major change in the School's departmental organization. This change, aimed at the better integration and coordination of certain departments, organized the School into two large divisions and four separate departments. The divisions were: Elementary, Secondary, and Higher Education with eight subordinate departments (Adult Education; Art Education; Business Education; Elementary Education; Higher Education; Music Education; Physical Education, Health Education, and Recreation; and Secondary Education); and Psychology, Guidance, and Exceptional Children, a division which encompassed those departments. Departments which remained as separate entities were: Administration and Supervision, Instructional Technology, Social and Philosophical Foundations of Education, and Teacher Training. Under the reorganization, the number of chairmen was reduced to six: chairmen of the two divisions and of the four separate departments. Chiefs of the subordinate departments were referred to as "heads."

In 1966, following changes in California's credential requirements, the departments of Business Education, Fine Arts Education, Music Education, and Physical Education were discontinued within the School of Education, as were all programs for special secondary credentials in these areas. With their discontinuance, the Division of Elementary, Secondary, and Higher Education was

---

11. The name proposed by the department was "Instructional Technology, Instrumentation and Systems." At the faculty's suggestion, the words "Instrumentation and Systems" were omitted (*Minutes,* March 12, 1962).

renamed the Division of Curriculum and Instruction, and its departments reduced in number to three: Elementary Education, Secondary Education, and Higher Education.

In 1968, the division organization was abandoned, and separate departments, each with a chairman, were restored. As of 1968, the departments numbered ten: Administration and Supervision, Counselor Education (formerly Guidance),[12] Elementary Education, Higher Education, Instructional Technology, Educational Psychology, Secondary Education, Social and Philosophical Foundations of Education, Special Education,[13] and Teacher Education (formerly Training).[14]

Faculty. From 1960 to 1968, the number of faculty members of the School of Education, including dual appointments, increased from 90 to 158. (See Appendix E for faculty statistics, 1953–73).

Faculty losses during the period included the death or retirement of a number of distinguished educators connected with the School of Education. Taken by death were three: Leonard Calvert,[15] at the time of his death, December 18, 1964, director of

---

12. The change of name reflected the new emphasis in the field of guidance and new theories of counselor education.

13. Special education was the term adopted nationwide for the education of pupils (such as the deaf, blind, mentally subnormal, gifted, etc.) who deviate so far, physically or mentally from the comparatively homogeneous groups of normal pupils that the standard curriculum is not adaptable to their educational needs. The standard curriculum is modified in content, method of instruction, and expected rate of progress to provide optimum educational opportunity (English and English 1958).

14. The change of name was approved by the faculty at the recommendation of the Department in 1965 (*Minutes,* December 6, 1965).

15. A descendant of Leonard Calvert, younger brother of the second Lord Baltimore and the first governor of Maryland (1633–47), Leonard Calvert was born in Wabeno, Wisconsin, January 21, 1909. He earned his A.B. (1929) at Carroll College, Waukesha, Wisconsin; his M.A. (1933) at Northwestern University; and his Ed.D. (1953) at the University of Southern California. For 25 years a teacher, counselor, and administrator in the public and private schools of the Midwest, Hawaii, and California, Calvert was appointed to the faculty of the School of Education in the Department of Secondary Education in 1954. In 1959, Melbo selected him to direct the High School Specialist Teacher Education Program, a

86

the High School Specialist Teacher Education Program, and about to take a well-deserved sabbatical leave; Sophia Tichnor Salvin, principal for many years of the Washington Boulevard School for Handicapped Children and clinical professor at the School of Education, October 17, 1967;[16] and Osman R. Hull, September 3, 1968.[17] Representing the faculty at Hull's funeral, Cannon made moving tribute to his friend and colleague of many years:[18]

Added during the years 1960–68 to the list of emeritus

five-year project funded by the Ford Foundation's Fund for the Advancement of Education. Calvert had applied for sabbatical leave at the conclusion of the project, in order to do research in the junior college area. In his memory the Leonard Calvert Memorial Seminar Room was established in Waite Phillips Hall.

16. Sophia J. Tichnor Salvin (1904–67) was an internationally recognized authority in the education of handicapped children. For many years she was principal of Washington Boulevard School, the oldest school in the United States for handicapped children. In 1969, the school was renamed in her honor the Sophia T. Salvin School. She had also been associated for many years with the School of Education as lecturer, adjunct professor, and, at the time of her death, clinical professor. In her memory the Sophia Tichnor Salvin Memorial Seminar Room was established in Waite Phillips Hall, and the 1967 issue of the School of Education's Distinguished Lecture Series in Special Education was dedicated to her memory.

17. Hull's death brought to a close the long and active career of one of California's best known educators. Born August 21, 1890, he earned at the University of California, Berkeley, his B.S. (1913), M.S. (1914), and Ph.D. (1924). Prior to his appointment to the faculty of the University of Southern California in 1924, he served in the public schools of northern California, as principal of the high school, Crescent City, 1914–18; district superintendent of schools, Sebastopol, 1918–20; and district superintendent of schools, Napa, 1920-24. He was dean of the School of Education, University of Southern California from 1946 to 1953, when, at his own request, he returned for reasons of health to full-time teaching in the Department of Administration and Supervision. Among his many honors were the national presidency of Phi Delta Kappa (1946–48) and chairmanship of the editorial board of the *Phi Delta Kappan.* Educational administrative offices in Waite Phillips Hall were furnished as a memorial to him.

18. Cannon said, in part: "At a time like this, one is baffled by the terrible gulf between what one would wish to say and one's ability to say it. Those faculty members at the University who have worked with him would rate Dean Hull as indeed a great administrator, teacher, colleague, and friend. I have known many administrators, but no other whom no one wished to have replaced; many teachers, but few whom all students remember with both professional admiration and personal pleasure. Through the years there have been many colleagues for whom I have had extraordinary respect; but if I were forced to choose among them all, Dean Hull would be in the frontmost rank. Without a doubt, the keystone element

87

professors were Louis P. Thorpe in 1965,[19] and D. Welty Lefever in 1966.[20] Both were honored by an honorary degree from the University of Southern California: Lefever in 1966, and Thorpe in 1970.[21]

Promotions from within the faculty over the preceding eight

---

in all these superb human relationships was Osman Hull's stature as a man. While he adhered to standards of personal conduct difficult for most of us to achieve, he found so much good in the worst of us that affection for him was the automatic response of student, staff, or fellow-professor. He tended to minimize our faults and build on our minor successes, deemphasize our frustrations and suggest ways out of whatever difficulty. . . . To honor him, we need not promise to remember him, since he has left an indelible impression upon us all. Perhaps a more appropriate promise is to declare our continuing allegiance to the kind of life he lived, whether or not we can in truth achieve it, and to pledge ourselves to continue as effectively as possible the task he believed to be so critically important. Thus, to his memory, we do, indeed, so dedicate our efforts as long as we are privileged to live and to work together toward those ends." (Cannon, *Tribute to Osman R. Hull*, 1968).

19. Louis Peter Thorpe, one of the University of Southern California's most eminent professors and author of 12 textbooks and innumerable articles in the field of psychology, was born May 15, 1893, in Battle Creek, Michigan. He earned his A.B. (1925) at Emmanuel Missionary College; his M.A. (1929) and his Ph.D.(1931) at Northwestern University. In 1937, he was appointed to the faculty of the School of Education, where he served until his retirement. Greatly honored during his lifetime, Thorpe was one of the founders of the Southern California Psychological Association, Fellow of the American Psychological Association, and Diplomate in clinical psychology of the American Board of Examiners in Professional Psychology. His collection of rare books in psychology, presented by him to the Education Library, forms the Louis P. Thorpe Collection of that library. In his honor, the Louis P. Thorpe Seminar Room was established in Waite Phillips Hall in 1968. In 1970, Dr. Thorpe was awarded the Honorary Degree of LL.D. by the University of Southern California. Dr. Thorpe died November 29, 1970.

20. Born in Ephrata, Pennsylvania, June 13, 1901, David Welty Lefever earned his A.B. (1921) at La Verne College; his A.M. (1922) and his Ph.D. (1927) at the University of Southern California. For 40 years a distinguished member of the faculty of School of Education and well-loved teacher, he was also the author of numerous tests in the field of psychological measurement. Lefever also served as consultant to the State Department of Education and to many school districts in southern California. His dedication to the improvement of teaching and to basic research marked him as a pioneer in the advancement of educational science. In 1966 Dr. Lefever was awarded the Honorary Degree of LL.D. by the University of Southern California, and in 1968 the D. Welty Lefever Measurement Laboratory was established in Waite Phillips Hall.

21. A number of distinguished members of the faculty were recipients of

years and new appointments brought to 28 the number of full professors (excluding dual appointments). Promoted from within were: Brown, Carnes, Georgiades, David W. Martin, Metfessel, Muelder, Naslund, and Donald E. Wilson. Newly appointed were Stephen Abrahamson (1963), and Dan T. Dawson (1965); reappointed in 1967 after several years' absence was William B. Michael; and changed in 1966 from status as visiting professor to professor was Jane Warters.

As of 1968, associate professors were, with year of initial appointment to the faculty: James F. Magary and Merle B. Marks (1960); William F. O'Neill (1961); Robert B. McIntyre (1962); Edward C. Kelly (1963); Paul A. Bloland, John A. Carpenter, William H. McGrath, Mavis D. Martin, and Donald Schrader (1964): Leo F. Buscaglia, Laurence J. Peter, and Leslie E. Wilbur (1965); Joseph G. Coss (1966); and Bert MacLeech (1967).

The number of assistant professors increased from two in 1960 to 14 in 1968. They were, with date of initial appointment: Joyce B. King (King-Stoops) (1963); Richard H. Berg (1964); William Ofman (1965); Paul W. Fischer, Nathaniel Hickerson, and Grayce A. Ransom (1966); Roy Adamson, Robert D. Glasgow, Mabel E. Hayes, Herbert Miller, and Joseph F. Rudloff (1967);

---

honorary degrees during the 1960s. "At the time," recalled Dean Melbo in 1973, "I was a member of the University's Committee on Honorary Degrees. I had argued in the committee that distinguished and eminent faculty should be honored by the University. There was agreement, and I had the privilege of proposing both Lefever and Thorpe, and also Chen and Trillingham, who was an alumnus of distinction in addition to having served at various periods on the faculty of the School of Education." The Honorary Degree of Doctor of Science was presented to Lefever in 1966, at the time of his retirement. In 1967, Theodore Hsi-En Chen, professor of Education and of Asiatic Studies at the University of Southern California since 1938, was awarded the Honorary Degree of Doctor of Laws, as was also C. C. Trillingham, who retired that year after 25 years as superintendent of the Los Angeles County schools. Dr. Trillingham had received his Ed.D. from the University of Southern California in 1933. Thorpe was awarded the Honorary Degree of Doctor of Laws in 1970, as was also Jack Page Crowther, a distinguished alumnus of the University of Southern California, who retired that year as superintendent of the Los Angeles city schools.

89

and Myron H. Dembo, William B. Lee, and Robert A. Smith (1968).

Visting faculty as of 1968, included: Professors Lionel De Silva, Paul V. Robinson, John Allan Smith, and James H. Williams; associate professor A. Jean Ayres; and assistant professors Robert L. Calatrello; Frank H. Fox, and Donald G. Perrin.

In adjunct status were: Professors William H. Allen, Charles C. Carpenter, E. Maylon Drake, Jefferson L. Garner, Robert C. Gerletti, Chester E. Gilpin, Leonard L. Murdy, Harry W. Smallenburg, and John W. Stallings; associate professors Vincent E. Alexander, Elena Boder, Truman N. Case, James E. Gardner, Jerry C. Garlock, Harry Handler, and Richard Koch; and assistant professors Bill A. Adams, Norman B. Eisen, Stuart J. Mandell, John R. McCarthy, Samuel J. Rowe, Alathena Smith, Marguerite Stoner, and Ivor Thomas.

Clinical professors during the period were Marianne Frostig[22] and Sophia T. Salvin (deceased 1967); associate professor William Hirsch; assistant professor George F. Wilson; and a number of clinical instructors.

Among the lecturers were Virginia R. Archer, Wallace F. Cohen, Vincent Crowell, Robert H. Fisher, Logan Jordan Fox, Glenn G. Gooder, Schuyler C. Joyner, Bernard Kirsch, Robert D. Leland,

---

22. Founder of the Marianne Frostig School for the Neurologically Handicapped, Los Angeles, Marianne Frostig was an internationally recognized authority in this field. Born in Vienna, Austria, March 31, 1906, she received training there in child social work, and served from 1932 and 1937 as director of the rehabilitation program, Psychiatric Hospital, Zofiowka, Poland. Coming to America, she received her A.B. (1946) from the New School for Social Research, New York City; her M.A. (1949) from Claremont Graduate School; and her Ph.D. (1955) from the University of Southern California. Her international reputation took her during the 1960s and 1970s to many states throughout the United States and to a large number of foreign countries as lecturer and participant in workshops. The Marianne Frostig School was a demonstration school for the School of Education. In 1962, she presented a lecture in the first annual series of distinguished lectures in the field of special education conducted by the School of Education (Frostig, Marianne. "Education of children with special learning disabilities." *Distinguished Lectures in Special Education,* Volume 1, 1962, Los Angeles: University of Southern California, 1962).

90

Margaret H. Miller, Mary S. Reed, Vivien E. L. Teubner, Starla C. Warburton, Allen P. Webb, and Alfred H. Williams.

Educational Placement Office

In 1959, Edith Weir retired as director of the Bureau of Teacher Placement, a position she had held for 36 years.[23] Following her retirement, the Bureau of Teacher Placement was incorporated into the School of Education at the Educational Placement Office.[24] Melbo, who was committed both by position and by

---

23. Weir had been appointed in 1923, when President von KleinSmid established an appointment registry within the Office of the President of the University and named her appointment secretary. A graduate of the University of Southern California (1912), she came to her position with several years' experience in appointment work. During the First World War, she had been one of the most popular "American girls" in the overseas service of the American Red Cross, making a name for her unusual tact and efficiency as director of the Bureau of Permits and Passes in Paris. No American soldier on leave could enter Paris without her permission. Following the war, she had been employed by the United States Veterans Bureau as its director of rehabilitation in Palo Alto. At the University of Southern California, from 1923 to 1926 she had charge of all University placement services. With the establishment in 1926 of a University-wide employment office, the Appointment Office restricted its assistance to students and graduates of the University who desired to obtain assistance toward teaching positions. Miss Weir thus became an integral part of the School of Education's services, although the office remained within the University's structure. At the time of her retirement, she is said to have registered 60,000 applicants. Known throughout the state of California for her wide command of educational placement, she was, perhaps, the most trusted person in the entire state for her recommendations of candidates, including supervisory and administrative positions as well as teaching assignments. "She ran it from her head," said one who had had much experience with the Bureau of Teacher Placement, "and she seldom made a mistake."

24. Over the years, responsibility for teacher placement had vacillated between the University and the School of Education. A Teachers' Appointment Registry was first established in 1917, under the auspices of the University. With the establishment of the School of Education in 1918, it took over the registry and maintained this service in its own offices until 1923. In that year, President von KleinSmid returned the appointment registry to the University, moved it to his office, and named Edith Weir appointment secretary. Said von KleinSmid: "The new work to be established in the University by Miss Weir will embrace the appointment work heretofore carried on for teachers and graduates by the School of Education of the University as well as parttime and vocational work for stu-

91

philosophy to the concept of a strong placement office appointed Robert E. Cralle director, effective December 1, 1959.[25] Cralle was assisted by Paul Fisher as associate director, Rodman F. Garrity as administrative assistant, and Paul J. Avery as placement assistant. The Educational Placement Office was moved in 1961, to more ample quarters in the service building across from Bovard Administration Building. In the new quarters, it was reported, "There are five comfortable rooms where more than 300 school district representatives can interview 1,500 candidates annually for teaching and administrative positions."[26]

On June 30, 1962, Cralle was succeeded by Avery, who continued as director until February 1964, when he was appointed superintendent of public schools, Winnetka, Illinois. In May 1964, Melbo selected Richard H. Berg and persuaded him to become director. As of 1968, Berg was assisted by David Baker and Jerry Gibson. In that year, the Educational Placement Office was moved to Bruce Hall, 663 West 34th Street, a significant improvement in the housing of the office.

From 1964 to 1968, a total of 8,512 registrations for placement were processed, the yearly total rising from 1,640 in 1964–65, to

---

dents. It will also include the employment work heretofore carried on by the College of Commerce, Y.M.C.A. and Y.W.C.A. of the University as well as the associated women students, combining all these departments under the direction of the office of the president." (*Alumni News* 4(1), p. 7) After the University-wide Bureau of Employment was established by the General Alumni Association in 1926, the Appointment Office restricted its assistance to students and graduates of the University seeking teaching positions. In 1936, the Appointment Office was redesignated the Bureau of Teacher Placement, with Miss Weir director. No change was made in organizational structure, and the Bureau remained under University control. Transfer of the responsibility to the School of Education, as effected by Melbo in 1959, represented a forward step in strengthening the position of the School of Education as an autonomous professional school within the University structure.

25. Cralle came to the position from seven years as Executive Secretary, California Association of School Administrators. He had also served as deputy superintendent and business manager for various school districts, as district superintendent, and as Superintendent of Inglewood city schools. He had been lecturer in school administration at the School of Education since 1942.

26. *EDUCARE Newsletter* 1(1), p. 4.

VISION AND ACCOMPLISHMENT: 1960–1968

2,138 in 1968–69. A total of 45,858 papers were transmitted for job placement, averaging more than 9,000 each year. The number of candidates placed exceeded 1,525. While the majority were placed in positions within California, placement was national and international in scope, particularly at the college and university level, where 35 per cent of the candidates obtained out-of-state positions. Berg attributed a large measure of the success of the Educational Placement Office to the caliber of candidates and their excellent performance. "The reputation of our graduates for excellence in teaching," he reported, "is a tremendous asset . . . in the placement competition."[27]

Important feedback was gained by the Educational Placement Office from alumni, school administrators, and employing officials. Of particular assistance was the annual budgetary allocation of funds by the Education Alumni Association for the support of hospitality centers at several major educational conventions held throughout the nation. Funds were used to rent a room at the convention site, to pay the cost of coffee and cookies, and to offset the cost of furnishing materials about the School of Education. As director of Educational Placement, Berg directed the centers on each occasion. Faculty of the School of Education attending the convention also attended the coffee hours to greet those who visited the hospitality center. "The rooms," reported the Education Alumni Association's newssheet, the *Trojan Bell,* "have been filled beyond capacity and many USC graduates have advised us that they find these centers invaluable."[28]

Melbo had initiated these convention coffee hours as a means of assuring the School of Education a continuing role in every major national and state administration conference, and as a rallying place where faculty and alumni could meet. "It is a device," he told alumni groups, "for building group solidarity, and for extending mutual confidence and loyalties." In later years he

27. *EDUCARE Newsletter,* 11(1), p. 4.
28. *Trojan Bell,* Spring 1971, p. 4.

pointed to the broader implications of the hospitality centers:[29]

> One way by which we attempted to express our continuing interest and support of those persons who were on the 'firing line' in school administration was by the simple practice of being readily available to share their problems and successes.

> As dean of a professional school, I attempted to develop the concept with our faculty that we are loyal to our students, and that we maintain a continuing interest in our graduates throughout their entire career span. It is our responsibility to help advance their careers in all ways possible, and this in turn builds loyalty on the part of our alumni to the School of Education.

Accreditation

During the period 1960 to 1968, the School of Education was visited twice for accreditation purposes. In 1961, a joint accrediting committee of the State Board of Education of California and the Western College Association was joined by a team from the National Council for the Accreditation of Teacher Education (NCATE).[30] This was the first time the University of Southern California's School of Education had been visited by an NCATE accrediting team. In May 1961, on the basis of the visit, the California State Board of Education recommended the reaccreditation of all credential programs at the School of Education for a five-year period.[31] In September 1961, the following clarification of certain points, the NCATE reported to President Topping that the council had granted full accreditation

---

29. MS comment, May 1973.

30. NCATE, a voluntary agency founded in 1952, makes its appraisal of teacher training institutions on the basis of nationwide criteria. As of 1970, about three-fifths of the states recognized NCATE accreditation by offering reciprocity of certification to institutions certified by NCATE.

31. *See* University of Southern California (1961) for the School of Education's report to the accrediting committee, prepared under the direction of Cannon, appointed by Melbo for this task.

94

to the University of Southern California for the preparation of elementary and secondary teachers and school service personnel through the doctor's degree. This action covered a period of 10 years (1960–70).[32]

In 1965, the School of Education was again visited by the State Board of Education's Committee on Accreditation. All credential programs were accredited for the maximum term of five years, except that related to teaching the physiological handicapped, which was accredited for three years.[33]

Credentials

The question of credentials and their requirements, the initial stages of which were described in the preceding chapter, grew to climactic proportion during the early 1960s. Nor had the troubled waters been stilled by the 1970s. Beneath the surface, and dividing educators nationwide, were deep philosophical and historical issues concerned with the proper preparation of the nation's teachers. In a paper entitled, "On the State of Disunion," presented before the California Council on the Education of Teachers, of which he was then president, Cannon referred to the historical background of the issue:[34]

> Our present situation in California, as it relates to teacher education and certification, can best be understood in terms of its historical development here and elsewhere. The conviction that scholarship in a traditional discipline would automatically assure teaching competence was the greatest obstacle to the establishment of systematic programs of teacher education over a hundred years ago. Not until the products of these programs proved superior to academy or college graduates with only a course or two in the philosophy of pedagogy did comprehensive

---

32. Letter, W. E. Armstrong, Director, NCATE to President Norman H. Topping, dated September 15, 1961 (*Agenda,* November 6, 1961).

33. *Agenda,* November 14, 1966.

34. Cannon (1964).

95

programs of each education, including practice teaching, find their way into universities. While the first Chair of Pedagogy was established nearly a century ago at Iowa, there have always been dissenters. The occasional outbursts of certain California academicians, against both teacher education and all things practical or applicational, are a part of this tradition.

Now added to the traditional conflicting points of view was the furor in America which attended the launching into orbit in 1957 of the Russian *Sputnik*. Popular concern for the quality of public education in the United States rolled like a tidal wave over the nation. Much public sympathy was engendered for critics of the public schools. Fired by these critics, came the popular outcry against the public school teachers, the schools of education which produced them, the state departments of education which certified them, and the state legislatures which set the requirements for their service. Sensitive to the people's discontent, politicians entered the fray. Crash political solutions were frequently proposed and sometimes carried out. In California, credentials became a political football.

The credential question had, of course, already been raised among the educators. It will be recalled that in 1954, the superintendent of Public Instruction and the president of the California Council on the Education of Teachers had jointly appointed a 14-member statewide committee on credential revision. This committee had rendered its report in November 1957, to the Council on the Education of Teachers. During the next two years, from 1957 through 1959, the superintendent of Public Instruction, then Roy E. Simpson, had arranged for a series of public meetings throughout the state. Immediately after the public meetings, the staff committee of the State Department of Education analyzed the information, suggestions, and recommendations and formulated a credential structure which it believed would receive the greatest support of the education profession as well as that of the citizens' groups that had evidenced special interest in the problems. In February 1960, the State Board of Education approved the credential structure proposed for the certification of professional employees for California's public schools. With some changes, the standards approved by the State Board in its February 1960 meeting were those incorporated by State Senator Hugo Fisher of San Diego in Senate Bill 57, introduced into the legislature in January 1961. Said Superintendent Simpson:[35]

> No bill received greater legislative committee scrutiny than the one introduced by Senator Hugo Fisher, Senate Bill 57, Chapter 848, which implemented the recommendations of the five-year study on the revision of our credential structure, undertaken by the California Council on Teacher Education at the request of the Superintendent of Public Instruction. Nor did any other bill presented at this session of the Legislature receive as much organized opposition from certain segments of the profession.

The "Fisher Bill," as it was familiarly called after its author, was passed by the California legislature and signed into law by Governor Edmund G. Brown as "The Licensing of Certificated Personnel Law of 1961." Under its provisions, the legislature established five separate types of credentials;[36] made five, rather than four, years of college preparation for elementary teachers and certain secondary teachers; and required a subject matter major and minor, one of which must be academic, for every elementary, junior high school, senior high school, and junior college teacher whose teaching service was authorized by the standard teaching credential. The State Board of Education was directed to prepare specific requirements for the credentials, within the mandatory provisions of the law. It was also authorized to promulgate additional requirements. Said Cannon, on behalf of the California Council on the Education of Teachers:[37]

> Our council agreed that Senate Bill 57 was now the law of the land ... and we should attempt to implement it as intelligently and enthusiastically as possible.

---

35. Simpson (1961), p. 383.

36. Standard teaching credential with specializations in elementary teaching, secondary teaching, and junior college teaching, respectively; standard designated subjects teaching credential; standard designated services teaching credential; standard supervision credential; standard administration credential.

37. Cannon (1964).

97

A 10-member State Central Coordinating Committee on Credential Revision was appointed to design a procedure for development of the requirements for credentials which would be recommended to the State Board of Education. The central committee, in turn, requested appointment of four resource committees. The School of Education was represented by four members on these committees. Melbo, appointed to the central committee, also served as cochairman of the resource committee on standard administration-supervision credentials. Cannon was appointed to the resource committee on the standard teaching credential; and Carnes and Smallenburg (then Director of Research and Guidance, Los Angeles County Schools, and adjunct professor of the School of Education) were appointed to the resource committee on standard designated services credential.

In April 1962, the central committee rendered its final report to the California Council on the Education of Teachers and, in May 1962, to the State Department of Education. Hearings on the report were held throughout the state. Said Superintendent Simpson in October 1962:[38]

> I can think of no educational problem which has received a comparable amount of study and consideration by all segments of education in California as has the credential revision issue. We want to implement Senate Bill No. 57, so as to accomplish its two major purposes: (1) increased subject matter preparation for all teachers; and (2) assignment of all teachers to teach subjects for which they have adequate preparation.

Unexpectedly, further delay was occasioned in November 1962, when Rafferty was elected California's superintendent of public instruction.[39] Eventually, the State Board of Education

38. Simpson (1962), p. 288.

39. Maxwell Lewis Rafferty, Jr., owed his election in part to his conservative stand on matters of public education and to his attacks on current trends in education as deleterious to the acquisition by students of basic education. Born May 7, 1917, in New Orleans, Louisiana, Rafferty received his A.B. (1938) and his A.M. (1949) from the University of California, Los Angeles; and his Ed.D. (1956) from the University of Southern California. Prior to receiving his doctorate, Rafferty had been teacher at Trona, California (1940–47); principal at Big Bear (1948–

published its requirements, and the new credentialing system was placed in effect as of January 1, 1964. Teacher education institutions in California were authorized to continue until September 14, 1966, to recommend, with certain provisos, candidates for all credentials for which authorized programs were in effect at the institution prior to January 1, 1964.

In credential parlance, credentials under programs in effect prior to January 1, 1964, became known as "old credentials" to distinguish them from those issued under the Fisher Bill. Difficulties experienced by some institutions in the state in meeting the criteria of the Fisher Bill resulted in passage by the California legislature of special legislation successively in 1967, 1968, and 1969, which extended the period at the end of which the "old credentials" were to be phased out. During the period 1964–69, the School of Education at the University of Southern California granted credentials under both systems, as appropriate.

Departmental Activities

Administration and Supervision. The Department of Administration and Supervision was one of the oldest and most firmly established of the departments of the School of Education. As a result of its preeminence in the field of educational administration, the School of Education of the University of Southern California was recognized nationwide as the ranking training center for administrative roles in the public schools of California, and as one of the ranking centers in this field for the entire United States.

In addition to the major program leading to the doctorate in educational administration, the department had developed a number of specialities. These included: personnel administration,

---

51); superintendent of elementary schools at Saticoy (1951–54), and superintendent of schools, Needles (1955–61). In 1961, he became superintendent of schools of the La Canada Unified School District, from which in 1962, he was elected California superintendent of public instruction. Rafferty was defeated in his bid for reelection in 1970. In 1971, he became dean at Troy State University, Troy, Alabama.

99

business administration, elementary administration, secondary administration, administration of higher education, schoolhouse planning, organization and control, and public relations. Thus it was possible for the doctoral candidate to major in the field of educational administration with a wide choice of specialization.

The faculty of the department had developed over many years unusual expertise in both the practical and theoretical dimensions of school administration, with one or more major professors responsible for each specialization within the total program. As of 1968, full-time faculty members, with year of appointment to the faculty, were: Professors Melbo (1939), LaFranchi (1946), Nelson (1947), Stoops (1953), Mueder (1958), Dawson (1965); and assistant professors Berg (1964) and Adamson (1967). Visiting professor was De Silva. Adjunct professors as of 1968, were: Charles C. Carpenter, E. Maylon Drake, Jefferson L. Garner, Chester E. Gilpin, Leonard L. Murdy, and John W. Stallings.[40]

---

40. Because of the geographical location of the University of Southern California in the greater metropolitan area of Los Angeles, the Department of Administration and Supervision was particularly fortunate in having a large number of highly successful school administrators, many of them its own alumni, available as adjunct professors. As of 1968, but typical of all years for quality of staff, Carpenter was the former deputy superintendent, Los Angeles County schools; Drake was superintendent, Alhambra City School District; Garner was superintendent, Centinela Valley Union High School District; Gilpin was associate executive secretary, California Teachers' Association, Southern Section; Murdy was superintendent, Fullerton Union High School District; and Stallings was superintendent, Corona Unified School District. De Silva, the visiting professor, was executive secretary, California Teachers' Association, Southern Section, 1947–67.

Others who served in adjunct status with the Department of Administration and Supervision during the 1970s included: Richard M. Clowes, superintendent, Los Angeles County schools (1967–   ); Robert H. Fisher, personnel director, personnel commission, Los Angeles city schools (1951–70); and Darcy A. Skaggs, superintendent, Baldwin Park Unified School District (1954–70) and after 1970, attorney-at-law, Baldwin Park. Serving in visiting professor status in the European Program for courses in administration were James H. Williams, retired superintendent, Glendale Unified School District; and C. C. Trillingham, retired superintendent, Los Angeles County schools (1942–67).

100

In general, students in educational administration were mature persons, with clear-cut professional goals, considerable experience as teachers, and some experience in administration. Approximately 90 percent were employed and were pursuing the doctorate for professional growth and advancement.

In 1960, a new program was inaugurated for continuing leadership in, and upgrading of, the training of public school administrators. This program provided for special proficiency and training diplomas in the areas of superintendent of public schools; assistant superintendent—personnel services; assistant superintendent —business services; assistant superintendent—educational services; secondary principal; and elementary principal. Diplomas issued by the University of Southern California in these areas represented a formal background in course work in school administration, as well as significant practical field experience. Experience confirmed that these special training programs effectively aided the objectives of the profession in the continuous process of improving proficiency in the several professional areas of school administration. With justifiable pride, Nelson as one of the originators of the program noted that a diploma in school administration was valued in the field as much or more than the doctoral degree. School authorities and boards of education placed great confidence in those who held the diploma in administration, since its award signified not only acquired knowledge but demonstrated qualities of leadership desired in school administrators, such as assumption of responsibility, making of appropriate decisions, ability to work effectively in a negative environment, effective use of staff members, and infusion of effective research ino the school situation.

The department also gave special attention to building the theoretical-conceptual aspects of educational administration. In this effort, it provided guidance to the Education Library in maintaining the educational administration section of the library collection and, in addition, developed two special collections of its own for majors in education administration. These collections were located in seminar rooms adjacent to the offices of the De-

101

partment of Administration and Supervision. In the Schuyler C. Joyner Educational Administrative Laboratory[41] was housed a collection of administrative materials brought together with the assistance of the Institute of Administrative Research; and in the R. Bruce Walter Room[42] was housed a collection of educational administration dissertations and school surveys.

An important facet of the work of the department's faculty was their participation in the programs of the Advanced Study Centers both in the United States and overseas. Particularly active were Nelson and Stoops. Nelson and LaFranchi also played important roles in the Melbo school surveys, serving frequently as associate directors for the general surveys and as colleagues in the special surveys. Strong participation by members of the department in state and national associations of administrators and as consultants to local, state, and national committees on school administration provided the basis for the increasingly important position of the School of Education in school administration theory and practice. Typical of the interest of the department in the

---

41. The laboratory was furnished with funds provided by EDUCARE, the support group of the School of Education, and named by that society in honor of Schuyler C. Joyner, its second president (1962–63). Joyner, who was born in Indiana in 1903, received his B.A. (1929) from the University of Minnesota and his M.A. (1931) and Ed.D. (1941) from the University of Southern California. Following seven years as teacher and principal in the schools of St. Cloud, Minnesota (1922–29), he was assistant superintendent, Pasadena city schools (1930–34). In 1934, he joined the Los Angeles city school system, serving as deputy business manager (1934–55), business manager (1955–64), and deputy superintendent, Business and Educational Services (1964–68). Joyner was Delta Epsilon Lecturer for 1963. Coauthor of a book on school insurance and author of numerous articles on school management, he was an outstanding authority in the business aspects of school management, serving as consultant after his retirement from the active field.

42. Robert Bruce Walter was born in 1895, in Bedford County, Pennsylvania, and was graduated from the State Normal School, Millersville, Pennsylvania, in 1916. From 1913 through 1921, he was teacher in the schools of Pennsylvania; and from 1921 on, he was associated with the school systems of California. He received his B.S. in Ed. (1929), his M.S. in Ed. (1939), and his Ed.D. (1951) from the University of Southern California. Appointed assistant superintendent, Los Angeles County Schools in 1939, he was named by C. C. Trillingham chief deputy superintendent in 1942, and continued in that position until his retirement, 1965.

102

profession were annual spring field conferences on public school administration sponsored by the School of Education and held at the University of Southern California. At these conferences prominent authorities presented addresses of timely importance to school administration.

Counselor Education. At the master's and doctoral level, the Department of Counselor Education identified certain objectives that pervaded its program, regardless of the occupational setting for which the individual was preparing. The objectives were: to improve student self-understanding in order to facilitate counselor-counselee relations; to broaden and refine student understanding of the dynamics of behavior as influenced by psychological and sociological variables; to develop among students a philosophy of counseling consistent with modern theory and research, and congruent with the counselor's self; to increase, through supervised experiences, student counseling competence; to improve student skills in methods of obtaining information about counselees, including the use and interpretation of standardized tests; to provide students with the statistical and research tools necessary to the production, evaluation, and utilization of research data; and to develop understanding and skills in the roles, relationships, and management problems involved in personnel service programs.

Full-time members of the department as of 1968, with date of appointment to the faculty, were: Professors Wagner (1941), Carnes (1949), and Warters (1951); associate professors Bloland (1964), Schrader (1964); and assistant professor Ofman (1965). In adjunct status were: Professor Smallenburg and assistant professors McCarthy and Thomas.

The largest number of students in the department aspired to become public school counselors. During the 1960s, in response to growing social concerns, an increasing number selected for their specialty some phase of college personnel work, vocational rehabilitation, and work with youth, adults, and family groups in noneducational settings.

An important facet of the work of the department was the

103

Counseling Institute, established in 1960. Funded under Title V-B of the National Defense Education Act (NDEA) and directed by Carnes, the institute had its origin in the summer counseling institute conducted in 1959. Continuing NDEA contracts on a yearly basis from 1960 through 1965 were received for the holding of academic-year and summer institutes. As the only NDEA Counseling Institute in eleven Western states, including Hawaii and Guam, the institute had a broad range of students and wide influence. In addition to Carnes, for whom the management of the institute was a full-time assignment, part-time faculty included Thorpe, Wagner, and Warters.

Each academic-year institute comprised approximately 30 high school teachers who were preparing to become counselors. Trainees received a program equivalent to the California standard designated services credential, with specialization in pupil personnel services. Supervised field experience in high schools in the Los Angeles city schools and campus laboratory experiences were provided.

Summer institutes involved 50 counselors from the public schools who did not meet California credential requirements, or who wished to pursue further work in the counseling field. The intent of the program was to upgrade the trainees' competencies through intensive course work and highly supervised counseling experience.

A specialty area within the department was the Vocational Rehabilitation Counseling Program, funded as an on-going training grant from the Rehabilitation Services Administration, Department of Health, Education and Welfare. As of 1968–69, the grant provided support monies for teaching staff, program administration, and student tuition stipends. Under this grant, an interdisciplinary Rehabilitation Counseling Curriculum and Development and Program Planning Committee, composed of specialists on a University-wide and community-wide basis, developed a comprehensive program at the graduate level. The program encompassed a curriculum for a two-year master's degree program in rehabilitation counseling, and a curriculum for an

104

Ed.D. and Ph.D. program in rehabilitation counseling and rehabilitation counselor education. It also arranged for field work stations for practicum in appropriate agencies, and identified sources of supply and means for providing trainees with subjects for counseling. Under the direction of Schrader, by 1969 eight students had completed the two-year training program. Other staff for the rehabilitation program included Carnes, Wagner, Ofman, Donald R. Hoover, Everett Stude, Ivor Thomas, Kathryn Lewis, and Betty Walker. In 1969, in recognition of the need to focus on the applied aspects of rehabilitation counseling, Fred A. Moore was added as assistant coordinator for administration and teaching responsibilities, and Rosemary Callahan as clinical instructor for field supervision of agency internships.

Elementary Education. The Department of Elementary Education had the distinction of being the only department within the School of Education with multiple reponsibility at both the undergraduate and graduate level. Operating as a service department for teacher education, the department played an important role at the bachelor's level in providing courses leading to the standard teaching credential with specialization in elementary education, the standard supervision credential, and the standard administration credential. At the graduate level, it offered a major for the M.S. in Ed. degree, supportive courses for the M.E. degree, and a major or supplementary field for both the Ed.D. and the Ph.D. in Education. Specialization in elementary education at the doctoral level included, as of 1968, curriculum, curriculum theory and development, language arts, mathematics, reading, science, social studies, and teacher education.

As of 1968, faculty of the department, with date of appointment and specialty, were: Professors Adams (1929), social studies; Perry (1945), mathematics; Naslund (1950), social studies and curriculum theory and development; and Brown (1955), reading and curriculum; assistant professor Ransom (1966), reading; and, as Director of the Early Childhood Institute, Smart (1968). In adjunct status were associate professors Vincent Alexander and James E. Gardner, and assistant professor Samuel J. Rowe. Lectur-

105

ers were Vincent Crowell, Bernard Kirsch, Margaret Miller, Mary S. Reed, Vivien E. L. Teubner, and Alfred H. Williams.

A new facet of specialization, which was to see a strong development during the 1970s, was that of early childhood education. In June 1967, at Melbo's urging that this field must be developed, the School of Education received an NDEA grant of $80,000 to fund a program in preparing teachers in early childhood education. From December 1967 through March 1968, an NDEA-funded Institute for Early Childhood Education for School District Teams was conducted under the supervision of Wilson of the Department of Teacher Education, with Jeannette Veatch as director. Sagaciously foreseeing the importance which this phase of education would play during the next decade, Melbo placed the 1968 institute in early childhood education under the Department of Elementary Education and appointed as its director Margaret E. Smart, specialist in this area, and a person of proven experience and strong potential.[43]

The other specialty of the department was the Reading Center. Until 1964, the on-campus Reading Center was the only center of the School of Education for reading problems. In March 1964, Melbo announced that the Reading Center program was being expanded to occupy space facilities made available by the Nation-

---

43. Smart obtained her B.F.A. (1936) and her M.S. in Ed. (1960) from the University of Southern California, and her Ed.D. (1969) from the University of Arizona. Her professional experience included six years as elementary school teacher, Redondo Beach City Schools; two years as reading consultant, K-8, in that system; reading consultant and curriculum coordinator, K-14, Orange County Schools Office; program assistant, Tucson District I and the University of Arizona; and, in the fall of 1963, instructor, audio-visual course, University of California, Los Angeles, Extension Division. Following her appointment to the USC faculty, Smart served from November 1972 through April 1973, as a member of the advisory committee to the Assembly Education Committee, whose purpose was to formulate recommendations for state legislation which would authorize the inclusion of four-year-olds in the public school system of California. She had also served as consultant to the California State Department of Education on such matters as compensatory education, program development, and Project Follow-Through, and as consultant on early childhood education to a number of school districts in California.

106

al Charity League.[44] This action followed a series of discussions between Melbo and officers of the league, as a result of which the league's Board of Directors entered into contract with the School of Education for financial support of the Reading Center. Members of the Los Angeles Chapter of the league undertook to supply the modern building facilities and to underwrite part of the center's annual budget. Thus, in September 1964, was established the NCL-USC Reading Center, a modern facility located at 5000 Hollywood Boulevard, Los Angeles.

With the completion of Waite Phillips Hall in 1968, the Campus Reading center was transferred to a suite in that building. Under Brown's direction, the staff of the centers included several reading specialists. Among these was Mavis D. Martin, appointed in 1964 as Visiting Professor with assignment to the Reading Center. Martin resigned in 1967, to accept a research assignment in the Southwest Regional Laboratory at Albuquerque, New Mexico. At that time, Ransom, who had been appointed in 1965 assistant professor of education and assistant director of the NCL-USC Reading Center, was named associate professor and director of the NCL-USC Reading Center.

The two centers shared certain common program strands. Their central purpose was to educate and train reading specialists and resource leaders at all curriculum levels. Together they formed the clinical component of the professional preparation for graduate students who planned to become specialists in reading. They provided a situation and facilities to implement instruction in the professional aspects of the teaching and study of reading; encouraged, organized, directed, and sponsored research in the field of reading; provided reading improvement services to persons of

---

44. The National Charity League was a nonprofit corporation composed of mothers and daughters, designated Patroness and Tick-Tocker Groups. The League's purpose was to initiate and encourage charitable endeavors and to foster the mother-daughter relationship in social, cultural, and philanthropic projects. Chapters of the organization were largely in southern California. The Los Angeles Chapter, incorporated in 1947, had as its major philanthropic project the support of the NCL-USC Reading Center.

107

public school age and counseled parents on related matters; and provided professional leadership in the field of reading. Each center, however, had its specific program, differing from but complementing the other.

At the NCL-USC Reading Center, a complete school program, with emphasis on reading, was offered to boys seven to 14 years of age. Class size was limited to a maximum of nine pupils. An important facet of the center was the development of a plan of behavior modification and group counseling. Under this plan of "academic reorientation," the weekly visits to the center by Gardner, a specialist in children's learning disabilities, were followed by a faculty seminar jointly conducted by Gardner and Ransom.

The Campus Reading Center, in addition to other remedial programs, held classes in reading improvement for University students, high school seniors, ninth grade pupils, and interested adults. Adult reading classes, introduced in 1968, were relevant to the training of reading specialists who wished to serve a wide spectrum of reading needs, including those for adults who performed only slightly above the functionally literate level.

Both centers offered an accelerated and enlarged summer program. Particularly useful for graduate students who needed to work with larger groups of children was the cooperative arrangement between the Reading Centers and the Valley East Elementary Area. Under this arrangement, a group of children from the Los Feliz Elementary School were diagnosed and organized for demonstration classes.

Research, which was emphasized as a regular part of the programs of the centers, also encompassed special projects. A Diagnostic and Prescriptive Reading program, developed by Ransom in 1965, was being field tested and evaluated as of 1969 in a cooperating school of the Los Angeles city school system. The thrust of the project was to assess the effect of supplying from a central school resource center appropriate diagnostic and prescriptive materials for teacher-pupil use. Efficient use of learning centers, cost analyses, and dispersal and retrieval of materials were among the factors under study.

108

Higher Education. Although courses in higher education had been offered by the School of Education for many years, a major leading to the doctorate in that area was for the School of Education, as for the nation at large, a late development. Perceiving the need for this specialization, Melbo in February 1958, invited a scholar and administrator of note to join the faculty in rank of full professor and assigned him responsibility for developing a program which would eventually provide a major for the doctorate in higher education. The scholar and administrator was Earl V. Pullias, then Dean of the Faculty at Pepperdine University.[45] Not all shared the Dean's optimism in initiating the new program, recalled Melbo:[46]

> For some time I had felt that there was a real opportunity, as well as a need, to develop a program in higher education, with enough scope to make it a major field. By a rare stroke of good luck, I learned that Dr. Pullias, then Dean of Pepperdine, had expressed a wish to return to the professorial role. I went to see him and came away convinced that he could develop a good solid program in higher education.
>
> I then went to talk with Dr. A. S. Raubenheimer, then Vice-President for Academic Affairs, to broach the idea of expanding our program in this field and to request a modest fiscal allocation for the position. "I believe the position will pay for itself by tuition receipts within the first year," I told him. He was skeptical. "If it doesn't, you can take the difference out of my salary," I countered. He replied, "I will."

---

45. Born March 12, 1907, at Castalian Springs, Tennessee, Pullias took his A.B. (1928) at Cumberland University, his M.A. (1931) at the University of Chicago, and his Ph.D. (1936) at Duke University, where he was Teaching Fellow, 1931–36, and instructor, 1936–37. Following a year of postdoctoral study in Oxford, England (1937–38), he joined the faculty of Pepperdine, where he was professor of psychology (1938–57) and dean (1940–57). A member of the Los Angeles County Board of Education from 1954 on (president 1956–57, 1962–63, 1967–68) and of the Commission on Membership and Standards of the Western College Association (1958–61), as well as author of a number of books on college teaching, Pullias was one of the most respected authorities in the field of higher education.

46. MS comment, May 1973.

109

So I appointed Dr. Pullias, whom Dr. Raubenheimer also liked and respected greatly, and from that beginning the program has become one of the best in the country, with graduates holding positions all over the nation.

At first the work in higher education was carried on in cooperation with the Department of Secondary Education, and as part of the Division of Elementary, Secondary, and Higher Education. With the establishment of separate departments, each headed by a chairman, the Department of Higher Education was established in 1968, with Pullias as chairman. The area of higher education in the School of Education had been greatly strengthened in 1965 with appointment of Leslie E. Wilbur in rank of associate professor.[47] In 1969, Clive L. Grafton was appointed in rank of assistant professor, adding to the department's repertoire a specialist in student personnel.[48]

The first doctorate with major in higher education was awarded in 1961. By 1969, a total of 59 doctorates had been awarded in the field, 15 during the academic year 1967-68. Other departmental services included a special program for preparation of instructors at the junior college level, and the conduct of minors in higher education for students of other departments, both of the School of Education and the University.

Under the broad philosophical lines developed by Pullias, the

47. Wilbur brought to his position long experience in higher education and a background in the liberal arts. A veteran of World War II, he had studied in 1945 at the University of Paris; had obtained his B.A. (1948) at the University of Illinois in French and English; his M.A. (1951) at the University of California, Berkeley, in English; and his Ph.D. (1962) at the University of Southern California. He had served as instructor of English (1950–60) and assistant dean (1962–65) at Bakersfield College; and as president of Barstow College (1962–65).

48. Grafton, who bore the distinction of having been the first to have his oral examination for the doctorate conducted in Waite Phillips Hall, received his A.A. (1950) at Compton College; his A.B. (1956) at Pepperdine College; his M.S. in Ed. (1958) and Ed.D. (1968) at the University of Southern California. He had been teacher and administrative assistant at Compton College (1952–58); teacher and dean of men at Cerritos College (1958–65); and assistant dean of students at the University of Southern California (1965–69). with part-time teaching in the School of Education. His published articles included one on the community college and the foreign student, and two on the changing college student of the 1960s.

110

objective of the department was not only to develop an area of special competence within higher education but to provide the type and quality of experience that promotes growth toward excellence in scholarship and educational leadership (statesmanship) in whatever areas of education the student entered. To achieve this objective, special emphasis was placed on the solution of major problems which seem to influence the quality of teaching and learning in colleges and universities (the "climate of learning"), and on the concept of the teacher as mediator of experience who himself is continually growing in perception and knowledge.

As part of his overall philosophy of education, Dean Melbo had always been convinced of the great contribution the profession of education could make to the teaching and learning of the other professions. This philosophy he was able to put to practical test through the development of a program at the School of Education in cooperation with the University's School of Medicine. In 1967, Dean Loosli of the School of Medicine and Dean Melbo of the School of Education originated the program which was to develop into a highly successful venture. Recalled Dean Melbo in 1973:[49]

> One day Dr. Clayton Loosli, then Dean of the School of Medicine, came to me with the purpose of finding a way to improve the teaching and learning of medicine. To do this, Dr. Stephen Abrahamson, a Ph.D. from New York University, then on the faculty of the University of Buffalo, was appointed as a professor of education and assigned to the Medical School, which had obtained a grant for this purpose.

The courses developed by Dr. Abrahamson, a specialist in curriculum and evaluation,[50] were continued into the next decade, with continuing grants from the United States Public Health

---

49. MS comment, May 1973.
50. Abrahamson had obtained his B.S. in Ed. (1942) in mathematics, and his Ed. M. (1948) in curriculum at Temple University; and his Ph.D. (1951) in evaluation at New York University.

111

Service.[51] To encourage this aspect of the students' professional training, the School of Education gave due recognition to the fact that those entering the program from the medical profession were highly educated and competent persons in their own right, whose prior training and experience were relevant to an advanced degree. With the firm support of Dean Melbo and the School of Medicine, the programs developed by Dr. Abrahamson proved highly successful and were noted by the dean as a prototype for improving education in almost any professional school:[52]

> A year or so after the program started, I asked Dr. Abrahamson how things were going. "Fine," he said, "If I can get those medics to define their objectives, the rest is easy."

> Since that beginning, Dr. Abrahamson has helped to prepare several dozen young men and women taking doctorates in the Department of Higher Education and having an intern-type of experience in Medical School. Many of these have gone out to improve teaching in other medical schools of the country. This is a prototype for improving education in almost any professional school.

Encouragement to all who studied with the Department of Higher Education was provided by two remarkable collections of volumes in that area: the Jean Burton Clark Browsing Shelf in Higher Education, housed in the Education Library, and the Clara Duer Marble Memorial Reading Shelf, housed in the Higher Education Seminar in Waite Phillips Hall.[53]

Instructional Technology. The Department of Instructional Technology was established in 1962, as an outgrowth of the previous audio-visual department. The new department repre-

---

51. Under the grant, the Department of Medical Education, School of Medicine, undertook to train health professions teachers holding medical degrees in matters pertaining to the improvement of teaching and learning in health professions. The grant provided that the Fellows might pursue graduate study in a school of education, including study for the master's and doctor's degrees.

52. MS comment, May 1973.

53. The Higher Education Seminar Room was dedicated to the memory of John Malcom Pullias (1939–57), son of Dr. and Mrs. Pullias. Collections in the area of higher education were increased from time to time by grateful pupils of Pullias and friends of higher education.

112

sented in curriculum and level of instruction a new conceptual design in the field of instructional technology. The first of its kind in any school of education in the United States and probably in the world, the new department was the direct expression of Melbo's long interest in the promise which technology holds for education. Even as a faculty member, as Levitt notes in his history of the earlier years of the School of Education, Melbo had consistently advocated the use of film and related media for instruction long before his colleagues were ready for such innovations. They responded to his suggestions, according to Levitt, with "alarm over initial costs."[54] Now, as dean, Melbo was convinced that educators must move from their narrow concept of instructional technology as "audio-visual aids" to the broader consideration of modern technology as it affects society and its entire educational system. Reminiscing on this subject in 1973, Melbo said:[55]

> I had had some experience with "training aids" (film and other specially designed learning aids) in the U.S. Navy during World War II. The slogan "more learning in less time" was intriguing and, although hard evidence to that effect was lacking, I became convinced that the audio-visual media were worth developing.
>
> As a faculty member, I encouraged the beginnings of "audio-visual education" in the School of Education, and later, as dean, the movement to a broader base, namely instructional technology. In pressing for faculty approval of a doctoral major in this field, I had two objectives: (1) to eliminate any "second class" departments, i.e., those so limited in curriculum that they could offer only the master's degree, thus giving the new field of instructional technology a higher status, at least at USC, and in short time other universities followed our lead; and (2) hopefully, that with a doctoral major there might be some significant research which would move instructional technology away from its built-in "hardware" emphasis and result in a theoretical base and a unique methodology for learning.
>
> The first objective was readily achieved, and USC became

---

54. Levitt (1970), p. 432, n. 5.
55. MS comment, May 1973.

the number one provider of doctoral graduates with an instructional technology specilization. The second objective has not yet been realized, although there are some promising approaches growing out of the research.

To head the new department, Melbo appointed Finn, who had headed the Department of Audio-Visual since its establishment in 1949, and who continued as head of the Department of Instructional Technology until his untimely and unexpected death in 1969. In addition to Finn, other members of the department during the 1960s were: assistant professors F. Roy Carlson (education and electrical engineering) and Herbert Miller; and, in adjunct status, professors Gerletti and Allen; assistant professor Rudolph; and as lecturers George D. Booth, Mona B. Kantor, Robert Kaufman, Stanley Levine, Edgar R. McGregor, and Leo E. Persellin. Visiting assistant professor was Donald G. Perrin.

More than most departments of the School of Education, the Department of Instructional Technology was centered in one man and the projects he directed as chief investigator. To large extent, Finn was the department. Born March 7, 1915, in Great Falls, Montana, Finn earned his B.S. (1937) at Montana State College, and was appointed that year to the faculty of Colorado State College. In 1938, he was awarded a Rockefeller Fellowship for graduate study in educational radio and motion pictures under Charles J. Hoban, Jr., and Edgar Dale. In 1941, he was awarded his M.A. at Colorado State College, and in 1942, entered the military service. As Captain, Signal Corps, United States Army, he developed all instructional aids at the U.S. Army's Command and General Staff School, Fort Leavenworth, Kansas. Having obtained his Ph.D. degree in 1949 at Ohio State University, again under Edgar Dale, Finn was appointed to the faculty of the School of Education, University of Southern California. During the 1960s, he rose to national and international fame as president, Department of Audio-Visual Instruction, National Education Association, president, Educational Media Council (1963–65), and director of many federally funded projects in the field of instructional media. Finn died April 2, 1969. Memorial services were conducted by the

114

Department of Instructional Technology April 5, 1969; and by the University of Southern California, April 8, 1969. At the latter service, eulogies were given by both President Topping and Dean Melbo. In Finn's memory, the James D. Finn Instructional Technology Memorial Seminar Room was dedicated in Waite Phillips Hall.[56] Of him Dean Melbo said: "For more than 20 years, James Donald Finn served the University of Southern California with great distinction. He served with the brilliance that entitles a university to speak pridefully, for one true measure of an institution of higher learning is the greatness of its faculty. Greatness in thought, greatness in deed, greatness in spirit were characteristic of Jim Finn." At a special memorial service held by the Department of Instructional Technology on April 5, 1969, when his colleagues and associates had gathered at the University of Southern California to deliberate on how they might adjust to the void his death on April second had left, Finn's lifelong friend and mentor, Charles F. Hoban, characterized well his influence on all who knew him:[57]

> After taking his Ph.D. under his good friend and mine, Dr. Edgar Dale, at The Ohio State University, Dr. Finn came to this great University and remained here—teaching, thinking, writing with the great felicity of his Gaelic heritage, and, in general, stirring the waters. Wherever he was, with colleagues or students, he always created intellectual ferment of the highest order.

Important projects undertaken by Finn during the 1960-68 period included the Technological Development Project (TDP), the Instructional Technology and Media (TTM) Project, Special Media Institutes (SMI), and the Medical Information Project (MIP).

The Technological Development Project (TDP) was undertaken in 1960, when Finn, who was the newly named president

---

56. Finn's photograph was placed in the seminar room in his memory by the U.S. Army Pictorial Agency. See illustration.

57. Quoted from Memorial Services for Dr. James D. Finn, Department of Instructional Technology, University of Southern California, April 5, 1969.

of the Department of Audio-Visual Instruction (DAVI) of the National Education Association (NEA), was named principal investigator for a $102,980 NEA project to determine the future impact of technology on education. The study was funded by the United States Office of Education, and headquartered at the University of Southern California. At the University Finn, who had been granted an extended leave of absence from his duties in the School of Education in order to conduct the three-year project, maintained an office at 924 West 37th Street and a second office in the NEA Headquarters, Washington, D.C. Acting as representative and associate for the project in Washington was Lee Campion, television consultant to the NEA.

The primary purpose of the TDP, which was conducted from October 1960 to February 1963, was to assess the relevance of traditional instructional aids (television, language laboratories, teaching machines, and other devices) to the teaching-learning process. Essentially a task of synthesis and prediction, project findings were disseminated in a series of occasional papers, monographs, and articles in various professional journals, as well as in several audio-visual presentations.

The outstanding work done under the TDP led to the creation in 1963, of the Instructional Technology and Media (ITM) Project. This project was carried out under contract between the United States Office of Education and the University of Southern California, with Finn again named principal investigator. Initially funded with $296,173 from the federal government, the two-year contract had a three-pronged purpose: to procure a series of 10 monograph manuscripts for the U.S. Office of Education, synthesizing research findings in the new media; to produce several motion pictures on the role of the new media in education; and to continue the monitoring, assessment, and predictive functions relating to technological developments in education. Again, two offices were maintained, with Donald Rucker and Emanuel Lombard assisting Finn at the University, and Clarice Kelley in the Washington office. William H. Allen was appointed *Monograph*

116

editorial director, and Bernard Kantor was appointed associate director for film production.

As a further means of disseminating the instructional technology findings, during the academic year 1965–66, the Department of Instructional Technology, in conjuction with the Instructional Media Center at Michigan State University and the Center for Instructional Communications at Syracuse University as subcontractors, conducted at the University of Southern California's School of Education a pilot program for a volunteer group of directors of instructional media centers. The pilot program, which consisted of a series of one-week Special Media Institutes (SMI), drew 121 college professors and educational specialists. Following a favorable review of the pilot program by James Brown of San Jose State College, an expanded program of SMI was conducted during the academic year 1966–67, with the Teaching Research Division of the Oregon State System of Higher Education joining the consortium of participating institutions. These institutes were attended by 228 participants. Again, after a favorable independent review by Phil C. Lange of Teachers College, Columbia University, SMIs were conducted during the academic years 1967–68 and 1968–69. In all, more than 600 institute directors and educational specialists attended the institutes.[58]

A byproduct of the institutes was the compilation of sets of materials relating to the cognitive domain of the educational process. These were developed in a symposium conducted by the Oregon group. These materials were later used in Behavioral Sciences Institutes, which were also conducted for directors of institutes in educational media.

The number of participants who were trained in the SMI and the frequency with which they were held, as well as the physical requirements for their support, placed a drain upon the resources of the School of Education. Like "The Man Who Came to Din-

58. The SMI were funded under Title XI of the Education Professions Development Act of 1967, and hence were referred to in the jargon of the day as "Title XI Institutes."

117

ner," institute members tended to possess the house and all therein. Commented Dean Melbo, somewhat wryly, in 1973:[59]

Adequate housing was a persistent problem for I.T., as it began to expand. I fortunately managed to get several large classrooms in the west end of the old Annex Building allotted to the School of Education. These were remodeled for I.T., including a television studio, offices, preview rooms, laboratory, etc. The facilities were really quite good. But in a very short time, Dr. Finn's I.T. crew had overflowed into several adjacent classrooms, occupying them by a kind of academic "squatters' rights." Other space later was obtained for various I.T. projects. Their space requirements seemed to me and most of the faculty to be insatiable.

In October 1966, the Department of Instructional Technology, in cooperation with the University of Southern California's School of Medicine, began work on the Medical Information Project (MIP), under a large grant from the United States Public Health Service.[60] Under the supervision of Abrahamson, newly appointed as professor of education and of medical education, and Finn, the project was concerned with the application of instructional technology to the problem of continuing medical education. It was designed to assist general practitioners in keeping abreast of the information explosion in medical technology. As an initial step, appropriate self-instructional hardware was identified. Sixteen programs were then produced, covering a variety of topics of importance to general medical practitioners. By 1970, more than 200 physicians had participated in the field testing of the programs and the associated hardware.

Finn was a man of enormous ideas who was naturally impatient with the slow acceptance by education of the new

---

59. MS comment, May 1973.

60. The 1963 Health Professions Educational Assistance Act, followed in 1967 by the Education Professions Development Act, indicated the interest in forwarding professional education. In the medical field, cooperative arrangements between the School of Education and the School of Medicine were highly successful.

118

technology.[61] In a speech delivered at a meeting of the John Dewey Society at Las Vegas, Nevada, March 3, 1962,[62] he said:

> I mentioned a slow development of these approaches to instruction. . . . It has not notably influenced the theory of school administration or the education of superintendents. In preparing this paper, I had occasion to examine a number of recent books on educational philosophy. With one or two exceptions, they are so little concerned with these developments that, using the philosophers as a source, one must conclude that a technology of instruction does not exist . . .

Within the last five years this discontinuity has ended and the possibilities of a technology of instruction have suddenly thrust themselves into the educational mainstream. The philosophers have begun to cluck, if not in books, then in speeches, articles, and conversation; the curriculum specialists have been seen running about throwing up barricades to protect the child from the machine monster; and educational statesmen have

---

61. An incident, more amusing in retrospect than at the time, occurred in 1960, when Finn attended the convention in Cincinnati of the NEA's Department of Audio Visual Instruction. Reported *Time* magazine for March 14, 1960: "After studying the eye-boggling machines that flashed answers across screens, taught foreign languages in deep, resonant voice, lit up with a cheerful 'very good' when fed a correct answer, the audile educators were quick to prophesy a revolution in the art of teaching. "It is now possible," declared James D. Finn, professor of education at the University of Southern California and incoming DAVI president, "not only to eliminate the teacher but the school system." In a letter to *Time's* publisher, Henry Luce, Finn protested the misquotation. "You chose to emphasize one sentence out of a paper that occupies over 20 pages in its published form. By taking this sentence out of context, you have implied that I suggested that the possible elimination of the teacher and/or the school system by technology is a good thing. On the contrary, I was suggesting exactly the opposite, merely pointing out that, in the wrong hands, instructional technology poses a threat to certain basic values." On his return to campus, Finn asked to address the Faculty Club at its luncheon. A club flyer announced somewhat facetiously to its members that Finn would speak on the topic: "Will the Machine Replace the Professor?" and stated that Finn had "requested an opportunity to clarify his position, and so we are providing this forthcoming Faculty Club Meeting as a forum before which he can defend himself."

62. Finn, James D. "A Walk on the Altered Side." Printed in the October 1962, issue of the *Phi Delta Kappan.*

managed to raise the adrenalin of their constituents with speeches that sound as if they were ghostwritten by Ned Ludd or Jean Jacques Rousseau. We are urged to destroy the weaving machines and return to nature—all in the same breath. That the deeper philosophical questions raised by instructional technology were still of concern to him was shown in an address presented at a Lake Okoboji Educational Media Leadership Conference in 1968:[63]

What is this dialogue? It is a dialogue between higher-order technological organization, the industrial state, impersonal controls over people and spokesmen, no matter to the degree that they are right or wrong, for men as human beings—for man in microcosm. Some educators, at least, ought to see the thousand dilemmas present in this confrontation and seek solutions which are first, educative, and secondly, human, without reducing our culture back to some primitive stage where we live in the hills in shacks.

Summing up Finn's life and influence, Dean Melbo said:[64]

Dr. Finn was at heart a philosopher. Regretably, he never achieved what we used to talk about as being most essential in the field—a firm theoretical base for the media-oriented learning.

Educational Psychology. The Department of Educational Psychology participated in five important teaching activities, which reached out to every department within the School of Education. It furnished instruction in foundational as well as specialized courses for students who identified primarily with other departments, but who needed a basic orientation in the major areas of the psychology of education. It provided specific training for graduate students in all departments in statistics, research design, and measurement techniques, as well as consultative assistance on theses, dissertations, and research-related activities; and offered didactic courses and supervised field experiences in the training of school psychologists, pupil personnel specialists, and remedial specialists, as well as contributing to the formal preparation of

---

63. Quoted from *Memorial Services for Dr. James D. Finn,* Department of Instructional Technology, University of Southern California, April 5, 1969.
64. MS comment, May 1973.

VISION AND ACCOMPLISHMENT: 1960–1968

school counselors and personnel in special education. With the aid of the Department of Teacher Education, the Department of Educational Psychology prepared prospective teachers in psychological foundations of education by designing and staffing courses in learning, development, and measurement and evaluation. For majors in educational psychology working on advanced degrees, it presented specialized course work, including individualized programs.

During the 1960s, the department lost through retirement two of its most distinguished members: Thorpe in 1965, and Lefever in 1966. In 1967, the return to the faculty after an absence of some years of William B. Michael, distinguished psychologist and nationally recognized expert in testing, greatly strengthened the department, as did also the appointment to the faculty of a number of additional members. As of 1968, department members, with date of appointment, were: Professors Meyers (1947), Metfessel (1956), and Michael (1967); associate professors Magary (1960), McGrath (1964), Robert A. Smith (1968); and assistant professors Dembo (1968), Fox (1968), and Kirnser (1968). In adjunct status were associate professors Garlock and Handler, and assistant professor Mandell. In addition, there were a number of lecturers and research associates.

Most of the faculty of the department were actively engaged in research and in publishing. A notable example of research conducted during the 1960s was Metfessel's Project Potential. This major research project, funded by a large grant under the Cooperative Research Program of the U.S. Office of Education had as its full title, "An Investigation of Critical Attitudinal and Creativity Factors Related to Achieving and Nonachieving Culturally Disadvantaged Youth." Centered on the enhancement of creative activities in culturally different groups, the project was conducted by Metfessel with a sizeable staff and in cooperation with the Los Angeles city schools. The final report, rendered in 1968, resulted in the completion of a series of interrelated doctoral dissertations and in important work experience for graduate students as well as in a number of publications. Significant products included a bat-

121

tery of measuring instruments developed for special purposes, and the sharpening of the sensitivities of teaching and administrative personnel in many school districts to the learning potentialities of minority groups.

Secondary Education. The Department of Secondary Education collaborated with the Department of Teacher Education in the preparation of secondary teachers by providing the required-for-certification fifth-year course, *The Secondary School.* It also offered a master's and doctor's degree in secondary education. Field participation continued to receive its traditional emphasis in the work of the department. Secondary school specialists from the area of teacher education, reading, music education, business education, and physical education taught departmental courses featuring their respective specializations and capitalizing on their constant contacts with public education.[65] This phase of the department's work became particularly important following the discontinuation in 1966 of these departments within the School of Education and of their programs for special secondary credentials in these areas.

The Department of Secondary Education maintained constant and intimate contact with the practice of the profession of teaching. Visiting and adjunct professors such as Jefferson L. Garner and Truman N. Case, and lecturers taught courses which made unique contributions because of the dual roles of these instructors in the university and the field. The three generalist professors of the department, Olson, Georgiades, and Cannon, consistently served as field consultants and "critics of the profession" in such ways as to remove any impracticality from their instruction, while affording practitioners the benefit of their specialized knowledge. Olson served as general curriculum development consultant in a

---

65. Members of the department with dual appointment were, as of 1968: Professors James R. Hanshumaker (education and music) and Lenore C. Smith (physical education); and associate professors Phyllis W. Glass (education and music) and Richard H. Perry (physical education). Instructor-Coordinators in these areas were William M. Triplett (music education) and Lynn Turner (physical education).

122

variety of districts and was honored for his extraordinary contribution work experience programs in Santa Barbara County and at the state level. Georgiades was a key figure in the move of the National Association of Secondary School Principals (NASSP) toward such innovations as team teaching, flexible scheduling, study-group size variation, and independent study. In 1967, he was recognized by being appointed to President Topping's all-University Committee on Academic Excellence.[66] Cannon, who had joined the department in 1966, at his own request, from the Department of Teacher Education, was appointed by Melbo coordinator for University assistance to the joint University-School of Education-Los Angeles City project, Project APEX.

Project APEX, first entitled, "Mid-City Secondary Education Project,"[67] was an innovative program initiated in the Los Angeles city schools under the provisions of Title III of the Elementary and Secondary Education Act (ESEA) of 1965. Under the provisions of this act, thousands of local school districts in every part of the United States developed special programs to improve the educational opportunities and experience of millions of boys and girls. Project APEX was a joint venture of the Los Angeles city schools, the University of Southern California, and the School of Education. "APEX started," said Melbo in 1973:[68]

when Isaac McClelland, Assistant Superintendent of Area

---

66. The committee interviewed the dean of each school within the University, the vice-presidents, selected faculty, and students in order to formulate recommendations to be presented to President Topping, and eventually the Board of Trustees, for the establishment of a master plan for academic excellence. Georgiades' commitment to the concept of excellence later gave rise to his establishment within the School of Education of the Center for Excellence in Education.

67. The project was renamed APEX (acronym for Area Program for Enrichment Exchange) when two members of the Los Angeles Board of Education encouraged student leaders from all the Los Angeles city schools involved to find a more unique title than "Mid-City Secondary Education Project." The board members in question felt that a more intriguing name would kindle the kind of student enthusiasm which would help transform a good program into an exciting and inspirational experience. (*Agenda,* May 15, 1967).

68. MS comment, May 1973.

123

D,[69] Secondary Schools in L.A. came to my office to inquire how the University could help in developing better education for mid-city high schools. I said we could and would. There followed a series of "brainstorming" sessions in my office—Isaac McClelland and his assistants, Eugene Olson and Eugene McAdoo and myself. With a give-and-take of ideas fueled by our experience and enthusiasm, we hammered out in three or four work sessions the basic proposal which was later submitted by the L.A. Board for funding under Title III. I am still proud of our joint creation.

The purpose of the project was to make midcity high schools so excellent that no one with school age children would wish to move to the suburbs in search of better educational opportunities. Director for the Los Angeles city school system was Eugene Olson, assistant to McClelland. To coordinate resources of the University and to represent it on the APEX Executive Committee, Melbo appointed Cannon.

Los Angeles city high schools involved in the project initially were Dorsey, Fairfax, Hamilton, and Manual Arts. Crenshaw was added after its opening in February 1968. These high schools, with their feeder junior high schools, formed an educational complex designed to offer talented students from any school the advantages of unique and extraordinarily excellent programs or courses presented at any school within the complex. The unique programs were planned and carried out with the cooperation of the University of Southern California. University participation included lectures to APEX pupils in such subjects as African history, computer programming and data processing, aerospace engineering, drugs and narcotics, sciences, cinema, social work, medical education,

---

69. Isaac H. McClelland was Area D superintendent, Division of Secondary Education, Los Angeles city schools 1965–70. From 1970 to his retirement in 1972, he was assistant superintendent, Instruction. McClelland (A.B. and M.A., University of California, Berkeley, with graduate work at the University of Southern California) was a member of the Los Angeles city school systems from 1938 to 1972, and a distinguished public citizen. A member of the Board of Directors of the NAACP and the Urban League, he was one of the organizers of EDUCARE and its sixth president (1966–67).

124

psychology, human development, and audio-visual services. Groups of APEX pupils were also brought to the University campus for library experience, computer practice, and sports. An added feature was the participation in the program by various international students at the University, particularly those at the School of Education, who presented informal talks on their respective countries.

From January 1967 to July 1970, the program was operated under federal funding and thereafter, on a much reduced scale, by district funds. In July 1970, the deputy superintendent of instruction of the Los Angeles City Unified School District, expressed to Dean Melbo the Los Angeles city schools' appreciation of the University's cooperation in Project APEX and of Cannon's assistance in coordinating University resources:[70]

> The enthusiastic endorsement by the University of Southern California of Project APEX for the past three and one-half years is indeed gratifying, and the constructive suggestions included in each evaluation have been greatly appreciated by the Project Staff and the members of the APEX Advisory Council.
>
> We are especially indebted to Professor Wendell Cannon of the School of Education for the outstanding professional services he has rendered as coordinator of the University's resources, and for his active participation as a member of the APEX Advisory Council.

Social and Philosophical Foundations of Education. The Department of Social and Philosophical Foundations of Education developed during the 1960s a course of studies at the graduate level in four fields: philosophy of education, sociology of education, history of education, and international education. In a broader sense, however, the department regarded its primary function as that of performing a service for the entire School of Education. Since each of the department's specialties was regarded as a "foundation"

---

70. Letter, J. Graham Sullivan, deputy superintendent, Instruction, Los Angeles City Unified School District, to Dr. Irving R. Melbo, dean, School of Education, dated July 30, 1970.

125

subject in other fields of education, the majority of students enrolled were majoring in other fields of education.

While an effort was made to employ personnel qualified to teach in several of the foundation fields, the various specialties tended to be taught more frequently by certain members. The two professors who most often taught courses in philosophy were Brackenbury and O'Neill. Sociology of education was primarily offered by David Martin, Norman L. Friedman, Robert D. Glasgow, and Bernard Sklar, all of whom were involved during the 1960s in programs for disadvantaged youth.[71] History of education was taught by Ellis Oneal Knox, visiting lecturer and Professor Emeritus of Howard University.[72] By far the greatest development in the department was in the area of international education which, by 1968, had coalesced in the Center for International Education under John A. Carpenter.[73]

---

71. During the summers of 1967 and 1968, Martin was director of two federally funded institutes for teachers of disadvantaged youth. Glasgow served as consultant for Science Research Associates on education for the disadvantaged, and, in 1969, conducted an evaluation of the busing program of the Los Angeles city schools. Sklar trained business executives in human relations and at Chicago City College had previously taught human relations to Neighborhood Youth Corps for upgrading skills.

72. Knox, first appointed in 1969, had a distinguished record as educator and writer. He obtained his A.B. (1922) at the University of California; and his A.M. in Education (1928) and Ph.D. in Education (1931) at the University of Southern California. In addition to his years as professor of education, he had served as consultant to the Peace Corps and to the U.S. Commission of Civil Rights.

73. Carpenter received his A.B. at Catholic University of America in 1955, and a Certificate from the University of Paris, 1960. From 1960 to 1963, he served as Director, International Education and Foreign Language Programs, Department of Defense Schools in the European Area. Author of many articles in popular as well as professional journals and contributing editor to the *Overseas Educators Journal,* he had won wide acclaim for his innovative programs in international education. In 1963, *Time* magazine described him as "the energetic coordinator of foreign languages" for the Department of Defense school system, who believed that "to allow American children to live among foreign people without coming to know that people, its problems and greatness, is a national loss." In 1963, while attending a course at the Advanced Center of the School of Education in Europe, he was persuaded by Stoops to enter the graduate program on campus, specializing in international education. Prior to obtaining his Ph.D. in Education at the University of Southern California in 1968, he assisted in the coordination of a number of

VISION AND ACCOMPLISHMENT: 1960–1968

The Center for International Education developed from two separate but related activities in the School of Education. One was the traditional emphasis of the Department of Social and Philosophical Foundations on comparative education; the other was the presence in the School of Education of a comparatively large number of international students of education.

For many years the Department of Social and Philosophical Foundations (until 1956, the Department of History and Philosophy of Education) had offered work in comparative education. Under both Thompson and Brackenbury high interest in this specialty had been maintained.[74] Particularly important were the courses in Asiatic education offered within the department by the internationally recognized authority in Asiatic education, Theodore Hsi-En Chen.[75]

For many years, also, foreign students had been welcomed at the University of Southern California, drawn in large measure by President von KleinSmid's cordial receptivity and interest in in-

international projects, notably the Malawi Polytechnic Project, and gave courses in comparative education. He was appointed by Melbo in 1967 director of the Center for International Education.

74. Thompson (head of the department, 1932–52) had been director (1911–14 and 1919–21) of the Methodist Episcopal Mission Schools in Peru, South America. His interest in comparative education was the basis for his doctoral dissertation on the educational philosophy of Giovanni Gentile, Minister of Education in Italy under Mussolini, which had been published as the first of the Education Monographs of the University of Southern California. Brackenbury (head of the department from 1952 on) served as professor in Brazil, 1961–62, with the United Nations Educational, Scientific, and Cultural Organization (UNESCO). Other members of the department evinced similar interests in comparative education, teaching in international seminars and participating in international teacher programs.

75. Chen was born July 14, 1902, in Fukien, China. In 1922, he was awarded his A.B. from Fukien Christian University, and from 1922 to 1924 he taught English at the Anglo-Chinese College, Foochow, China. In 1929, he received his M.A. from Teachers College, Columbia University, and returned to China as Dean and Professor of Education, Fukien Christian University. In 1938, he received his Ph.D. from the University of Southern California, and joined the faculty of the University that year. In 1968, Chen presented to the Education Library his collection of documents relating to Asiatic education, probably the best in the world on this subject, and containing valuable insights into Chinese education both before and after 1949, the date of the founding of the Chinese People's Republic. Dr. Chen retired as Professor Emeritus, 1973.

127

ternational education. During the 1950s, Melbo, with U.S. government support and also with some funding from other countries, brought to the University an increasing number of foreign students and educators for visits or as participants in international teacher exchange programs. To meet the needs of these students and to provide them with tutorial and counseling assistance, Melbo organized in 1964, the Center for Intercultural Studies. He placed the center in the Department of Social and Philosophical Foundations as a natural concomitant to the comparative education courses presented by that department. The Center for Intercultural Studies, working closely with the Office of the Dean of Students and other divisions of the University concerned with foreign student assistance, met with a positive and enthusiastic response from them. The foreign students discovered that the center gave them a real sense of identification with the University and its School of Education.

In 1966, the Center for Intercultural Studies was renamed the Center for International Education and, in 1967, Melbo appointed John A. Carpenter its director. With the firm support of the dean, whose long-standing interest in international education and enthusiastic endorsement of intercultural activities found in Carpenter "the right man for the right job," Carpenter developed the center swiftly and efficiently. As an administrative and service agency of the School of Education, the center initiated and administered intercultural programs domestically and abroad. Its three major functions were: to provide study, orientation, and field internship programs in international education; to support research and publication projects related to international education; and to organize service programs focused on educational needs overseas and among different cultural groups in the United States.

In executing its first function, the center directed a program of academic and professional development for foreign students in the School of Education. This program sought to assure that the studies and activities of international students were especially designed to be relevant to their career needs in their own countries. Fundamental concepts of the program were observation and

128

internship intrinsically related to the students' course of study. Academic counseling involving frequent contact between students and their professors was another major aspect.

The center also designed and administered short-term programs for groups of visiting international and community leaders or students. In 1967, a 10-day program of seminars, professional visits, and community activities was arranged for eight administrators of the University of Michoacan, Morelia, Mexico. This visit, sponsored by the U.S. Office of Education and the U.S. Department of State, was coordinated by Wilbur of the Department of Higher Education, with the assistance of Carpenter and Vera Young of the Center for International Education. In 1968, a 60-day professional activities program, beginning February 1, 1968, was arranged for eight Italian educators.

Another program arranged by the Center for International Education was that of the Volunteers to America.[76] In 1967, the University of Southern California was designated the Western Regional Office for the Volunteers to America Program and the locale for providing orientation to volunteers who were to be assigned west of the Mississippi River. Orientation began July 24, 1968, and was conducted through August 19, 1968, for 17 participants, of whom 15 were from Latin America and 2 from Africa. The orientation program, devised by the Center for International Education, included intensive instruction in the English language, a seminar in American education and society conducted by Dr. Hickerson of the Department of Teacher

---

76. Often described as the "Peace Corps in Reverse," Volunteers to America was a program proposed by President Lyndon B. Johnson in his message to the Congress on international education in February 1966. Said President Johnson: "Our nation has no better ambassadors than the young volunteers who now serve in 46 countries in the Peace Corps. I propose that we welcome similar ambassadors to our shores. We need their special skills and understanding, just as they need ours." In a pilot program conducted during 1967, volunteers who were to work in community development and education-remedial projects west of the Mississippi were trained at the University of Southern California.

129

Education,[77] and close cooperation with Temple City Unified School District for classroom observation and participation.[78]

A perceptive comment on the program was made by one of its participants, Samuel Kwashi Dogbe, teacher of English and African history at the Presbyterian Training College in Ghana, whose assignment in the United States was to be in the Temple City Unified School District. "The whole USC program," said Dogbe:[79]

> ... has been, no doubt, a great success and every praise must go to its directors who very tactfully and efficiently met all the problems of the "unprecedented" program, especially in the field of housing. They have done much and gained a lot for the next program, just as we have been prepared well for our assignments.
>
> Yes, our assignments: now I look forward to my assignment in Temple City. I feel this is a great challenge to me for the whole "Peace Corps in reverse" is a baby project. Its growth, maturity, and success are in my hands. I have been given the tools; the chipping and shaping of the wood into a masterpiece must be my great concern. My hope is that by the time I leave Temple City we must all have come to the realization that parochialism and stereotypes are a threat to everlasting peace. The right hand washes the left, but the right must also learn to accept help from the left.

77. Over a great number of years, the Department of Social and Philosophical Foundations of Education cooperated with the Department of Teacher Education in staffing the initial courses which undergraduates took when pursuing a teaching credential. The course on "The Teacher, The School, and Society," was regularly presented by Hickerson of the Department of Teacher Education.

78. Temple City Unified School District had launched in 1963, an international program with exchanges with schools in Ensenada and Magdalena, Mexico. The program won in 1966, the National Education Association's Pacemaker Award for the most innovative program in California. Notable support for the international emphasis was rendered by Superintendent M. John Rand (M.S. in Ed. (1948); Ed.D. (1952), University of Southern California). Rand's experience in international education later made him a valued member of the survey team for the Soche Hill College survey, Malawi, Africa.

79. University of Southern California, School of Education, Center for International Education (1968).

VISION AND ACCOMPLISHMENT: 1960–1968

The program instituted by Dogbe in Temple City met with great success, as was recorded in an article in *American Education* for July 1968:[80]

> Far from the slums of New York, another Volunteer to America, Samuel Kwashi Dogbe of Ghana, is teaching the children of Temple City, Calif., about the people and cultures of Africa. He laid out a semester course for the elementary-grade children, starting with maps showing the ethnic as well as political divisions of Africa, and moved on to the farming and fishing that most of the people there live by. He described family life in the villages, towns, and the games, music, and dances, and the important art of storytelling. He illustrated his talks with slides and movies, and for the folksongs accompanied himself on the banjo. The ground nut soup he prepared for the school lunch one day made such a hit that the children's parents clamored for meetings in the evening to learn how to make it. Before long he had a major role in an adult course in African culture and customs.

Providing courses for international students in the United States was only one aspect of the work of the Center for International Education. On the other side of the coin was the provision of courses for Americans who wished to know more about foreign cultures. In 1968, two such institutes were held, both supported by NDEA funds and both conducted overseas. One was an Institute on African Studies held in Ghana for 22 elementary school teachers, mostly from American schools overseas; the other was an Advanced Asian Studies Institute held in Taiwan for 38 secondary school teachers, again mostly from American schools overseas. The latter institute was codirected by Carpenter and Chen, assisted by Roger Benjamin, political scientist at the University of Minnesota, and Yu-Kwang-Chung, professor at the National Taiwan University.

Special Education. For many years the School of Education had trained teachers of the mentally retarded and, in conjunction with the John Tracy Clinic, teachers of the deaf and hard of hearing.

---

80. Pearse (1968), p. 25.

During the 1960s, however, federal funding and public interest in this area of education, far-sighted planning by Melbo, and the dedicated work of a number of specialists in the field, brought this specialty to a high level of achievement and won for the School of Education national and international acclaim in this field.

The program began with a seed planted by Sophia Salvin in the late 1950s. Said Melbo in 1967:[81]

> Some ten years ago Sophia came to talk to me about an idea, and there is still nothing more powerful in the world than a great idea. Her thought was that it was time to build a program in the field of special education which would prepare teachers, researchers, and administrators in this field.
>
> I wondered at first what she wanted for herself, but as I came to know her better I soon understood that what she did for others was all for love and nothing for reward.
>
> So it all began to build.

The next step was funding. Again the dean takes up the story:[82]

> I made a trip to Washington to talk with Dr. Romaine Mackie, at that time the one-woman Department of Special Education in the U.S. Office of Education.[83] There had just been funded a small program to stimulate the development of university training programs in special education. I applied for a "stimulation grant" of $10,000, the maximum allowable, received it, and used it to employ Dr. Magary.[84]

---

81. Melbo, I. R. "Tribute to Sophia," *Sixth Annual Distinguished Lecture Series in Special Education and Rehabilitation,* Summer 1967, p. v.

82. Tape recording, April 1973.

83. Romaine P. Mackie entered the U.S. Office of Education in 1947 as specialist in the education of the handicapped. For ten years she was chief, Exceptional Children and Youth, U.S. Office of Education. Prior to her going to the U.S. Office of Education, she was consultant for education of the handicapped in the California State Department of Education. She received her Ph.D. from Columbia University in 1943. Author of books, government publications, and many published articles and reports, she was internationally recognized in her field.

84. Magary had received his A.B. (1954) at the University of Michigan; his M.A. in Clinical Psychology (1956) at Wayne University; and his Ph.D. in Educational Psychology (1960) at Indiana University. Prior to his appointment to the faculty of the School of Education, he had been school psychological coordinator

132

The next year I applied for another $10,000 stimulation grant, received it, and from that beginning we went on to request and obtain other federal funding as our program (and federal support) grew together.

Melbo's appointment of Magary proved to be a seminal influence in the development of special education at the School of Education. Magary's enthusiasm and professional competence soon made it apparent that again, with unerring accuracy, Melbo had picked the "right man for the right job." The growth of the specialty quickly made necessary establishment of clinical facilities for teacher education in this field and, in 1961, at Melbo's request, the Los Angeles Board of Education officially designated the Washington Boulevard School for the Multiple Handicapped as a demonstration school for the School of Education. Again, the idea had arisen with Sophia Salvin. Said Dean Melbo in his moving tribute to her at the time of her death in 1967:[85]

> One day Sophia came and offered the thought that Washington Boulevard School, of which she was principal, might well become a demonstration school. The idea was eminently sound, and I communicated with the Los Angeles Board of Education, and the Board approved, and so we had a demonstration school which still serves us magnificently.[86]

In 1961, an interdisciplinary planning committee was formed for the development of a doctoral program in special education. The committee, with Meyers as chairman, included representatives from the many disciplines encompassed by special education.[87] The program devised by the committee, and approved by the faculty, drew in many courses previously offered

---

with the Devereux Foundation, Devon, Pennsylvania. In 1960, he published a book, *The Exceptional Child: A Book of Readings.*

85. Melbo, I. R. "Tribute to Sophia," *Sixth Annual Distinguished Lecture Series in Special Education and Rehabilitation,* Summer 1967, pp. v, vi.

86. In 1969, the school was renamed the Sophia T. Salvin School.

87. Other members were Elena Boder, M.D., associate clinical professor of pediatrics, School of Medicine; A. Jean Ayres, Ph.D., occupational therapy; William Perkins, A.M., Ph.D., speech pathology; Edgar L. Lowell, Ph.D., John Tracy Clinic; and Sophia T. Salvin.

133

by other departments, and introduced new courses leading to advanced degrees in special education. In 1962, with Melbo's enthusiastic support, Magary inaugurated the summer series of distinguished lectures in special education, a series which was to become an annual event of outstanding importance and success.

With a grant in 1962 from the U.S. Office of Education which assured the continuation of funds in the area of leadership training in special education, Melbo established the Department of Exceptional Children, with Magary its head. In 1964, the Department of Exceptional Children was subordinated to the Division of Psychology, Guidance, and Exceptional Children. In 1966, it was established as the Department of Special Education.

By 1968, the department offered a complete series of programs in teacher training in special education, as well as graduate programs through the doctorate. Clinical facilities had been expanded to a wide range of institutions, including six for the mentally retarded, three for the physically handicapped, five for the emotionally disturbed, three for the visually impaired, and several for the deaf and hard of hearing. Teacher education programs were accredited in mental retardation, speech correction and lip reading, deaf and hard of hearing, and physically handicapped. In addition, a complete sequence was offered for teachers of the educationally handicapped, emotionally disturbed, and neurologically handicapped, although credentials to teach in these areas were not specified in California, as of 1968.

To provide instruction in this wide range of specialties, a number of specialists had been added to the faculty: Buscaglia in learning disabilities; MacLeech in mental retardation; Coss in physical handicapping conditions; and Peter in prescriptive teaching. Laurence J. Peter was another of Melbo's "finds." Recalled Melbo in 1973:[88]

> I found Laurence J. Peter at the University of British Columbia, and found that he was somewhat discontented with his future prospects. He had recently written a professional book on

134

88. Tape recording, May 1973.

prescriptive teaching. It was this book, and its emphasis on the diagnosis of learning capabilities and the subsequent "prescription" of an individualized learning program that particularly appealed to me. I interviewed him, and incidentally enjoyed his dry and droll sense of humor, replete with bits of satire, and appointed him to the faculty. While at USC, he developed his book, *The Peter Principle,* the success of which would ultimately take him out of the University world.[89]

As of 1968, Peter was also director of the School of Education's Evelyn Frieden Center for Educationally Handicapped Children,[90] a facility designed and equipped for the precise study of teacher-child interaction, and a laboratory for research and development of materials and methods for prescriptive teaching.

In cooperation with the John Tracy Clinic, the School of Education continued to offer a program designed to prepare teachers for the deaf and hard of hearing. The program included course work in the methods of teaching the deaf, directed teaching ex-

---

89. Born in Canada, Peter received his A.B. (1957) and his M. Ed. (1958) at Western Washington State College, and his Ed.D (1963) at Washington State University. Prior to his appointment to the faculty of the University of British Columbia, he had served for 22 years in the school systems of British Columbia, principally at Vancouver. His professional book, *Prescriptive Teaching* (1965) was followed in 1969 with the semi-serious *The Peter Principle,* a penetrating analysis of administrative stultification; and in 1972, with *The Peter Prescription,* in similar vein.

90. The center (formerly designated the USC Educational Therapy Clinic for Emotionally Disturbed Children) was named in memory of Evelyn Fargo Frieden (1921–1967), who died while a graduate student in special education at the School of Education. Born in Chicago, she had worked her way through junior college while employed by the American Can Company. Immersed during the depression years in trade union movements, in later years she was active in peace and civil rights movements. In 1946, she married Mike Frieden, by whom she had four children. In 1957, she took a B.S. degree with honors at the University of California, Berkeley, in child development, and received a grant to finish a master's degree in special education at San Francisco State College. Prior to entering the School of Education for doctoral work in special education, she had taught eight years in the San Gabriel Valley School District, working with emotionally disturbed and retarded children.

135

perience with preschool children and their parents, and with elementary-level deaf children in public school programs.[91]

Lowell and his highly specialized staff[92] had earned for the John Tracy Clinic a national and international reputation. As Melbo noted, the Tracy Clinic was "beyond doubt the best clinical facility of its kind in the world." Research, which had always been an important phase of the clinic's services, received much federal support, beginning in the 1960s, both in the form of fellowships and research grants in the education of the aurally handicapped. Segments of the research which had a direct bearing on teacher education included the Speech Project[93] and the Teaching Machine Project.[94]

During the 1960s, the John Tracy Clinic, in cooperation with

91. The specialized preparation required a full-time academic year, beginning with the fall semester. Completion of the program led to certification by the Conference of Executives of American Schools of the Deaf. Admission preference was given to students who had had previous course work in education and who would be eligible for a teaching credential upon completion of the program. The program could be included either as a part of the California standard teaching credential with specialization in elementary teaching, or the special education credential restricted to teaching in classes for the deaf.

92. As of 1968, in addition to Lowell, the staff included Joseph S. Rudloff, assistant professor of education and appointed in 1968, director of the John Tracy Clinic Demonstration School; Alathena J. Smith, in clinical psychology; Marguerite Stoner, specialist in the profoundly deaf; Charlotte B. Avery, specialist in audiology and coordinator for a speech project for the profoundly deaf; Starla Warburton, coordinator for practice teaching in deaf education; Sammie Kay Barnes, supervisor of teachers in training; and Mary Tidwell, specialist in speech.

93. The federally funded speech project had among its objectives the preparation of materials for teaching speech to hearing impaired children and adults. The first phase of the project, which began in June 1966, concerned itself with the production of a series of 52 ten-minute films on teaching speech to the profoundly deaf. By 1969, 22 films had been completed and 10 more were in various stages of completion, with 20 more to be completed before the end of the five-year project. In addition, a series of listening and transcription exercises, including audiotape, were developed for sharpening the listening skills of prospective teachers of the deaf.

94. The objective of the Teaching Machine Project was the development of an auto-instructional machine which could be used in classrooms for the deaf, with film strip projection. This objective had been achieved by 1969, and the first machines were in preparation. By 1971, it was announced that the first production run of the Program Master teaching machine had been completed by General Electric, under license from the clinic.

the School of Education, organized an effort for teacher recruitment. From 1967–70, a total of 25 teachers of the deaf were prepared, and 115 teachers and graduate students were enrolled in the summer sessions.

One of the most important developments in the area of special education was the establishment in 1964 of the Instructional Materials Center for Special Education. This center, funded by the Bureau of Education for the Handicapped of the U. S. Office of Education, was established at the University of Southern California as a pilot project of the U. S. Office of Education. Located first at 17 Chester Place, in the former residence of President von KleinSmid, the center was a member of the nationwide USOE Instructional Materials Center Network for Handicapped Children and Youth. The center at the University of Southern California served the three-state region of California, Arizona, and Nevada. Said Melbo in 1973:[95]

> When this opportunity came, it was almost too good to be true. Here was an opportunity to translate theory into materials and procedures, and a ready-made three-state laboratory situation in which to work. I was enthusiastic then—and now!

Originally designed as a means of getting information regarding teaching materials for the handicapped into the hands of professionals in these three states, the center soon broadened its objectives to include preservice teacher instruction in the use of the Instructional Materials Center; development of model preservice teacher education packages; development of model field inservice instructional packages; intensive, short-term, inservice instruction in special areas; training of graduate students and field professionals in techniques of modifying teacher behaviors; development of instructional materials and models for training school administrators in program evaluation; and inservice education in media production and use with the handicapped.

In 1967, the center, in coordination with the California Special Education Bureau, cosponsored a conference for 250 ad-

---

95. MS comment, May 1973.

137

ministrators of special education programs. In 1968, in cooperation with U.S. Office of Education's Bureau for the Education of
the Handicapped and the California Special Education Bureau, it
sponsored the western United States conference on the use of
ESEA funds for handicapped children and youth.

The budget for the center in 1968–69 was for more than
$250,000 and its membership more than 5,000, or approximately
50 per cent of all special education personnel in the three-state
region served. With a staff of 31 persons, it circulated in 1968
more than 1,000 items each month on two-week loans, was host
to more than 200 educators each month, including individuals and
groups from school districts, educational institutions of higher
learning, and visitors from out-of-state and out-of-country. Staff
personnel made an average of 15 field presentations a month to
school districts throughout the region. Operating the center under
Melbo's supervision was McIntyre as director; Charles A. Watts,
associate director; and Cara Volkmor, librarian.

Teacher Education. Development of teacher education programs during the 1960s was stimulated by the needs of a rapidly
growing and changing socio-economic climate in both the nation
and in southern California. The University of Southern California, as an institution of higher learning located in a large metropolitan area, sought to serve the needs of the city schools and,
at the same time, to use the situation as a laboratory in which both
to learn and to develop appropriate programs in many fields. As
a professional school of the University, the School of Education
was vitally concerned with the educational scene in southern
California. It participated to full extent in the various appropriate
programs of the University and devised special teacher education
programs of its own to meet the new requirements.

Faculty and staff were persons of long experience in teacher
education. Cannon headed the department from 1948 to 1966,
Wilson, a member of the department since 1954, succeeded Can-

138

non in 1966.[96] Others in the department as of 1968, all with teaching experience, were: associate professor Marks; assistant professors Fischer, Hayes, Hickerson, King (King-Stoops), Lee; adjunct assistant professors McCarthy and Rowe; nine instructor-coordinators; 12 clinical instructors; and nine lecturers. Subordinated also to the department were the members of the Teacher Corps units of the University of Southern California. Invaluable assistance was rendered the department by its administrative assistant, Gladys S. Caywood, who had been with the department since 1952.[97]

The core curriculum of the department, basic to all programs of teacher education, included academic preparation, professional preparation, specialization in teaching, observation, and directed participation. The basic program for elementary teachers was designed for undergraduates and graduates to complete requirements for the California standard teaching credential, with specialization in elementary education. The basic program for secondary teachers was designed for the college graduate, so that the student could complete the requirements for the standard teaching credential, with specialization in secondary education at the end of two semesters and one summer of graduate work.

In 1968, the School of Education was offering five specially designed teacher education programs: Specialist-Teacher Program, Internship Program, Teacher Assistantship Program, Vocational Teacher Program; and the Teacher Corps. Each program

---

96. Wilson, who came from five generations of teachers, received his B.S. (1947) at Central Missouri State College; and his M.S. in Ed. (1948) and Ed.D. (1951) at the University of California, Los Angeles. In 1954, Melbo appointed him to the faculty of the School of Education as Visiting Professor to participate in the Ford-funded Southern California Education Project. In 1958, he named Wilson to the faculty in the Department of Teacher Education. Active in many educational and civic activities, Wilson was a prominent citizen of Torrance, where he held elective office. In 1967, he was elected president of the California Association for Student Teaching.

97. An invaluable member of the Department of Teacher Education, Mrs. Caywood attended the normal (teacher) training program at Coe College, Cedar Rapids, Iowa, and was for four years a teacher in the elementary schools in Iowa. Prior to coming to California she had held various positions in the business field.

139

combined in a unique fashion the School of Education's traditional emphasis on campus and field experience, internship concepts as developed over more than a decade of experimental programs, and the teacher-assistant role in teacher preparation.

The conceptual design of these programs was Melbo's creation. In 1973, he summarized the basic plan thus:[98]

In terms of its *conceptual design,* I urged and advocated, with excellent faculty and field support, that the theory component and the methods component be taught *concurrently* with the field experience components: actual classroom-school observation and participatory teaching under supervision.

The conceptual design also provided that each student would have one semester of student-teaching experience at each of two levels: e.g., primary and middle grades or high school sophomores and the high school seniors.

Further, the design provided for experience with two levels of socio-economic pupil population, e.g., in a school with "disadvantaged" children and a school with children from more favored or affluent community groups.

Finally, there was the concept that a contemporary professional school of education must have, not one, but a number of different teacher preparation programs, each organized to prepare teacher "specialists" in various categories, e.g., kindergarten, reading, English as a Second Language, the mentally retarded, etc.

In 1961, Melbo succeeded in having introduced into the state legislature a bill, which was subsequently passed, authorizing county superintendents to issue certificates to qualified persons to serve as teacher assistants, and also authorizing governing boards throughout the state to employ teacher assistants and to make such payment as they deemed proper for services rendered.[99] This

---

98. MS comment, May 1973.

99. The internship concept was incorporated in Assembly Bill 442, sponsored by the School of Education to clarify the employment relationship growing out of the Specialist-Teacher Program. Introduced during the 1961 legislature, the Bill passed both houses and was signed into law by Governor Edmund G. Brown. It changed those portions of the Education Code of the State of California pertaining to matters affected by it.

140

legislation was, of course, an all-important adjunct to the internship program and the other programs, since it afforded the possibility of fiscal support for these programs and the students involved.

It would be difficult to overestimate the importance of the conceptual design to the whole structure of teacher education at the University of Southern California's School of Education. It underlay all of the special teacher programs and, indeed, set the stage for the later development of the Teacher Corps programs, both urban and rural-migrant.

It will be recalled that the Specialist-Teacher Program had been launched in September 1960, after a year's planning. Said Melbo:[100]

> The faculty, having had considerable experience with high school teacher education programs requiring a fifth year of collegiate work and having enjoyed prior experiences with successful pilot programs, has found most rewarding the year of development.... As a result of the year's time and effort, the new program has been established as an operating and promising member of our family of programs in teacher education.

The program was conducted from 1959 through 1965. Calvert, director until his untimely death on December 14, 1964, was succeeded by Marks, who had been associated with the program from its inception.[101] Assisting Marks in bringing the program to

---

100. Letter of transmittal, University of Southern California, School of Education (1960).

101. Merle Byron Marks was born in 1925 in Cleveland, Ohio. Following World War II service with the U.S. Navy (1943–46), he obtained his A.B. (1948) and his A.M. (1949) at Western Reserve University. From 1949 to 1952, he was a teacher in the elementary schools, Los Angeles County; from 1952 to 1955 teacher in the secondary schools of Los Angeles City; 1955–56 assistant vice-principal, Narbonne High School, Los Angeles; 1956–57 coordinator, Student Body Programs, Narbonne High School; 1957–60 coordinator, New Teacher In-Service Program, Fleming Junior High School, Los Angeles; and 1960–65 on leave from Los Angeles city schools as assistant in the High School Specialist-Teacher Program. In 1967, he was appointed associate professor of education, School of Education; and in 1972, associate dean, Graduate Studies, School of Education.

141

a successful conclusion were Hugh W. Chock, coordinator;[102] James W. Hall, research and evaluation specialist; and Catherine Clark, administrative assistant and secretary.

During the period of its operation, the program was expanded from cooperation with the Los Angeles city schools only to the Los Angeles greater metropolitan area and to junior high schools. The final report on the program, issued in 1965, indicated that, during the program's life span, a total of 3,200 inquiries had been received, 1,000 interviews conducted, 400 applications received, 150 accepted, and 125 persons admitted. Of these, 105 had completed the rigorous training.

The full impact of the program could only be assessed by the eventual success of its participants. As early as 1963, however, Calvert expressed his confidence of the program's value:[103]

> We are confident at this point that the employment of the TA's benefits high school pupils, the district personnel, the participants themselves, the cooperating academic departments, and the School of Education's parallel programs. We are furthermore convinced that the product of the entire program is in a very real sense a superior and specialized teacher.

---

102. Chock, a doctoral candidate at the School of Education on leave from the Los Angeles city schools, died July 25, 1966. At the time of his death he was immediate past president (1965–66) of the USC Chapter of Phi Delta Kappa, and in his memory the Phi Delta Kappa Office in Waite Phillips Hall was designated the Hugh Chock Memorial-Phi Delta Kappa Office. Chock, a native of Hawaii, where he was born July 30, 1921, served during World War II in Okinawa, the occupation of Japan, and did surveying in the Palau Islands for the Photographic Mapping Service of the United States Army. He was graduated from the University of Minnesota, later obtaining a Master of Science degree at the University of Southern California. A well-loved teacher of science and mathematics at Westchester High School, Los Angeles, from 1952 to 1956 and at Hamilton High School from 1957 to 1961, Chock came to USC as instructor-coordinator in Teacher Education Projects. Although ill, he continued his work, his studies, and his duties as president of the Alpha Epsilon Chapter of Phi Delta Kappa to the end of the school year, 1965–66. Wrote Henry Barnhart, president, Alpha Epsilon Chapter 1963–64, "Hugh Chock will continue to live in the hearts and minds of those who knew him. . . . He entered into life wholly with an affirmative approach which inspired progress . . . It will not be easy to fill the void left by this man [*Alpha Epsilon News Letter*, September 1966, p. 3]."

103. *Specialist-Teacher Program Newsletter*, February 1, 1963.

142

All will not survive what is thought to be one of the most arduous and extensive programs in the nation, but those who do will attribute much of their success to the resident teachers and staff coordinators with whom they worked while teacher assistants.

Evaluation of the program by members of the Los Angeles school district and disinterested teacher-training experts,[104] bore out Calvert's estimate. Resident teachers and administrators considered the teacher assistants to be of considerable help in the school. All were willing to have more in the future. Participants evaluated their extended parallel academic courses, professional theory, and field experiences as very rigorous, but of considerable practical value. Programmed teaching and learning showed great possibilities both for the instruction of teachers and for use by practitioners. The value of the expanded sequences of experiences from teacher assistantship to full-time specialist-teacher appeared to have great possibilities. In retrospect, Melbo said in 1973:[105]

> The program was eminently successful. The numbers involved were never great but we had not expected they would be. The concept was a very sound one and was much appreciated by the cooperating school systems. The program is still in effect, and it continues to be one of the several and distinct teacher education programs which the School of Education currently maintains.

The 1961 legislation had made the program financially viable. An amusing anecdote in this connection was related by Melbo:[106]

> At or near the end of the fourth year of the program, it became apparent that there was enough interest and support on the part of the cooperating school systems to permit the program to continue without the fiscal support from the Ford Foundation's $660,000 grant. So, one day, after this had become apparent, I decided it would be no more than fair and honest to return the unused portion of the Ford grant.

104. Peter Mickelson, University of Wisconsin, formerly of the University of Hawaii, and Hubert Everly, dean, School of Education, University of Hawaii, were assigned by Melbo to evaluate the program in all its aspects.
105. Tape recording, May 1973.
106. Tape recording, May 1973.

143

I wrote a letter explaining that the program was now self-supporting and, thanks to Ford's generous funding, it had been possible to develop the program, and it could now stand on its own as a successful pattern of teacher education. I was therefore returning the balance in the account and a check was enclosed in amount—as I recall it—of $140,000.

No sooner had the letter reached Ford Foundation offices in New York than one of the officers, whom I happened to know personally, was on the telephone, wanting to know what was the matter with their money (although he didn't put it quite like that). But apparently it was an absolutely new phenomenon that any institution that had received a grant would return it or any portion of it. I suppose I thereby became the only person in the history of the Ford Foundation ever to return voluntarily a portion of an unused grant after the program had been established on its own.

I quickly assured my friend that there was nothing wrong with the Ford relationship. It was one we cherished very much. Our position simply was that the program was now on its own and was self-supporting. In all good faith we should return the unused portion of the money. We had been modest and careful in the expenditures involved, and had used other funds where they were available in order to conserve the Ford Foundation resources. I also made special point in telling him over the telephone, as, indeed, I had in the letter accompanying the check, that we would feel free to call upon Ford Foundation for support for other programs at other times. Perhaps they might recall, when such an application was made, that we had, indeed, been prudent in the management of their funds. We regarded the funds as investment capital and proposed to handle them in that manner.

Melbo's prudent use of the Ford Foundation's funds was typical of his overall prudence and careful management in the fiscal area. "During my years as dean," he noted in 1973:[107]

... the School of Education has been a consistent contributor

144

to the University's fiscal solvency. Without exception, I have operated in the "black" every year, and turned in a substantial balance to the General Fund.

I have never believed that a "deficit" operation is any evidence of academic excellence. Instead, it is probably an indication of academic obsolescence or administrative irresponsibility.

The Internship Program, instituted following the conclusion of the Southern California Teacher Education Program of 1954–59, was a continuation of that program, in cooperation with public school districts in the Los Angeles area. Like its predecessor, the program was designed to recruit, and train for teaching responsibilities, selected mature men and women who had not previously been formally prepared. Candidates were required to hold a bachelor's degree, with acceptable scholarship; to have attained the degree at least two years before admission to the program; and to be acceptable to the University for admission as graduate students. They must also be selected by a cooperating school district, in accordance with the district's own personnel standards and qualifications, to serve a year as a classroom teacher under a "partial fulfillment of requirements" credential. The course of study was so arranged that, upon its completion, in combination with a year of successful teaching experience, the candidate was qualified for the standard teaching credential with a specialization in either elementary or secondary teaching.

In 1960, a pilot program was initiated in the Teacher Assistantship Program. This pilot program, designated the "Specialist Elementary Project," was a graduate experimental program to recruit, prepare, and induct into elementary school teaching selected persons who had at least a bachelor's degree but who lacked the professional preparation necessary for a teaching credential. An inhouse project, undertaken without outside funding, the pilot project was conducted in cooperation with the Torrance Unified School District. "Torrance," pointed out Dean Melbo in 1973:[108]

... was a rapidly growing school district with a strong and

---

108. MS comment, May 1973.

145

forward-looking superintendent, Dr. J. H. Hull.[109] In addition, I was often called upon as a consultant to advise with the superintendent and board. Then, too, Dr. Wilson was serving at that time as a member of the Torrance Board of Education, and was instrumental in helping the Board to see the value of the proposed program.[110]

The pilot program concentrated first on training teachers for service in the seventh and eighth grades. With the approval of the Torrance Board of Education, qualified students were employed as teacher assistants during the training program, receiving compensation for their services. The 20 candidates successfully completed the program and entered the Torrance Unified School District as teachers.

In 1962, this program became the Teacher Assistantship Program, conducted by the School of Education with various local school districts. Designed on lines similar to those of the pilot project, emphasis was given to the preparation of the candidate for a specific teaching assignment, although no guarantee of future employment was asked or granted.

B.S. in Education—Technical Studies. In 1968, the School of Education began a new program which was designed to prepare teachers of vocational and technical studies for worldwide service in secondary schools and colleges which maintained vocational-

---

109. J. Henry Hull (Ed.D., USC, 1948) retired as Superintendent, Torrance Unified School District in 1970. Author of more than 40 articles on professional subjects, he was the recipient of an American Educator's Medal, a Freedoms Foundation Award, and prominent member of EDUCARE.

110. Wilson, a highly regarded citizen of Torrance, was a member of the Board of Education from 1965 to 1968. In 1968, he was elected to the Torrance City Council, by the second largest voter plurality achieved to that time, reflecting the citizens' confidence in him. He was also chairman of the North Torrance Lions Club committee on education. Extending the municipality into the international educational field, during his 1972 visit to Israel, Kuwait, Lebanon, Egypt, and Jordan as participant in the U.S. State Department's Contemporary Pedagogue Program, Wilson met with municipal representatives in each country to present the resolution prepared for his visit by the Torrance City Council, and arranged on a number of occasions for exchange of professional texts between the institutions of learning in those countries and the University of Southern California and Torrance school district.

146

technical curricula. The program was instituted by Melbo in order to meet a demand for supervisors and teachers of vocational specializations in foreign and American institutions. "I became aware," Melbo commented in 1973:[111]

> ... of the need of such a program and degree during the early years of the Malawi project.[112] We began to get a considerable number of foreign students from Malawi and elsewhere—mostly African and Asian nations—and they were expected to return as instructors in various polytechnic schools. They also needed the prestige of an American degree to be "respectable" as a faculty member of such schools, which were often associated with national universities.

The curriculum, which led to the degree of Bachelor of Science in Education—Technical Studies included a sound liberal arts foundation, a relevant diversified academic major, and professional training.[113] Said Melbo:[114]

> The program design was simple. I arranged with Los Angeles Trade and Technical College (a community college) to give the technical courses which then became transfer credit to USC. We gave the academic and professional courses at USC, provided the advisement and counseling, and gave the degree.

As of 1973, this program remained restricted to international

---

111. MS comment, 1973.

112. From 1962 through 1967, the University of Southern California through its School of Education undertook, under contract with the U.S. Agency for International Development (AID), the establishment of a Polytechnic School in the new African nation of Malawi (formerly Nyasaland). In addition to construction of the school and establishment of the curriculum, in a later contract, the School of Education undertook the training of selected Malawians at the campus of the University, in order to train them for positions of responsibility upon their return to their homeland. The Polytechnic was incorporated as one of the schools of the multicampus University of Malawi.

113. In addition to certain general requirements, the academic major was diversified to include three of the following areas: humanities (excluding art, music, and the foreign languages), social sciences, mathematics, natural sciences, fine arts (including, art, music, and drama) and foreign languages. Eight upper division units were required in each of the three areas chosen. Course work totaling no more than 20 units might be selected from business education or administration, engineering, and vocational subjects.

114. MS comment, May 1973.

147

students. Educational trends of the 1970s, however, gave reason to foresee a receptive market in American schools, as Melbo foresaw the situation:[115]

> To this date (1973), this program has been restricted to the international market. It really ought to be developed along similar lines to provide well trained technical and vocational teachers for the domestic market. I am sure it would be successful, but there are those in the University who frown upon anything "vocational" at the Bachelor of Science level.

Teacher Corps. Teacher Corps training began at the University of Southern California in 1966, when the University was selected as one of the 84 Teacher Corps university training centers located in 34 states, Puerto Rico, and the District of Columbia.[116] At the University, Melbo placed the Teacher Corps in the Department of Teacher Education under the general direction of Wilson. Immediate direction of the Teacher Corps activities at the University of Southern California was provided by associate director, Annette Gromfin.[117] As developed at the University, the

---

115. MS comment, May 1973.

116. The Teacher Corps was a federal program created by Title V-B of the Higher Education Act of 1965. It became operational in the spring of 1966. On June 19, 1967, provisions for the Teacher Corps were amended and extended as a part of the Education Professions Development Act of 1967. As stated in the enabling legislation, the purpose of the Teacher Corps was to serve to strengthen the educational opportunities available to children in areas having a concentration of low-income families, and to encourage colleges and universities to broaden their programs of teacher preparation. The first national director was Richard Graham, who took his post in November 1966. Graham had been a Peace Corps director and member of the Equal Opportunity Commission. The federal government paid corpsmen throughout the two years of training in the corps at the level of a beginning teacher approximately 90 per cent of their salaries, as well as the salaries of their supervising teachers. It also paid all administrative costs of the colleges and universities that sponsored training program. From 1966 through 1973, an average of 39 new Teacher Corps projects was funded each year, and all but three of the 50 states, as well as the District of Columbia and Puerto Rico, had or had had Teacher Corps projects.

117. Gromfin's academic and professional background were peculiarly suited to the problems of the urban areas. A graduate of the University of Illinois in political science, she had had two years of graduate work in the Law School of De Paul University, and special graduate work in the administration of social services

148

Teacher Corps program was a cooperative effort between the University and two clusters of school districts, each with its unique problems.

The first cluster, to which the program was confined during its first two years of operation, consisted of certain school districts in the Los Angeles and Riverside county school systems. As of 1966, cooperating school districts were Enterprise City, Garvey, Jurupa Unified, and Willowbrook. In 1967, three more school districts were added: Compton City, Compton Union High School, and El Monte. The communities of these districts were "pocket ghettos" and "ports of entry" for migrants to the urban area from Mexico, the South, and Appalachia. Their populations were ill-equipped to cope with the demands of urban life, and their children unable to compete in local educational institutions. As of 1968, corpsmen were working in 20 schools in these seven districts.

The second cluster, added in 1967, consisted of two school districts, Cutler-Orssi Unified and Woodlake Union High School, in Tulare County. This area, situated some 220 miles north of Los Angeles, formed part of the rich farming land of the San Joaquin Valley. There the migrant stream had been affected by automation, and a new type of resident population was emerging on the fringes of local communities, but with little involvement in rural society. The recent residents, who were almost entirely Mexican-American, were settling in localities where few or no bilingual-bicultural educational programs existed to accommodate their needs.

With the addition in 1967 of the second cluster, the Teacher Corps program was divided into two parts: "Teacher Corps: Ur-

at the University of California, Los Angeles. Her professional experience included service as vocational employment and educational counselor, Cook County Department of Public Welfare; deputy probation officer, Los Angeles County Probation Department; project associate, Community Education for Delinquency Prevention, Youth Studies Center, University of Southern California; senior project associate, Crenshaw Community Study Project; and coordinator and consultant, Community Action Programs, Los Angeles.

ban" under Gromfin, and "Teacher Corps: Rural-Migrant" under Patricia Heffernan Cabrera.[118] Both efforts functioned similarly in response to federal guidelines. Participants in both programs were selected on the basis of National Teacher Corps criteria, and on the basis of personal interviews with Teacher Corps staff at the University of Southern California and with participating districts. Both were administered as "cycles" of the National Teacher Corps program, a cycle being defined as a two-year period. Cycle I began in the summer of 1966 and terminated in the summer of 1968; Cycle II began in 1967 and terminated in 1968, etc., through the various cycles. Both programs were designed as a two-year graduate studies program leading to the degree of Master of Science in Education, with specialization in education of the disadvantaged. Successful participants in the program received the California standard teaching credential, and, if applicable, the Certificate in the Teaching of English to Speakers of Other Languages (TESOL).

In general, Teacher Corps programs provided generic principles and practices of teacher education as well as specialization and adaptation to unique cultural, economic, and educational differences, with special emphases upon the Mexican-American and Negro. An interdisciplinary approach was used in both programs to interrelate and synthesize the knowledge from related fields of sociology, psychology, social work, and teacher education. The

---

118. Cabrera's intense interest and competency in the rural-migrant area stemmed in part from her life experience. "I was an Army brat, and in a way I learned the same things children of migrants learn—to overcompensate to establish yourself all over again.... We lived in Alabama, in the country, with no electricity, no running water. I bathed in the creek, washed my hair in the creek, cleaned kerosene lamps." (*Los Angeles Times,* April 19, 1970). At 16 years of age she entered Jacksonville State College (now University), from which she graduated in 1949. A number of years of marriage brought her first-hand knowledge of English as a second language. Highly regarded by Teacher Corps and the U.S. Office of Education, she lectured at the invitation of the U.S. Department of State on English as a Second Language at the University of Vizoveci and Oloumec in Czechoslovakia during the summer of 1970. In 1971, she was awarded a Ph.D. from the Union Graduate School, an experimental program incorporated under the state of Ohio, of largely self-directed study and experience.

150

basic objective was the production of a more comprehensively trained teacher and one who was sensitive to cultural differences and able to apply varied skills. Included in both programs were the most relevant educational theories in child development, school socialization, community environment, and teacher-learner relationships. Core content was supplemented by related field experiences, special workshops with specialist and community resource personnel, demonstrations of practical application of theory, and participation by corpsmen in innovative and experimental programs.

An important facet of both programs was the team concept. Corpsmen worked in teams of four to seven trainees, with one team leader. The team leader was a teacher employed by the cooperating school district who had been released from her usual tasks to work with the Teacher Corps program. A major thrust of both programs was the encouragement of jointly working through problems and the use of other corpsmen as resource persons in the design and execution of teaching strategies.

During the 1966–68 period, "Teacher Corps: Urban" operated in three cycles: Cycle I (1966–68) completed its program; Cycle II (1967–69) and Cycle III (1968–70) entered it. For each cycle, the two-year training program was divided into a preservice and an inservice phase. The preservice phase consisted of an intensive 10-week training effort, which included relevant academic work on the University campus as well as a heavy concentration of field experiences in poverty communities. During the inservice phase, which covered two academic years, corpsmen moved to the school to which they were assigned for this part of their training. The first semester was spent as teacher assistant, the second and third as student teacher, and the fourth in supervised responsibility for the classroom. Field experiences were concentrated in the Watts and East Los Angeles areas where were to be found concentrations of Blacks and Mexican-Americans. Field experiences included an extended live-in with Black and Mexican-American poverty families, team tutorials in a nonschool setting in a poverty area, meetings with various community action groups, and field trips

151

to unusual and experimental school programs, such as the Juvenile Hall schools.[119]

"Teacher Corps: Rural Migrant" was the National Teacher Corps' first venture into the education of children of migrant and seasonal agricultural workers. As developed by Cabrera as a pilot program for the U.S. Office of Education, the program was designed to develop in the interns the kind of personal resources and sense of commitment necessary if they were to "reach and teach" the child of the rural-migrant. Inservice training was preceded by a 12-week preservice phase, the basic purpose of which was to provide an indepth perspective of the Mexican-American farm worker.[120] Interns then received their inservice training in Tulare County, where a "flying faculty" carried the University courses, seminars, and workshops to the field teams. Consultative services were also made available to the rural communities, with certain programs open to district teachers and administrators, and other special programs for community leaders and other interested persons.

The success of the program was indicated in numerous ways. Statistics as of 1969 indicated that of the 17 members who completed the program, all continued in the field of education, 14 as public school teachers mainly in rural communities.[121] The program's success was also recognized by the U.S. Office of Education, which has identified it as a model effort for

---

119. Juvenile Hall schools were special schools operated by the superintendent, Los Angeles County schools, to provide education for boys and girls who were wards of the Juvenile Court.

120. Guest lectures presented during the preservice phase were incorporated and issued by Cabrera as *First Papers on Migrancy and Rural Poverty: An Introduction to the Education of Mexican Americans in Rural Areas.* Subtitles included: "Agencies and the Migrant: Theory and Reality of the Migrant Condition"; "The Mexican American Heritage: Developing Cultural Understanding"; and "Attitudinal Characteristics of Migrant Farm Workers," the last a lecture presented by Horacio Ulibari, professor of sociology, College of Education, University of New Mexico.

121. Others included a junior college instructor, graduate student in instructional technology, and administrator of Teacher Corps/Vista Program.

152

bilingual-bicultural teacher training and an exemplary program for Mexican-Americans. Said Cabrera, with justifiable pride:[122]

> It coupled pragmatism with idealism and proved that teachers, as innovators and change agents, can make education meaningful and relevant.

In a communication to officials of the program in Washington, D.C., the county superintendent of schools, Tulare County, expressed his appreciation of the program as a "very progressive teacher training program," and one whose motto, "To reach and teach," had met with success in Tulare County.[123]

New Graduate Programs

Mid-Career Program. In 1965, the School of Education launched a new graduate program for inservice education. Known as the Mid-Career Advanced Development Program for Practicing Professionals, the program had as its purpose the provision of an indepth understanding of current and future problems pertinent to the career educational leader who desired to become an accredited and certified specialist in the particular field of service, and to assist the practicing professional to avoid obsolescence at a critical point of the professional career.

In 1973, Dean Melbo perceptively observed:[124]

> I strongly urged the mid-career idea not only as a "different" program for graduate study, but as a means of mutual identification—practicing professionals and professors in a professional school. One aspect of the conceptual design was that the second half of one's career ought to be as important and productive as the first half. Thus the term, "mid-career," and the deliberate design of the program, not only to prevent professional obsolescence but to build upon the know-how, the insights, and the wisdom of the first half of a life career. Since that beginning,

---

122. University of Southern California, School of Education, "Teacher Corps: Rural-Migrant" (1969), p. 17.
123. Letter, Max Cochran to Dr. Don Davies, dated April 30, 1969 (Reproduced in University of Southern California, School of Education, Teacher Corps: Rural-Migrant (1969), following p. 17.
124. MS comment, May 1973.

153

Yale University and Ohio State University, and perhaps others, have borrowed both the name and the concept.

The Faculty Committee for the program comprised Brackenbury, Pullias, and Perry, as chairman. Specialized groups for which the program was developed were elementary school administrators, secondary school administrators, curriculum directors and coordinators, and pupil personnel directors. Admission was by nomination of the applicant's superintendent or by individual application, and subsequent invitation by the School of Education. All participants were required to be regularly admitted to graduate study in the School of Education and to hold an advanced professional license or credential representing at least one year of graduate work.

During 1965, three groups, with approximately 30 students each, were operating in the program. In 1966, two more groups entered. The rigor of the selection process is indicated by the fact that the 24 members of the first group admitted were selected from 150 applicants. The groups met in closed sessions, representing one full year of graduate study (24 semester units) distributed over a two-year sequence. Planned specifically for each entering group, the sequence followed a multidisciplinary approach under the guidance of regular faculty members of the School of Education. Completion of the program was recognized by award of a Specialist's Certificate, presented at the annual convocation of the University. The first certificates were awarded at the 1967 annual commencement to 45 persons.

As Melbo noted, members of each group developed unusual camaraderie:[125]

> The members of each Mid-Career group developed a truly wonderful *ingroup* morale and loyalty. Group members were very protective of each other, and generously helpful and supportive. When a new course began, the professor was the "outsider," who had to win his way into the group by demonstrating not only his competence but his understanding of the Mid-Career concept and its significance. Members of the Mid-Career groups still meet together, socially and professionally.

154

125. MS comment, May 1973.

All credits earned in the Mid-Career Program were transferable toward any advanced degree program of the School of Education. The program also provided an alternate route to entrance into the doctoral program, since the faculty approved in 1965 the recommendation of the Committee on the Doctoral Program that successful completion of the examination at the close of each semester's study might be acceptable as a replacement for the corresponding area of the comprehensive examination which was otherwise required for entrance to the doctoral program. In approving this alternative, the committee emphasized that it reserved the right not to be dominated in its judgment by the ratings, but to use them as judiciously as possible, and as only one factor in making the decision to admit or not to admit, as with the comprehensive examination scores. With these precautions, the committee believed that the alternate process could be used and that the dean and faculty could be assured that both the character and reputation of the doctoral program would be protected and, perhaps, enhanced.[126]

Advanced Study Center in Europe. The summer of 1963 saw the opening by the School of Education of graduate-level study in Europe for personnel employed there by the United States Government. At the request of the United States Air Force and the Department of Defense Dependent Schools in the European Area (USDESEA), Melbo authorized the establishment of a summer Graduate Center at Wiesbaden, Germany. The first courses were offered in educational administration, with Stoops the first member of the faculty to teach in this program.[127] Students in the four-week program consisted of chiefly principals and other administrators of schools in the USDESEA system, who were brought by the Department of Defense from such far locations as

---

126. "Report of the Committee on Doctoral Program: Relation of Mid-Career Program to the Doctoral Program in the School of Education." (*Agenda,* May 10, 1965; approved by faculty, *Minutes,* November 8, 1965)

127. While in Wiesbaden, Stoops also established the first Phi Delta Kappa chapter in Europe.

North Africa and the Scandinavian countries as well as from locations in central Europe to pursue the course as part of their professional duties. The program's success encouraged its repetition on a regular basis during the summers, with two full-time faculty members assigned from the School of Education.

Summer Institute in Japan. In 1965, in cooperation with the United States Air Force and the Department of Defense, Melbo arranged for a one-month institute to be conducted in Japan for administrators of Pacific Area Dependent Schools. The institute, which was held in Tokyo during June 1965, was directed by Melbo personally. Approximately 80 educational leaders attended the institute, which marked the first step of the School of Education into the Far East.

M.S. in Ed. Program in Europe. In 1964, Melbo responded to an invitation to consider the establishment of a graduate program in Europe leading to the degree of Master of Science in Education. As a result of his negotiations, the School of Education entered into contract with the United States Air Force, inaugurating what was to become one of the most successful overseas programs conducted by the University of Southern California.[128]

Centered at first in Wiesbaden, Rhein Main, and Ramstein Air Bases in Germany, by 1968 the program had expanded to five centers in Germany: Birkenfeld, Hahn, Ramstein, Rhein Main, and Wiesbaden; a center at Torrejon, Spain; and two centers in southeastern Europe: Athens, Greece; and Izmir, Turkey.

During the first two years of the program in southeastern

---

128. Other programs of the University of Southern California in Europe included a program leading to the Master's degree in Aerospace Operations Management, begun in 1964; and a program leading to the degree of Master of Arts in International Relations, begun in 1966. In 1969, the former program was being conducted at Bitburg, Hahn, Ramstein, Rhein Main, and Wiesbaden in Germany, and at Torrejon and Moron in Spain. The latter program was conducted at South Ruislip, Upper Heyford, and London, England. Combined graduation ceremonies were conducted for these programs in Europe by the University of Southern California, with full academic regalia and by officers of the University of Southern California who traveled to Europe for these occasions.

156

Europe, faculty members alternated weekly between Athens and Izmir, flying each week end across the Aegean Sea. While this proved somewhat hazardous and tiring to the professors, it also added variety.[129] From the students' point of view, attending classes every other week made possible large blocks of time for required reading and independent study. In the final two years of the program in Athens and Izmir, each center had its own resident faculty member.

All centers operated by the School of Education were staffed with regular faculty members of the School or by those of comparable rank and stature who were appointed in visiting professorial status for the special assignment. Among the "regulars on the circuit" were Nelson, Warters, Perry, and Wagner from the full-time faculty, and from the visiting professors Garner, Williams, and Trillingham, all retired superintendents of school districts in southern California, and C. R. Von Eschen, Professor Emeritus of Education, Beloit College, Wisconsin. Other members of the faculty of the School of Education who left their duties on campus to spend one or more semesters in the European program were Brackenbury, Carnes, McGrath, Meyers, Muelder, O'Neill, and Wilbur. By 1973, Melbo estimated that more than 60 members of the faculty had participated in the overseas program, either in Europe or the Far East.

Apart from the implicit responsibility of all universities to lend their resources to the accomplishment of goals in the national interest, the Dean referred to the European program, and later the Pacific program, as "his faculty development program." The as-

---

129. In an interview with the *Stars and Stripes,* Nelson, with his usual aplomb, denied any hardship from the frequent travel. "The switch-about makes it pleasant," he said, adding, "Mrs. Nelson uses the expression 'Mexican jumping beans' to describe our two-country schedule. But it's really a wonderful opportunity to see and do things that are not possible back in the States." Mrs. Nelson, with the good sense and good temper that characterized all of the wives of the faculty members, said: "We're in good health and we're curious about the way people live everywhere. We're not bothered by different kinds of food and we enjoy roughing it. So long as we feel well, we will continue to travel." (*Stars and Stripes,* November 18, 1968)

sumption was that a year of experience, working and living in another country and learning something of the educational system of another nation, would broaden the professor's base of understanding of worldwide educational, social, political, and economic factors, thus making him a better professor upon his return to campus. Sharing the professors' interests and experiences also were, in a number of instances, their wives. To the many students who came to know them well overseas and to appreciate their presence, these gallant women added verve and enjoyment to the program as they entered into the many activities with grace, humor, and the best of will.[130]

The first graduation ceremony in which students in the M.S. in Ed. program in Europe participated was held in Wiesbaden, Germany, July 30, 1967, with 72 graduates in Education. In 1968, two graduation ceremonies were held: one for 32 persons in Toledo, Spain; and the other for 110 graduates in Wiesbaden. General Horace M. Wade, Commander in Chief, United States Air Forces in Europe (USAFE) delivered both 1968 commencement addresses. Carl M. Franklin, Vice President, Financial Affairs, University of Southern California, assisted by Dean Melbo, conferred the degrees. As of that year, more than 500 military and civilian personnel were enrolled in the total USC European program, and by June 1969, more than 400 had received their master's degree.

On August 11, 1968, in a special ceremony held in the General von Steuben Hotel, Wiesbaden, the United States Air Force conferred upon Dean Melbo its highest civilian award, the Air Force Exceptional Service Award. The medal, with accompanying

---

130. The military made every effort to see to the well-being and comfort of the professors, as well as to administrative details, but there were inevitably some discomforts. When a strike of Turkish employees at the Kordon Hotel, Izmir, forced Professor and Mrs. Wagner to evacuate their rooms *sans* luggage, Mrs. Wagner's only comment was: "I'm so sorry it had to happen, but since it did, I'm so glad we were here to experience it." On another occasion, when Mrs. Von Eschen sprained an ankle, forcing her into a cast, she nevertheless made the planned trip to the interior of Turkey, limping around the ruins. "I've wanted to do this since college," she said, "and I just know I won't have another chance."

158

citation,[131] was presented by General Wade, officiating on behalf of the Honorable Harold Brown, Secretary of the Air Force.

Malawi Polytechnic Project

Probably the most significant, and certainly the largest, international project with which the School of Education was involved during the 1960s was the Malawi Polytechnic Project, which Melbo brought to the University of Southern California following a series of personal conferences with officials in the United States Department of State.

Participation of the School of Education in this project was part of the vast program of United States assistance to developing countries. Since the Second World War, aid to developing nations had become a fixed feature of American foreign policy and of the national budget. As a "have" or richly endowed nation, America gave generously, sharing its largesse with the world's "have-not" nations, with the ultimate aim of witnessing developed societies evolve from primitive ones and of fostering the more equitable distribution of the world's wealth and opportunities. In this effort, the colleges and universities of the United States played an important role. Said David E. Bell, Administrator of the Agency for International Development (AID):[132]

---

131. The citation reads: "Doctor Irving R. Melbo distinguished himself by exceptionally meritorious service to the United States Air Force from August 1964 to December 1967. As Dean of the School of Education, University of Southern California, Doctor Melbo's exemplary ability, perseverance, and imagination were instrumental factors in the establishment of graduate degree programs in education in the USAFE Command. During this period Doctor Melbo inaugurated graduate programs at Wiesbaden, Rhein Main and Ramstein Air Bases in Germany and at Torrejon, Spain; Athens, Greece; and Izmir, Turkey. Due to his efforts, Air Force personnel on duty assignments within the United States Air Forces in Europe are able to acquire a master's degree while performing their primary duties. The singularly distinctive accomplishments of Doctor Melbo reflect great credit upon himself and have earned for him the sincere gratitude of the United States Air Force."

132. Bell (1964), p. 5. The article cited in the text of an address delivered by Bell at the Education and World Affairs Conference, Michigan State University, October 11, 1963.

The Agency for International Development is, in a very real sense, simply the governmental expression of the national determination to extend a helping hand to less-developed societies struggling against great odds to modernize their societies. As such, we in AID are engaged in mobilizing the talents and competence that exist throughout the American society, and channeling them to the task of assisting in the building of nations.

Our colleges and universities are plainly a great reservoir of such talent, skill, and determination. In the past decade the colleges and universities have been valued partners in the foreign assistance program. This partnership must be expanded and strengthened in the years ahead. Perhaps no other group in our society gives so much, or has so much to give, as the academic community.

As of 1963, 69 universities of the United States were engaged in technical cooperation efforts abroad in 37 countries, and AID had committed more than $3 million in support of university contracts. No two contracts were alike. In each instance, the assignment was a highly specialized one, tailored to the local situation. In all countries, the objective was the same: the building of modern educational systems which would better equip that society to meet its own pressing need for highly specialized manpower.

The special contribution of the University of Southern California's School of Education to international development was carried out in the new African nation of Malawi (former Nyasaland).[133] There, from 1963 to 1969, the School of Education developed a viable, functioning polytechnic as one means of fostering the economic development of the country.[134]

133. In 1964, former Nyasaland was named Malawi in recognition of its newly won independence. Situated in southeast central Africa, the area was first visited by the famed missionary and explorer, Dr. David Livingstone in 1859. From 1891 to 1953, Nyasaland was a protectorate of the British Empire (Commonwealth). In 1960, Britain granted Nyasaland a constitution, and in 1963, Dr. Hastings Kamuzu Banda became prime minister under the new constitution. In 1964-65, Nyasaland became independent under the new name of Malawi, and in 1966, Malawi became a republic within the British Commonwealth, with Banda as president.

134. The economy of Nyasaland had traditionally depended, aside from re-

160

The first negotiations for University of Southern California participation in U.S. assistance to Nyasaland began in the spring of 1962, when Melbo made the initial contacts in Washington, D.C. Shortly thereafter, officials of AID visited the University's campus to confer with Melbo on a possible contract for establishment of a polytechnic in Nyasaland. Following allocation of project funds, and at the request of the host government, AID entered into contract October 1, 1963, with the University of Southern California for what Melbo was to describe as the "awesome responsibility of establishing a major educational institution in the new nation of Malawi."[135]

By the terms of the contract, the University of Southern California, through its School of Education, and under the general supervision of the Dean of the School of Education, agreed to design and implement a program to increase the school opportunities available for Malawians to develop and train themselves for useful employment; to plan, construct, and develop a comprehensive institution designed to provide commercial, technical, and general education on a full- or part-time basis; and to demonstrate, through this institution, the ways of planning more effective programs and improving the use of human and technical resources to train Malawians to staff the institution.

Immediately upon the signing of the contract, Melbo ap-

---

mittances, on agriculture and a few cash crops, such as tea, peanuts, and cotton, which did not earn enough to pay for imports. British aid had been the main means of offsetting the trade deficit and of balancing the national budget. Although Nyasaland had one of the lowest per capital incomes in Africa, Banda was confident that the country, which was rich in land and people, could be converted to one with higher incomes and better living standards. He looked to new growth of light industry and the development, with neighboring Mozambique, of hydroelectric power. The presence of bauxite deposits and considerable stands of timber also gave promise of an improved economic future, if these could be developed. The 1965–69 National Development Plan for Malawi emphasized four main fields: expansion of agricultural production, improved internal communications, expansion of secondary and postsecondary education, and encouragement of industrial development. Establishment of a viable, functioning polytechnic formed one of the most important elements in the national development plan for Malawi.

135. University of Southern California (1970), p. iv.

161

pointed Bruce J. Hahn as an adjunct professor of the School of Education and chief-of-party for the project.[136] On October 6, 1963, Hahn joined other educators for orientation in Washington, D.C., and in London, prior to departure for Malawi, where he arrived October 11, 1963.[137] Hahn was soon joined in Malawi by three American technical advisors whom Melbo appointed to comprise the first team fielded by the School of Education. Altogether, the School of Education fielded four teams, with overlapping tours, so that, until the final months of the contract in 1969, eight American specialists were always on site.

To achieve the contract's objectives, it was decided to construct, equip, and furnish at Blantyre, Malawi's largest city, a polytechnic facility to accommodate up to 600 full-time and upwards of 2,000 full- and part-time students; to staff the facility with a vice-principal and eight technicians with specialized skills; and to train, during the six-year contract, 3,000 Malawians in a comprehensive variety of subjects. Until Malawians could be suitably trained for positions of responsibility, the project chief-of-party was to serve as vice-principal and the American specialists as teachers and curriculum advisers. Specializations selected for emphasis were electricity and electronics, power mechanics, machine shop, metal technology, industrial training, science, woodworking, and mathematics. Team members were selected in accordance with these specialties.[138]

---

136. Hahn (B.S. (1930) and M.S. (1939) Oregon State College, and Ed.D. (1955, Colorado State College) had been instructor and assistant professor in industrial arts at Oregon State College (1947–57) and was an educational technician with AID (1957–63).

137. Under separate contract with AID, The American Council on Education fielded in 1963–64 a survey team to make a comprehensive assessment of Malawi's needs for educational institutions and curricular emphasis, and to formulate proposals for an educational plan required for Malawi's economic and social development in the next 15 years. Hahn joined the members of the survey team for preliminary orientation and later served as consultant to the team in the area of technical and vocational education.

138. Team members and their specialties were: Team 1 (1964–66): B. J. Hahn,

162

Construction of the facility began in November 1963, and was completed in December 1965, at which time the Polytechnic was incorporated into the newly inaugurated University of Malawi.[139] First classes began at the Polytechnic in January 1966, and the first students were graduated in July 1969. Throughout the period supervisory visits were made by Melbo, John A. Carpenter (who had been appointed by Melbo the project's first coordinator) and by other University representatives. Admirable on-site assistance was rendered by Jean McComas, who served 22 months as administrative assistant for the technical department. Expenditures, excluding building costs, totaled $1.325 million. The result of the total effort was that, in less than seven years, a modern, well-equipped school for polytechnical education of a high order had been built and was functioning within the system for which it had been built. That this accomplishment was no mean feat those experienced in similar projects overseas will readily attest.

---

chief-of-party; J. D. McMullen, metals; F. B. Barrows, electronics; R. B. Blackmun, auto; E. S. Foster, machine. Team 2 (1966–68): H. M. Lang, industrial training; W. L. Shaw, science; G. L. Sogge, woodworking; T. Upton, mathematics. Team 3 (1966–69): R. Moses, chief-of-party; T. Bowen, electrical engineering; P. Henry, mechanical engineering; R. Oetley, mechanics; E. Soper, welding. Team 4 (1968–69): F. Barker, technical drafting; R. Blackmun, auto; R. Hart, surveying; W. McComas, printing.

139. It was planned that constituent colleges of the multicampus University of Malawi would be: Bunda College of Agriculture, built with AID assistance 18 miles from Lilongwe in the central region of Malawi; Chancellor College, housed in 1968 in the Chichiri Secondary School between Blantyre and Limbe but planned for location at Zomba; The Institute of Public Administration at Mpemba, 12 miles from Blantyre; The Polytechnic, on the Kamuzu Highway between Blantyre and Limbe; and Soche Hill College, a teacher education institution on the outskirts of Limbe. As recommended by the survey team of the American Council on Education, objectives of the University of Malawi were planned to be limited but progressive and to rely on the general core of higher education, with initial professionalization in agriculture and education, and restraint for the time being from developing medicine, pharmacy, architecture, engineering, law, and similar specializations. (The American Council on Education 1964, p. 71)

163

What were the essential ingredients of the success of the Malawi project? First, in Melbo AID found a university administrator capable of mobilizing the resources necessary to carry out the contract. In the School of Education of the University of Southern California it found a professional institution capable of building on existing expertise and past experience. Melbo and field teams chosen by him were educators who could perform under overseas conditions. That this capability was not usual was made clear by Bell, AID's administrator, in discussing the type of personal and professional abilities required for "overseasmanship":[140]

> A decade of hard experience attests to the fact that the overseas American can profit greatly from advance preparation. The good engineering professor in a U.S. university is not necessarily a good engineering professor in an overseas university. The well-prepared and successful dean of a U.S. college of education does not always succeed as an education adviser overseas. Good intentions are not enough. New and unfamiliar demands are made on the overseas American. He functions, in the jargon of the sociologists, as a "change agent." He no longer simply does a task; his job is to change attitudes and even behavior—no mean task in any culture and an especially difficult task in strange surroundings and an unfamiliar culture. (Given the large obstacles, it's a miracle that so many overseas Americans do as well as they do.)

As the Malawi project drew to a close, Melbo took the necessary steps to insure the continuation of the Polytechnic as an ongoing institution. Through another contract, related to but not part of the original, he arranged, with AID funds, to train on the campus of the University of Southern California, a number of carefully chosen Malawians who would be capable with further education of assuming positions of responsibility in their own country. In September 1967, the first participants in this program were enrolled at the University of Southern California. On its campus they pursued curricula which would enable them to ac-

164

140. Bell (1964), p. 7.

quire either the bachelor's or the master's degree in a selected field of critical importance to the development of their country. By 1970, Arthur Kalambatore, one of the selectees, had finished his training at the University of Southern California, earned the M.S. in Ed. degree, and returned to the Polytechnic as lecturer in business administration. Others were midway toward degrees in various technical, business, and engineering fields. As noted previously, it was in view of this need and from his experience with the Malawi project that Melbo devised and instituted the vocational teacher training program leading to the B.S. in Ed.—Technical Studies.

In a paragraph he wrote for the final report of the Malawi project, Melbo eloquently set forth its deeper meaning to international relations:[141]

> The last of the teams has now returned to the United States from Malawi. The teams bring with them the satisfaction of a job well done, an outstanding facility built, a new curriculum designed, and the good feeling that comes with success. . . .

> The returning of the remaining participants will add yet another strand to the bond which has developed among Malawians and Americans in general—and between the Polytechnic and the University of Southern California in specific. . . .

> In a very large measure, this job of nation-building by the process of improving the capacities of its people is only begun. . . . In a larger sense the job of nation-building is never done, nor is the work of an educational institution ever completely accomplished. There are always goals ahead, and this is as it should be.

Soche Hill College Survey

In May 1966, Melbo directed, under contract with AID, a team survey[142] of the secondary school teacher training needs of

---

141. University of Southern California (1970), pp. 49–50.
142. Members of the survey staff were: Irving R. Melbo, director, Dean of the School of Education, USC; John A. Carpenter, director, Center for International

Malawi, with focus on Soche Hill College. Although not a specific part of the Malawi project, the survey provided valuable information regarding the total educational setting of which the Malawi project was a part.

Soche Hill College, on the outskirts of Limbe, Malawi, was a government teacher-training center built with an initial grant from the British government. It trained secondary school teachers, including homecraft specialists, and offered a three-year diploma course. It was expected that Soche Hill College, with other institutions of higher learning in Malawi, would become constituent parts of the multicampus University of Malawi.

The report of survey, which examined all facets of the college and its expected relationship to the University of Malawi, was in effect a comprehensive survey of the entire Malawi educational system and its teacher-training program, as well as a detailed plan for Soche Hill College in the light of Malawi's anticipated socio-economic development.

Inhouse Publications

Education Monographs. Education Monographs, the publications issued by the School of Education with the imprint of the University of Southern California, were few and were published only sporadically. None was published after 1963. Despite the annual contributions of the Alpha Epsilon Chapter to the School of Education-Phi Delta Kappa Publication Fund, the spiraling costs of publication, lack of a full-time editor, and the restricted sale of the monographs discouraged even those most interested in promoting their continuation.[143]

Education, USC School of Education; Donald E. Wilson, professor of education and director designate, Teacher Education, School of Education; and M. John Rand, superintendent, Temple City Unified School District and lecturer in educational administration, USC School of Education.

143. The *Education Monographs* were established in 1930, largely as a result of Dean Rogers' interest in broadening the base for the School of Education's professional reputation. From 1934 to 1936, nine monographs were issued, the first

In January 1970, the faculty approved the recommendation of the Research and Publications Committee, which had studied the problem for several years, that the School of Education monographs be discontinued. Funds spared were to be made available for support of faculty publications and research, through guidelines to be developed by the Research and Publications Committee.[144]

Distinguished Lecture Series. In 1962, Magary proposed, and obtained Melbo's enthusiastic support for, an annual distinguished lecture series in special education. These lectures, which were held each summer under the sponsorship of the School of Education and the Summer Session of the University, were open to the general educational public. They continued over the years to make a rich contribution to the field of special education, attracting by their importance an increasing number of national authorities as speakers and as audience a large number of distinguished teachers and research specialists. In 1967, the scope of the lectures was expanded to include outstanding leaders in rehabilitation.

A monograph containing the lectures was issued by Magary in 1962, and reinstituted by the Department of Special Education in 1967, with the publication of the lectures for the 1966 summer series. The attractive format and special informational items included in the publications made them welcome additions to the libraries of interested institutions and specialists in the field. After 1967, the publication was issued annually, with a success matching that of the lecture series.

---

of which was Thompson's study on the educational philosophy of Giovanni Gentile, Mussolini's Minister of Education. A revival of interest, despite the impingements of the Second World War, saw the publication of five monographs between 1940 and 1945. A second revival of interest in the late 1950s resulted in the publication of three monographs between 1960 and 1963. Thereafter financial strain, lack of an editor, and difficulties in the sales of the monographs, many of which were reedited dissertations with slight public appeal, gradually brought about their discontinuation.

144. *Agenda,* January 12, 1970.

167

Professionalism

During the 1960s, faculty participation in national and international aspects of education greatly increased. "I want the School of Education," said Dean Melbo, "to have a part in the program of every major professional organization at state, regional, and national conferences. You get on the program, and I'll find a way to get you there."[145] Too numerous to relate, these activities enhanced the professional reputation of both the individuals comprising the faculty and the School itself, as did also the numerous articles, books, and research projects undertaken by the faculty.

Through invitations from other countries or at the behest of United States governmental agencies, a number of the faculty served on educational missions abroad. In 1962, Magary, as representative of the U.S. Department of State, studied special education programs in the Soviet Union. In the spring of 1963, Melbo participated at the request of the Department of State in a month-long study of the Israeli educational system,[146] and in 1969, as guest of the government of Saudi Arabia reviewed the educational programs and facilities of that nation. Brackenbury, under the sponsorship of the United Nations Educational, Scientific, and Cultural Organization (UNESCO), taught in Brazil 1961–62; Muelder taught at the University of Ceylon the same year as Fulbright professor; Georgiades was consultant in 1964 to the Ministry of Education, Greece; McGrath was Fulbright professor in India in 1966; Meyers was designated first lecturer in the newly established William E. Blatz Memorial Lectures at the Institute of Child Study, University of Toronto, in 1966; and in 1968, Magary was a Fulbright lecturer at the Teachers' Training College,

145. MS comment, May 1973.
146. The survey, which included Israel's system of education from the primary grades through professional graduate studies at the university level, was made by a small group of American educational administrators. Others in the group included a college president from New Jersey, a university president from Michigan, and a dean of education from New York.

VISION AND ACCOMPLISHMENT: 1960–1968

Singapore. Lowell, an internationally recognized authority on the deaf and hard of hearing, lectured frequently abroad on problems of the aurally handicapped.

EDUCARE

Hailed as the most significant development for the School of Education during the year 1960–61 was establishment of the School of Education's support group, EDUCARE. With its establishment, the School of Education became the eighth professional school of the University of Southern California to form a support group.[147]

A special and unique creation by Melbo, whose ardent support of the School of Education now found in alumni and friends of the School an enthusiasm nearly equal to his own, EDUCARE became during ensuing years one of the most active and influential support groups of the University. In 1973, Melbo recalled that he had first proposed the idea at a luncheon given by him in a popular restaurant near the campus:[148]

> In 1960, having observed the success of the support groups in some of the other professional schools of the University, I invited a select group of education alumni to have lunch with me at Julie's, and proposed the idea, including a $100-a-year membership fee. "If those dentists and doctors and lawyers can do it," I told them, "we can, too. We're just as much a profession, even though we may not make as much money."

147. Other support groups of professional schools of the University of Southern California were, with year of founding: Century Club (1956), School of Dentistry; Legion Lex (1957), Gould School of Law; Salerni Collegium (1958), School of Medicine; Commerce Associates (1958), School of Business Administration; QSAD Centurions (1958), School of Pharmacy; Architectural Guild (1959), School of Architecture and Fine Arts; SCAPA Praetors (1959), School of Politics and International Relations; Archimedes Circle (1961), School of Engineering; and Libraria Sodalitas (1962), School of Library Science. The Latin nomenclature and the Greek background of most of the names reflects the Trojan theme, first introduced in 1912 to describe a USC team, and carried out on campus by the life-size statue of a Trojan warrior, dedicated at the University's Semicentennial Celebration, 1930.

148. MS comment, May 1973.

169

Doubt was expressed that 'persons in education' would support their school in such manner and degree. I argued, 'Our alumni really have a lot of loyalty to the School of Education. We are loyal to them, and try to maintain a lifelong interest in them, and I believe the relationship is reciprocal. I think I can get enough members myself to get the group started, but that isn't enough. It takes a commitment on a broader base—that every member in a profession owes something to those who will come after, and that this is one way of helping.'

The group agreed, and I set up a meeting to draft bylaws and to plan an initial membership drive. A subcommittee, consisting of Charles C. Carpenter, Earl Brown,[149] and myself, had the task of finding a name for the organization. Finally, with the help of the dictionary, which listed the word "education" as a derivation from the Latin *educere*, "to lead out," the name EDUCARE was proposed and adopted. "And if there are some who interpret this as meaning those who care about education, that's all right, too," I said. Later, when MEDICARE became a byword, I always explained that we had it first.[150]

At a meeting, April 5, 1960, the organization's bylaws were drafted and C. C. Trillingham was elected provisional president.[151] One year later, at the Charter Dinner, held April 28, 1961 with

149. William Earl Brown was then superintendent of the South Bay Union High School District, Redondo Beach, California. Born in 1904 in Birmingham, Alabama, he received his A.B. (1933) at the University of California, Los Angeles; and his A.M. (1934) and Ed.D. (1956) at the University of Southern California. He was superintendent of South Bay Union High School District from 1952 to 1970; third president of EDUCARE (1963–64); and Delta Epsilon Lecturer (1970–71).

150. The committee apparently chose to derive the name from the Latin *educere* because of the educational philosophy implied in that term. A second and perhaps more plausible derivation, from the ancient point of view, is the derivation from Latin *educare*, "to bring up or rear." Derivation from the latter retains, of course, the spelling selected by the support group, EDUCARE, as well as the Latin pronunciation of the term used by the organization. MEDICARE was established in 1966.

151. Clinton Conroy Trillingham was born in Clinton, Indiana, May 31, 1900. He received his A.B. (1921) at Southwestern College, Kansas; and his A.M. (1931) and Ed.D. (1933) at the University of Southern California. He was instructor at the University of Southern California, 1933–34, and then entered the Los Angeles county school system. He was appointed superintendent in 1942, and continued to hold that position until his retirement in 1967. In that year, the University of

VISION AND ACCOMPLISHMENT: 1960–1968

approximately 150 charter members in attendance, the charter was adopted and officers elected, with Trillingham president. Speaker for the occasion was Sterling M. McMurrin, then newly appointed U.S. Commissioner of Education in the Kennedy Administration.[152] "I suggested to him," said Melbo in 1973, "that he might use the EDUCARE dinner meeting as a 'platform' from which to announce the position of the Kennedy Administration on educational issues. He agreed." In succeeding years, the annual EDUCARE black-tie dinner meeting, held in the spring months, usually featured a speaker of national stature, either in the educational, political, or similar field. (See Appendix F for a list of EDUCARE speakers at the annual dinners.)

From its inception, EDUCARE was one of the most rapidly growing of the USC support groups. Beginning with 134 members in 1961, by 1969 it had increased its membership to 846. Special efforts to draw in new members included area "Get-acquainted Rush Parties," personal invitations to those whom members would like to sponsor, and a very active membership committee. One of the most energetic was Melbo, who worked closely with the EDUCARE Board of Directors to insure the organization's growth. Said one past president, "The dean has been personally responsible for about half of our membership."

Southern California conferred upon him the Honorary Degree of Doctor of Laws. Trillingham was Delta Epsilon Lecturer in 1962; and first president of EDUCARE (1960–62).

152. A graduate of Manual Arts High School, Los Angeles, McMurrin earned his A.B. and A.M. degrees from the University of Utah. He received his doctorate in philosophy from the University of Southern California in 1946, joined the USC faculty for two and one-half years, and then returned to the University of Utah as a professor and later academic vice-president. He was nominated by the late President John F. Kennedy as U.S. Commissioner of Education on January 28, 1961, confirmed March 29, 1961, and sworn into office April 5, 1961. On July 28, 1962, he resigned to return to teaching at the University of Utah. McMurrin's writings and studies in religion, philosophy, and the humanities distinguished him as a thoughtful, scholarly writer. Widely traveled, he was special adviser to the chancellor of the University of Teheran, Iran in 1958, the year in which Melbo directed a survey of that University, at the invitation of the chancellor of the University and the U.S. International Cooperation Administration.

171

There were many reasons for EDUCARE's popularity, most of them altruistic. Said one member in an article published in the EDUCARE Newsletter:[153]

> I believe that professional educators have an obligation to promote the field of education in the community. EDUCARE, with its program, establishes a positive image of the School of Education and indicates to the public that educators will support their own institution.
>
> I can think of no better use for one's expenditure of one hundred dollars per year, than to invest in the future expansion and development of the School of Education of the University of Southern California. . . .
>
> And—perhaps most important—no man is worthy of any exalted position, or any honor, or any accolade, who has not given considerably of his time, talent, and money, if need be, to a cause that far exceeds his own personal interest. Therefore, EDUCARE will fulfill this need.

In defining EDUCARE's role, Jack P. Crowther, president of EDUCARE, 1964–65, said:[154]

> I have heard many comments by individuals stating that EDUCARE is a "prestige" group. I would agree that it is a prestige group; however, not because of the caliber of the individual members, but a prestige group because of the great strides in progress and accomplishments for which EDUCARE is now becoming known, as the sponsor of the School of Educa-

---

153. Sadler, Jack. "What's in it for you?" EDUCARE *Newsletter,* 5(2), p.1. Sadler, who served during World War II (1943–46) in the United States Navy, received his A.B. (1949) from the University of California, Santa Barbara; his M.A. (1955) from Claremont Graduate School; and his Ed.D. (1959) from the University of Southern California. He died December 12, 1968.

154. Crowther was superintendent of Los Angeles city schools from 1962 to his retirement in 1970. In that year the University of Southern California conferred upon him the Honorary Degree of Doctor of Laws. The citation read in part: "Jack Page Crowther was a carpenter during the Depression of the Nineteen-thirties. In the decade of the Sixties, he was the master builder of superior educational programs for Los Angeles." A native of Utah, he received his A.B. from the University of Utah and his Master of Science from the University of Southern California. He was associated with the Los Angeles city schools from 1934 on, interrupting his career twice for active and distinguished service as an officer with the United States Army Reserve, in which he held, as of 1970, the grade of colonel.

VISION AND ACCOMPLISHMENT: 1960–1968

tion at the University of Southern California. So the "prestige" label for EDUCARE, now in its beginning stages, should do well to further enhance the fine reputation and spirit of our support group.

Projects of EDUCARE prior to 1968 were the funding, beginning in 1961, of annual allocations for a $2,400 fellowship and a $1,000 scholarship for graduate study at the School of Education; and a $1,500 grant made available to the Dean of the School to assist in attracting visiting professors or lecturers as part of EDU-CARE's faculty enrichment program. The first EDUCARE Distinguished Visiting Lecturer was Harold R. W. Benjamin, who was in residence at the University 1964–65.[155] In 1965, an EDUCARE professorship was established in the School of Education, to which John A. Carpenter was appointed in 1968. In 1965, also, EDUCARE initiated an annual invitational spring conference on problems confronting school systems, students, and educators.

In 1961, the Board of Directors of EDUCARE made a policy decision which committed 60 per cent of EDUCARE's annual income to assist in the funding of the proposed Education Building. By 1967, the fund thus accumulated and held in reserve amounted to $110,000. This money was made available in 1968, to supplement other funds which the University had for furnish-

---

155. Harold (Raymond Wayne) Benjamin was born March 27, 1893. He received his A.B. (1921) and A.M. (1924) from the University of Oregon, and his Ph.D. (1927) from Stanford University. During his long and distinguished academic career he had been professor of education and assistant dean of the College of Education at the University of Minnesota; dean of the College of Education at the University of Colorado; and from 1939 to 1957, dean of education and the summer session of the University of Maryland, where he developed that University's overseas program for military personnel. In 1951, he became professor of education at George Peabody College, Tennessee, from which he retired in 1958 as professor emeritus. Benjamin was an authority in the field of international education, having been first director of international educational relations of the U.S. Office of Education and a member of many governmental and international missions to foreign countries. Among teachers his two best-known works were *The Saber-Tooth Curriculum* (1939), a satire by the so-called Sage of Petaluma, J. Abner Peddiwell, Ph.D., and *The Cultivation of Idiosyncracy* (1949), the Inglis Lecture at Harvard University. Benjamin died in Baltimore, Maryland, on January 12, 1969.

173

ing and equipping Waite Phillips Hall. Rooms furnished and equipped by EDUCARE included the EDUCARE office, the EDUCARE graduate study room, the Schuyler C. Joyner Educational Administrative Laboratory; and, through personal contributions of the EDUCARE Board of Directors, a conference room in the administrative suite named in honor of Dean Melbo the Irving R. Melbo Conference Room. "The Dean," reported the EDUCARE *Newsletter,* in announcing the new conference room:[156]

> ... has been the adviser to EDUCARE since its inception in 1961, and has given evenings, weekends, and vacation time without stint to the development of the organization.

In recognition of EDUCARE's generous contributions and devoted support, a bronze plaque was permanently affixed to the wall in the foyer of Waite Phillips Hall.

Waite Phillips Hall of Education

That the School of Education desperately needed a building or buildings of its own had been evident for many years. The subject had become one which was, among some educators and alumni, whimsically referred to in educationese as a "long felt need." With perhaps more hope than confidence, plans had been drawn during the 1950s for a School of Education plant. The plans provided for an Education Center of six different space units, grouped together in a close working relationship. Each unit was to provide learning laboratories and other appropriate specialized space, together with offices for all of the professional training functions which could best be handled on campus. No provision for training school facilities was made, since it was considered that that training could best be found in the regular public schools. The first unit designated for construction was the Reading and Counseling Center.[157]

The Education Alumni Association was the first of the

---

156. EDUCARE *Newsletter* 8(1) p. 3.
157. Memorandum from Melbo to A. S. Raubenheimer, December 5, 1968 (*Agenda,* November 2, 1959).

School of Education's associated societies to take positive steps toward obtaining funds for the center's construction. In May 1955, Melbo reported to the faculty that a check in amount of $140.46 had been received from the Education Alumni Association to establish an Education Building Fund.[158] In October 1955, the Education Alumni Association began its campaign for funds to finance the first building in the proposed Education Center. With Grace M. Dreier as chairman of the drive,[159] the Education Alumni Association's annual spring conference, held March 15, 1956, was based on the theme, "Together We Build." Said Melbo in 1973:[160]

> In this fund-raising campaign, we featured a "deed," a printed form which recorded the number of square feet of building purchased at $15.00 per square foot. Thus, a $150 gift gave the donor a "deed" for 10 square feet of the proposed Education Building. Altogether, this campaign raised about $80,000 in gifts. At one point in the campaign, Tom Nickell (now Vice-President, University Affairs and chief fund-raiser) and I would drive out to various school districts and personally "sell" our square footage to alumni, mostly school administrators. The response was great, but it was a slow and time-consuming process.

Following the appointment of Dr. Topping as president of the University, new hope was engendered. In March 1958, Francis Doughterty was appointed Development Officer for the School of Education in the Department of Development of the University, and charged with responsibility to work on the Education Center Building Fund Campaign and related activities. In June 1958, Melbo announced that a report from Thomas P. Nickell, then Vice-President, University Planning, indicated that, as of May 5, 1958,

---

158. *Agenda,* May 5, 1955.

159. *Agenda,* February 13, 1956, and March 12, 1956. Grace Mogle Dreier was born April 25, 1894, and died July 12, 1967. As associate superintendent of schools in Los Angeles, she was an active member of the Education Alumni Association, of which she served at one time as president; and a Charter member of EDUCARE. The Grace M. Dreier Memorial Seminar Room in Waite Phillips Hall was furnished by friends in her memory.

160. MS comment, May 1973.

175

the amount pledged for the Education Center was $83,406.60, with a total participation of 1,465 donors.

Inclusion of the School of Education and Library Science Building in the facilities or "Enterprise" portion of the Master Plan of the University of Southern California, as incorporated in the President's Report of October 1961, was the next step toward the long-sought goal. The allocation for the School of Education and Library Science Building was $1,120,000, a fairly modest sum, as were the sums allocated to other campus life facilities, which totaled nearly $77.7 million. Yet there were many who believed it would take over a hundred years to raise the amount:[161]

> The magnitude of the physical and academic goals of the Master Plan, though inspiring to the University's community, caused many realists to wonder if such goals were attainable. The University had never had a completely successful moneyraising drive; it had never sought to achieve such a total concept of excellence. To raise $106.7 million in 20 years seemed impossible. The impossible, however, could and would be accomplished.

For the School of Education, the "impossible which was accomplished" came in the form of the bequest of an illustrious industrialist of the Southwest, the community leader and philanthropist, Waite Phillips. Born in 1883, he died in Los Angeles in 1964. The dedicatory program of Waite Phillips Hall, named in his honor, summarized his life and achievements:

> A descendant of the storied Captain Miles Standish, Waite Phillips' own life was a story of success in many fields. He worked hard with great zest and amassed a fortune. With equal energy and enthusiasm, he gave a fortune away to meet important needs of his fellow man.
>
> As an enterprising individual oil producer, he developed extensive and valuable oil producing properties, pipe lines, and marketing facilities throughout the midcontinent area. As a rancher and investor in real estate, he owned and operated farming lands and livestock ranches exceeding 300,000 acres, as

161. Servin and Wilson (1969), p. 259.

well as two large office buildings in Tulsa, Oklahoma. And, in addition, he served for several years as Chairman of the Board of Tulsa's First National Bank and Trust Company and of the Independent Oil and Gas Company, Tulsa.

During his life time, Waite Phillips was widely honored for his personal leadership and generous support of the civic and cultural life of Tulsa. In 1943, he was elected to the Oklahoma Hall of Fame. And, in 1959, the City of Tulsa honored him by naming a new public school the Waite Phillips Elementary School in recognition of his services to that community during the twenty-seven years he lived there. . . .

As a tribute to this great man, and, particularly, in recognition of special interest in young people, the University of Southern California is proud to place his name in perpetuity upon this outstanding new facility for the education of our future teachers.

In announcing the bequest, Melbo emphasized that it was through the special personal relationship and effort of President Topping that the grant had come to the University and to the School of Education. By unanimous motion, the faculty voted to send a special letter of appreciation to President Topping. The letter, which expressed the faculty's warm appreciation, said in part:[162]

No formal letter can begin to express the gratitude which Dean Melbo and the faculty of the School of Education feel for the balanced and statesmanlike leadership you are giving to the development of the University. We have rejoiced at each achievement on the road toward the goals that have been set. We are fully aware that each development strengthens the whole and thus makes it possible for each part to do its job better. As grants have come making possible the buildings and faculty so crucial to the greatness of the University, we have been pleased and have felt a keen pride in our institution.

However, our joy and appreciation are somewhat more per-

162. Letter to President Topping from Members of the Central Committee representing the faculty of the School of Education (Earl F. Carnes, Myron S. Olson, Earl V. Pullias), dated February 27, 1964 (*Agenda,* March 9, 1964).

177

sonal and intense in the case of the Phillips bequest. We are a large school with varied programs which we believe are vital not only to the University but especially to the society it strives to serve. We are concerned with all the problems of the education of man, from nursery school through higher education. As a faculty we are appreciative of the high esteem that has been accorded to the programs and activities of the School of Education. We are deeply committed to continue in this leadership role. Our plans and goals will be greatly advanced by the recent generous grant.

This letter then is a small expression of our appreciation for your confidence in and respect for the work of the School of Education. We, with the leadership of our Dean, will do everything in our power to use these new resources wisely and well. It is our fixed purpose that the School of Education be one of the great professional schools of the world.

On the same day, February 17, 1964, that the bequest was announced to the faculty, Melbo sent to the many alumni and friends of the School of Education an open letter announcing the gift and the plans to house the program and activities of the school. The letter read in part:[163]

The site area designated in the Master Plan is across University Avenue from Founders Hall in the very heart of the new University complex. Faculty and alumni committees will be asked to assist in the planning so that the new building may represent the most advanced development of professional ideas and the projection of our needs for a future time.

It is possible that individuals or groups may wish to memorialize some of the facilities within the new building, and this would indeed be appropriate.

The building itself will obviously be a recognition of the efforts of all who contributed in the past, and to those who are still contributing in numerous ways to the support and advancement of the School of Education. We are grateful for your loyalty and interest and for your limitless confidence in our future.

The architect chosen to design the building was famed Ed-

178

163. *Agenda,* March 9, 1964.

ward Durell Stone, who also designed the adjacent two-story Social Science Building and the nearby Von KleinSmid Center for International and Public Affairs. Stone used the same material, Norman brick, and the same architectural features for all three buildings, artfully joining the complex by a sunken garden and pool and by arched porticoes.[164]

With its lofty narrow windows appearing to span the full height of the towering structure, Waite Phillips Hall was a distinctive landmark on the campus of the University, soaring skyward 156 feet. Of the 78,250 square feet in the entire building, more than 12,000 were below grade level and connected with the Social Science building. Above grade level on the lower floors were classrooms, with offices nearer the top of the building. Among the features were innovative teaching and research facilities, individual offices for faculty, and more than 40 special-purpose areas and classrooms, including areas for instructional technology, a measurement laboratory, and a 100-seat lecture hall.

Between 1964 and 1968, numerous gifts were received from donors, some of whom wished to honor beloved professors or others who had been particularly interested in education. Such gifts, when so indicated, were memorialized in bronze plaques affixed to the particular rooms. In 1973, Dean Melbo inaugurated

---

164. Commenting in 1973, Melbo threw an interesting historical light on the construction of the Social Science Building. "The Social Science Building," he said, "was funded in a fortuitous way. As of 1964–65, the U.S. Government had some funds to assist universities with the funding of building construction projects. The principle was one of participation, of matching funds. I had a copy of the act (the Higher Education Facilities Act of 1965) and went one day to talk with Norman Topping about an idea to get more building area for the School of Education and related disciplines. My suggestion was that we use the money in the Phillips bequest as the University's share of the required matching funds. Dr. Topping approved the idea, and an application was prepared requesting over $1 million dollars. It was forwarded to Washington, where it received a favorable reading from the appropriate division in the U.S. Office of Education, which at the time was headed by Dr. Raymond S. Moore, who had been one of my doctoral candidates in 1947. A site visit to USC was scheduled, and Dr. Moore came as the head of the team. Soon thereafter we received approval of our application and the grant was made. (Tape recording, April 1973).

the tradition of placing a commemorative plaque in bronze on the door of the office of each professor who was named *professor emeritus.* The first recipients of this honor were La Franchi, Perry, and Wagner. Said Dean Melbo, "I really think this will mean much more to the professors, their families and their friends than the traditional watch." (See Appendix G for a list of the persons memorialized in Waite Phillips Hall as of 1973.)

As a result of the dean's personal efforts and those of the Education Alumni Association and many other societies, friends, and donors, Waite Phillips Hall of Education became one of the best furnished buildings on the campus. Understandably, envy was roused among those who did not know the tireless work it represented in personal solicitation on the dean's part. Said Melbo with good humor in 1973:[165]

> I recall a story that was relayed to me at the time by one of our faculty. It seems that some of the professors assigned to the adjacent Social Science Building were a little envious of the furnishings in the Education offices. "What are we?" some asked, "Second-class citizens?" Whereupon our Education faculty member explained that Dean Melbo had gone out and raised additional money to pay for the furnishing and equipping of the offices and rooms in Phillips Hall. "Why don't you get your dean to do that?" asked the Education faculty member. One of the replies was, "Dean Melbo didn't have any damn business to get more money!"

As the time drew near for occupancy, Melbo placed Muelder in charge of coordinating the planning and physical movement to the new building. A special Dedication Committee was also formed, with Wilbur chairman. Dedication ceremonies were held May 17, 1968. Present were Mrs. Waite Phillips (the former Genevieve Elliott), two Phillips grandchildren, and the son, Elliott Waite Phillips, who responded on behalf of his father and family to the expressions of appreciation from President Topping, representing the University; H. Leslie Hoffman, representing the University's Board of Trustees; Earl V. Pullias, speaking on behalf of

165. MS comment, May 1973.

the faculty; and Cheryl Trollinger, representing the student body. The Reverend John E. Cantelon, University chaplain, gave the invocation, and Dean Melbo presided as master of ceremonies.

Said President Topping:[166]

It is a source of great pride to us that Mr. Phillips selected the University of Southern California to be the recipient of his largest single bequest. And we are particularly proud and honored to have earned this significant recognition of our School of Education and its work. Waite Phillips Hall of Education is of inestimable value to the teaching and research program of the School. The training of the teachers and educational administrators of the future is among the most important functions of a university. Indeed, the advancement of the American educational system is essential to the continued strength and stability of our free, democratic society. Thus, Waite Phillips Hall of Education is a worthy tribute to a man whose own life exemplified the highest ideals of our nation.

On behalf of the School of Education, Dean Melbo spoke of a dream fulfilled, a vision become reality:[167]

For more than 50 years, students, alumni, and faculty of the School of Education have cherished a great dream. This dream was that some day they would have a home of their own on the campus of the University of Southern California.

Now through the generous bequest of Waite Phillips, this dream becomes a reality.

The new Waite Phillips Hall of Education stands tall and proud. It does honor to the man and the family whose wish to help humanity through education was so great.

It does honor also to the graduates and faculty of the School of Education whose achievements in their profession enable them to stand tall and proud. And it will inspire those who come as students to shape their own dreams for a great future; for what men can visualize they can also find the will and the means to accomplish.

---

166. University of Southern California. *Waite Phillips Hall of Education Dedication, May 17, 1968.*
167. University of Southern California. *Waite Phillips Hall of Education Dedication, May 17, 1968.*

NORMAN H. TOPPING

President, USC (1958-1970), Chancellor (1970-   )

IRVING R. MELBO

Dean, School of Education (1953-1973).

PROFESSORS, SCHOOL OF EDUCATION

Upper left: D. Lloyd Nelson (1947-   ); **upper right:** Theodore H. E. Chen (1938-73); **lower left:** Emery Stoops (1943-70); **lower right:** Wendell E. Cannon (1948-72).

IN
MEMORIAM

Leonard Calvert (1909-1964).

Sophia Tichnor Salvin (1904-1967).

CAREER AND INSERVICE PROGRAMS

Upper photo: Mid-Career Advanced Development Program, 1966. **Seated, left to right:** Martin Houdyshell, Virginia Mathews, Virginia Archer, Eli Vukovich, Walter Zebrowski, Claire Damewood; **standing, left to right:** Lane Teaney, unidentified.

Lower photo: Dignitaries, National Conference for Elementary School Principals, July 1969. **Left to right:** Roger Egeberg, Dean, USC School of Medicine; Norman Topping, President, USC; Edith Green, Congresswoman; Dean Melbo.

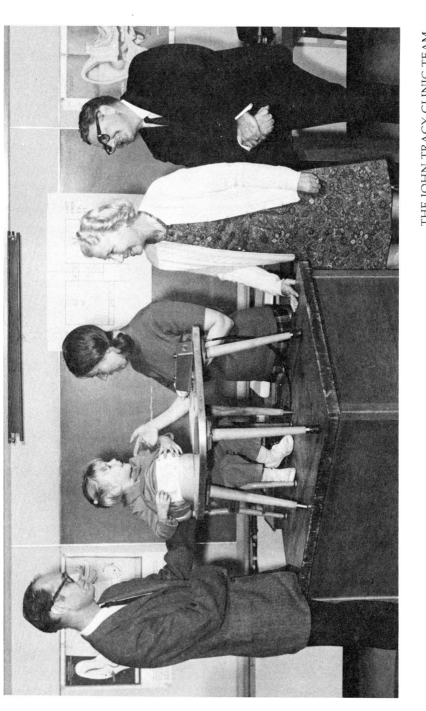

THE JOHN TRACY CLINIC TEAM

Left to right: Joseph Rudloff, Chairman, Nursery School; Tina DeWald, nursery school child (displaying hearing aid); Barbara King, teacher; Mrs. Spencer Tracy, founder of the clinic; Edgar L. Lowell, Administrator, John Tracy Clinic.

DISTINGUISHED SPEAKERS, EDUCARE

Upper photo: Left to right: Senator Wayne L. Morse (speaker); Tracey E. Strevey, USC Vice-President, Academic Affairs; Earl V. Pullias, Professor of Education. (EDUCARE Spring Dinner, April 19, 1963.)

Lower photo: Left to right: Tracey E. Strevey, USC Vice-President, Academic Affairs; Sterling M. McMurrin, U.S. Commissioner of Education (speaker); Mrs. McMurrin; Carl M. Franklin, USC Vice-President, Financial Affairs; Dean Melbo. (EDUCARE Charter Dinner, April 28, 1961.)

DISTINGUISHED MEMBERS, EDUCARE

C. C. Trillingham receives EDUCARE Citation of Merit, EDUCARE Dinner, April 27, 1962. At left is Dean Melbo, at right Schuyler C. Joyner.

DISTINGUISHED MEMBERS, EDUCARE

D. Welty Lefever receives EDUCARE Citation of Merit, EDUCARE Dinner, April 15, 1966. At left is C. C. Carpenter, at right Dean Melbo and Isaac McClelland.

MODEL, WAITE PHILLIPS HALL

Upper photo: C. C. Carpenter points to model. **Others, left to right:** Isaac McClelland, Daniel T. Dawson, Dean Melbo. (EDUCARE Fall Social 1965.)

Lower photo: Dean Melbo poses in front of model (1965).

EDUCARE
PRESIDENTS
AND
WAITE PHILLIPS
HALL OF EDUCATION

Upper photo: EDUCARE presidents at construction site. **Left to right:** C. C. Trillingham, Isaac McClelland, Jack P. Crowther, W. Earl Brown, Schuyler C. Joyner, C. C. Carpenter, Dean Melbo. (April 1967).

Lower photo: EDUCARE Dinner, April 14, 1967. **Left to right:** Schuyler C. Joyner, C. C. Trillingham, Dean Melbo, Robert Havighurst (speaker), Jack P. Crowther.

WAITE PHILLIPS HALL UNDER CONSTRUCTION
(September 1967)

WAITE PHILLIPS HALL NEARING COMPLETION
(December 1967).

WAITE PHILLIPS

Industrialist, philanthropist, humanitarian

DEDICATION
WAITE PHILLIPS HALL
MAY 17, 1968

President Topping,
speaker on behalf
of the University.

eft to right: Mrs. Waite Phillips, Dean Melbo, President Topping **(background),** Earl V.
'ullias, speaker for the faculty.

PLAZA, WAITE PHILLIPS HAL

Upper photo: Under construction, September 1967.

Lower photo: Dedication, May 17, 1968, showing portion of dedication assemblage.

THE LOUIS P. THORPE SEMINAR ROOM, WAITE PHILLIPS HALL

THE JAMES D. FINN INSTRUCTIONAL TECHNOLOGY
MEMORIAL SEMINAR ROOM, WAITE PHILLIPS HALL

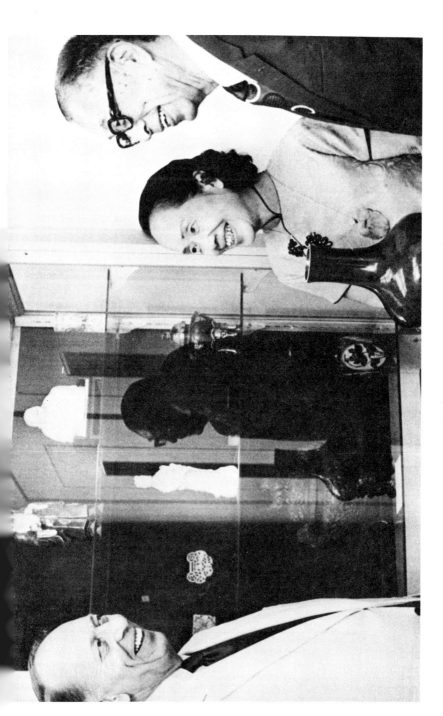

THE THEODORE HSI-EN CHEN AND WEN-HUI CHEN ROOM, WAITE PHILLIPS HALL

Left to right: Dean Melbo, Wen-Hui Chen, Theodore Hsi-En Chen (1973).

HIGHER EDUCATION READING ROOM, WAITE PHILLIPS HAL

Two views of the Higher Education Reading Room, dedicated to the memory of Joh Malcolm Pullias.

EARL V. PULLIAS

Professor of Education (1958-   )

STUDENT LOUNGES, WAITE PHILLIPS HAI

Upper photo: Sophia T. Salvin Memorial Seminar Room (International Student Loung

Lower photo: Student Lounge.

Donald E. Wilson, with McGuffey's Reader, a portion of the Wilson
Collection of Early American Textbooks.

Reading room and service desk, showing **(left to right)** Mrs. Elsie Harang, library assistant, and Mrs. Janet Harvey, education librarian. (Photograph taken in 1969)

SOUTHERN CALIFORNIA EDUCATORS WITH USC DOCTORATES IN EDUCATION

Left to right: Leonard Grandy (Ed.D. '59), Assistant Superintendent, Whittier Schools; Verne Steward (Ed.D. '34), Consultant, University School of Research; Aubrey H. Simons (Ed.D. '56), Superintendent, Pomona Unified School District; W. Norman Wampler (Ph.D. '47), Superintendent, Bellflower Unified School District; Heber H. Holloway (Ed.D. '59), Superintendent, Whittier Schools; Herman J. Sheffield (Ed.D. '51), San Bernardino Valley College. (EDUCARE Dinner, April 28,

SOUTHERN CALIFORNIA EDUCATORS WITH USC DOCTORATES IN EDUCATION

Left to right: Dale I. Glick (Ed.D. '54), Superintendent, Hermosa Beach City School District; Paul Fisher (Ed.D. '35), Assistant Superintendent, Siskiyou County Schools; W. Earl Brown (Ed.D. '56), Superintendent, South Bay Union High School District; Harry Smallenburg (Ed.D. '56), Director, Division of Research and Guidance, Los Angeles County Schools; Olaf Tegner (Ph.D. '58), Chairman, Department of Education, Pepperdine College. (EDUCARE Dinner, April 28, 1961)

CAMPUS, UNIVERSITY OF SOUTHERN CALIFORNIA

Showing (left to right): Von KleinSmid Center for International and Public Affairs, Social Science Building, and Waite Phillips Hall of Education.

CHAPTER 4

Change: 1969–1973

No social or educational revolution proceeds at an even pace or affects equally all segments of a society.

Like the inexorable tides which pound at our California coastline, there is an ebb and a flow. There are currents and cross-currents. There are little swirls and eddies, and still pools that remain as the tide moves out. But soon the restless surge of the sea mounts a new assault on the land, sometimes gently, sometimes in fury.

So it is with the patterns of a social revolution on the established institutions. There is impact and resistance, resistance and impact. And ultimately there is change.

I.R.M. THE SUPERINTENDENT OF THE SEVENTIES, 1969

The Scene of the '70s

In 1969, Melbo addressed the annual conference of the California Association of School Administrators and the California School Boards Association. With clear vision and accurate analysis of the current scene, he outlined for the school officials of California the problems he foresaw for the '70s and the kind of educational leadership which would be required to meet those problems. His was a clarion call for educational leadership that emerges by design rather than by accident or survival, a serious plea for that

183

type of educational statesmanship which, while facing squarely current critical issues, can yet meet with inner serenity and philosophic equanimity, the inexorable ebb and flow of social tides. Viewed from 1973, his words bear much weight both for the public school system of the United States and for institutions of the higher learning across the nation.

The principal problems Melbo foresaw he defined as the "5 R's": Rebellion, Race, Revenue, Relevance, and Reaction. Under *rebellion* he noted both student unrest and teacher militancy, both making necessary a new type of administration in which paternalism must give way to skill in conflict management. Integration-desegregation actions taken in enforcement of the Civil Rights Act would, he foresaw, have grave impact upon the public schools, some of it immensely destructive of public education as known in previous eras. In the economics of education, key factors would be society's willingness—or unwillingness—to support the educational enterprise; and the schools' productivity, both quantitative and qualitative, in response to public expectations. *Relevance,* a word so misused and so overworked in the '60s that many had come to hate it, would nonetheless be a problem area in the '70s, unless one were prepared to state that the curriculum was organized solely in terms of universals. Because no social or educational revolution proceeds at an even pace or affects equally all segments of a society, the educational leader must be prepared for the inexorable *reaction.* He must not be destroyed by infighting or lose direction in the storm's fury.

Nowhere in his published writings than in this address did Melbo more clearly set forth his personal philosophy of leadership or more succinctly state what he believed the role of the educational leader should be:

> If the prevailing societal reward system recognizes a perfunctory performance more than the courageous charting of a new course, then society will receive what it is really buying.
>
> If personal affability is an attribute more deserving of recognition than a high order of educational statesmanship, this is what will prevail.

184

Then there is no need for a new breed of superintendent in the '70s. The "good gray guys" will do the job.

Rather than the "good gray guys," replete with pragmatic compromises, tentative advances, and numerous strategic retreats, Melbo called for the leader who knew the reality of politics, who understood how confidence is gained and destroyed, how cooperation is enlisted and rewarded. The role he envisioned was that of the educational statesman. He would give, he said, "high priority to the ability of the superintendent to live and work in a negative environment." The leader, he asserted:

> ... must have more than a tough hide. He must be able to live without paeans of praise. He must have an inner security and be able to sense the emotional climate of his client publics, to respond with action prior to the creating of high emotion.

Melbo's analysis and challenge had their point of reference in the national and international events which had occurred during the latter '60s. Beginning in 1964, with the student rebellion at the University of California, Berkeley, campus after campus across the nation had been swept by student unrest. According to one study, in the first six months of 1968, 101 American colleges and universities were the scene of 221 demonstrations, involving nearly 40,000 participants. Within the next two years, hundreds of other student-activated campus disruptions took place, engendered by the unhappy involvement of the United States in Vietnam, by minority pressures, by a pervasive lack of institutionalized channels for expressing protest, and for many other social and political reasons. The student rebellion was supported not only by hard core activists but by vast numbers of moderate students and by many of the younger and more militant faculty. Campus unrest in turn engendered a lack of public confidence in institutions of the higher learning. Most college and university administrators found themselves caught between Scylla and Charybdis. On the one hand were the Congress, the state legislators, trustees, and the public—all highly irritated by the campus disturbances; on the other hand were the faculty and students, most of whom seemed to wish to deal with the disturbances in their

185

own way, through internal reform and changes in the national policy.

Election in 1968 of Richard M. Nixon as President of the United States also had vast implications for education. During his presidential campaign, Nixon had appealed to the nation's discontent over the Vietnam war and to public concern for preserving law and order in the face of urban unrest and lawlessness and campus disturbances. He promised high priority to combating inflation by slowing down the economic boom. Following his inauguration, the President began to move cautiously but firmly on programs dealing with hunger, ignorance, and disease, with a view toward reorganizing what he termed a wasteful hodgepodge of inherited programs. It was expected (and time confirmed) that, in accord with his basic philosophy, President Nixon would throw the weight of his influence toward state and local government action and toward private enterprise in preference to federal assistance.

All of these politico-socio-economic considerations, Melbo foresaw, would have their inevitable impact upon educational institutions and programs. No one was more keenly aware than he of the need to develop adequate responses to the new conditions. The direction of the School of Education in the 1970s was guided by Melbo's considered appraisal of the long-term effects of the expected developments at national, state, and local levels.

Organization and Governance

With respect to organizational structure, the School of Education remained unchanged from that of the 1967 reorganization. Broadly conceived, that organization consisted of the administration, as represented by the dean and his associates and assistants,[1] and the five "schedules": Faculty Council; Salary, Promotion and Tenure

1. Under the pressure of added and enlarged programs, the Office of the Dean was increased during this period by addition of a position of Associate Dean, Research and Development, and by two additional administrative assistant positions. Fiscal considerations, however, at the University level precluded the filling

186

Committee; Curriculum Committee; Departments; and Faculty Committees.

Within the established order, however, the philosophy of administration, and hence the governance of the School, underwent a fundamental change. Acting upon his own perception of the new role of the executive for the '70s, the dean, in concert with the Faculty Council, broadened participation in the decision-making process through the designed inclusion of both faculty and students in the structure of governance. If paternalism had existed, it now gave way to skill in conflict management. Details, which had previously been handled by the dean, were handed over to faculty committees, with student representation. The new arrangement freed the dean from many minutiae and permitted the full scope of his managerial ability to be devoted to the major objectives of the School as an educational institution of national and international scope. At the same time, it wisely recognized the new trends in management theory and the new activism among faculty and students.

Faculty Council. Under the chairmanship of Carnes (1968–69), Brown (1969–70), and Brackenbury (1970–73), the five-member Faculty Council continued to act as the representative, advisory, coordinative, and legislative agency within the School of Education. Among its major accomplishments were the appointment of a number of faculty committees; preparation, after long discussion and full coordination with faculty members, of a statement of responsibility of a faculty member to the School of Education and to the University; and adjustment of faculty loads in relation to professional contributions and restricted University funding.

---

of these positions. One position, that of Administrative Assistant, Public Relations, was filled, 1968–71, by John Allan Smith, through funds provided by EDUCARE. As of 1973, the administrative staff included Muelder, associate dean, Administrative Affairs; Marks, associate dean, Graduate Studies (who had replaced Kelly in that position as of 1972); and Jones, administrative assistant, Internal Affairs. Others in the Office of the Dean included Joan E. Allinson, secretary to the associate dean, Administrative Affairs; and Sondra M. Pocock, secretary to the dean.

187

Salary, Promotion and Tenure Committee. This committee had the unenviable task of treating matters most closely related, perhaps, to faculty morale, viz., salary, promotion, and tenure. Meeting frequently with the dean, the committee devoted long hours to the many intricacies involved in its task. Among the difficulties encountered were the limitation of total increments to a predetermined available amount as allotted to the School of Education for all positions in the regular budget; fiscal constraints imposed by the University; rise in cost of living; and inequities which at times resulted from "project" assignments as compared with "regular" budget positions. In November 1971, the faculty unanimously approved a proposal by the Faculty Council to change the membership provisions of the committee. Effective with the election of 1971, and in all subsequent years, the person receiving the most votes for membership on the committee was automatically elected for a two-year term. This change was predicated on the view that continuity of service was necesssary for at least one member of the committee. The term of office for all others continued to be for one year, and members might succeed themselves, if so elected.

Faculty Committees. Under the 1967 reorganization, faculty committees numbered five: Doctoral Program, Master's Program, Bachelor's Program, Research and Publications, and Library. As of 1973, seven more had been added: Admissions and Scholarship Standards; Appellate; Building and Facilities, Commencement, Honors Convocation, and Special Events; Credentials and Accreditation; Overseas Programs; and Student and Community Affairs.

The Admissions and Scholarship Committee was established in November 1968. Primary functions were to study and recommend admissions and scholarship standards for the School of Education; to review student petitions and appeals pertaining to admission status and to faculty action in assigning grades or credit; and to review recommendations relating to academic or other disqualifications.

188   In December 1968, the Buildings and Facilities Committee

was established as a standing committee. This committee, which had functioned as an *ad hoc* committee for the occupancy of Waite Phillips Hall, continued its supervision of regulations, security, and other matters pertaining to facilities occupied by the School of Education.

Newly formed in the fall of 1968, was a committee originally designated Student Affairs and Special Events Committee. Later, responsibility for special events was transferred to the Commencement, Honors Convocation, and Special Events Committee, and community affairs was combined with student affairs to form the Student and Community Affairs Committee. Meeting during 1968, with Wilbur as chairman, the committee drew in a number of faculty and students on an informal basis, addressing itself mainly to its functions and composition. Following a year's deliberation, the committee rendered a report to the faculty recommending: expansion of the committee's membership to include six student and seven faculty representatives, the former to be allotted among the graduate and undergraduate students and selected on the basis of desire to serve or at the recommendation of the faculty or students; and representation of students on all appropriate School of Education Faculty Committees, with the exception of the Salary, Promotion and Tenure Committee. These recommendations were approved by the faculty and in ensuing years were carried out.

The Appellate Committee was developed by the dean and the Faculty Council during the academic year, 1971–72. Operating informally and openly, the committee undertook to involve the appellant in steps toward a just solution of problems appealed to it, and to act within existing policies and rules, avoiding adversary relationships wherever possible and the treatment of problems involving rules of evidence.

In 1972, the Committee on Overseas Programs was established. Its purpose was to formulate plans, programs, and policies as required to fulfill the needs of the Overseas Program of the School of Education, and to serve in an advisory capacity to the Dean and faculty on that program.

189

The Committee on Commencement, Honors Convocation, and Special Events coordinated events and details pertaining to ceremonies and special events of concern to, or held by, the School of Education.

The Credentials and Accreditation Committee, formed at the close of the academic year 1972–73, was established by the dean and Faculty Council in order to assist in formulating policies and programs which would meet the anticipated requirements for credentials and accreditation to be promulgated by the California State Board of Education to assure conformance with the Ryan Act.

Departments. No change in departmental organization occurred, with the exception that in 1972, the Departments of Elementary Education and Secondary Education were merged, at their initiative, into the Department of Curriculum and Instruction, effective February 1973.

Faculty

During the 1968–73 period, the number of faculty members, including those with dual appointment, rose from 160 to 209. The bulk of increase was in the category of lecturers, whose number increased from 27 to 57 (See Appendix E for faculty statistics.)

Active and past members of the faculty who were taken by death during this same period includes: Eugenia G. Baker, November 9, 1968;[2] Harold R. W. Benjamin, January 12, 1969; James D. Finn, April 12, 1969; Marguerite Stoner, September 2,

---

2. Born May 9, 1914, in New York City, Eugenia Grace Baker received her B.A. (1936) from New York University; and her M.A. (1938) from Teachers College, Columbia University. From 1951 through 1966, she pursued doctoral level work at the University of Southern California. Her teaching career, which began in 1939, included teaching the orthopedically handicapped and mentally retarded in various schools in New York City, Michigan, and in the public schools of California. During the academic year 1966–67 she was visiting assistant professor, School of Education, in Special Education.

190

1970;[3] Ernest W. Teigs, November 14, 1970;[4] Merritt M. Thompson, November 27, 1970; and Louis P. Thorpe, November 29, 1970. On December 14, 1970, there was a single memorial service held on the campus for these three distinguished educators. Others who died during this period were: Charles C. Carpenter, March 15, 1971;[5] John Allan Smith, July 25, 1971;[6] Dan

3. An expert in teaching speech to the profoundly deaf, Marguerite Craun Stoner was born September 25, 1913, in Jefferson City, Tennessee. She earned her B.S. in Ed. (1933) at the University of Tennessee, and her M.A. in Education of the Deaf (1946) at Teachers College, Columbia University. Her professional experience included teaching at The Rhode Island School for the Deaf (1934–39); the Pennsylvania School for the Deaf (1939–45); the Lexington School for the Deaf (1946–49); and the John Tracy Clinic from 1949 to the time of her death. She was the author, with Edgar L. Lowell, of *Play It by Ear,* a book on auditory training. At the time of her death, she was engaged in a special research project which had among its objectives the preparation of materials for teaching speech to hearing-impaired children and adults.

4. Ernest Walter Teigs was born in Oconto, Wisconsin, July 25, 1891. He received his A.B. (1913) at Lawrence College; and his M.A. (1922) and Ph.D. (1927) at the University of Minnesota. In 1927, he was appointed associate professor of education, University of Southern California, and served from 1928 to 1946 as Dean of the University College and professor of education. From 1947 to 1953, he was editor-in-chief, California Test Bureau; and from 1953 to 1961 professor of education, Los Angeles State College. In 1949, he married Fay Greene Adams of the faculty of the School of Education. They were joint authors of the Teigs-Adams Social Studies Series and other books on elementary education. In his memory, and that of Merritt M. Thompson and Louis P. Thorpe, a memorial service was held by the University of Southern California December 14, 1970.

5. Charles Clifford Carpenter served in the public schools of California for 50 years and in the School of Education for 25, as lecturer, adjunct professor, and after 1970 Professor Emeritus. Born in Tulare, California in 1896, he graduated from Fresno Normal and State College in 1917, and then served (1918–19) with the American Expeditionary Forces in France. He received his A.B. (1927) from Fresno State College, and his M.S. in Ed. (1936) and Ed.D. (1948) from the University of Southern California. His professional experience included 12 years as superintendent of Azusa City Schools (1922–34); four years as superintendent of Downey Union High School (1938–42); and 25 years with the Los Angeles county school system, first as assistant superintendent (1942–65) and, after 1965, as chief deputy superintendent. He retired in January 1967. In 1957, Carpenter was named Delta Epsilon Lecturer. In his honor in 1951, the Alameda school district named an elementary school the C. C. Carpenter School.

6. Born in 1907, John Allan Smith received his A.B. (1932) at Santa Barbara Teachers College; his M.A. (1935) at Stanford University; and his Ed.D. (1948)

191

T. Dawson, October 20, 1972;[7] and Lenore C. Smith, April 27, 1973.[8]

Added to the list of emeritus professors during the 1969–73

from the University of Southern California. During World War II, he served as Captain, United States Marine Corps (1943–46). He was associated with Los Angeles city schools (1928–57). From 1957 to 1961 he was assistant superintendent, Paramount Unified School District; executive secretary, U.S. Educational Foundation in Pakistan (Fulbright Program) from 1961 to 1963; and from 1963 to 1966, was associated with Chapman College, the last year as dean of the Ship World Campus Afloat. From 1968 to 1971 he was visiting professor of education and administrative assistant to the dean, School of Education, University of Southern California. He was the author of a number of books, including an important study on school bond campaign techniques. The John Allan Smith Memorial Fund was established at the School of Education in his memory to aid in development of the Education Library.

7. Dawson, who died while still serving as professor in the Department of Administration and Supervision, was born March 12, 1914, in Port Townsend, Washington. He received his A.B. (1937) at San Diego State College; his M.A. in Education (1948) at Claremont Graduate School; and his Ed.D. (1953) at Stanford University. Prior to his appointment to the faculty of the School of Education, University of Southern California, in 1965, he was director of instruction, Merced County Schools (1947–48); vice-principal, Palo Alto Junior High School, (1948–49); assistant professor, Stanford University (1951–56); and executive secretary, California Elementary School Administrators Association (1956–65). At the time of his death, Dawson was also on the board of directors for the Institute of Teaching and the Editorial Advisory Board of the *CTA Journal.* A specialist in organizational behavior and personnel administration, in 1957, he received the Education Press's National Plaque for a series of articles in the *Palo Alto Times.* As the first executive secretary of the newly formed California Elementary School Administrators Association, he was instrumental in building that organization into one of the most respected and influential of educational associations. At memorial services held in Glendale, California, October 23, 1972, the tribute from the faculty and students of the School of Education was given by his friend and colleague, Robert A. Naslund, professor of Education, School of Education.

8. Lenore C. Smith, who died after long illness, was born April 2, 1909. She received her B.S. in Ed. (1929) from the University of Washington; her M.S. in Ed. (1937) from Stanford University; and her Ph.D. (1950) from the University of Southern California. From 1937 to the time of her death she was professor of physical education with dual appointment with the School of Education at the University of Southern California. Prior to her appointment to the faculty at the University, she had taught at Skagit Valley College in Mount Vernon, Washington. A delegate to the White House Conference on Aging in 1971, Smith was the author of *Recreation and Aging, New Dimensions on Programs for Senior Citizens,* and *Enriching Life for Senior Californians.*

192

period were: Adams (1969);[9] Stoops (1970);[10] Cannon (1972);[11] and

---

9. Fay Greene Adams retired after 40 years of service in the Department of Elementary Education of the School of Education. She was born in Dinuba, California, and received her A.B. (1926) and A.M. (1929) from the University of Southern California and her Ph.D. (1934) from Columbia University. Following five years' experience in the elementary and secondary schools of Los Angeles, she was appointed to the faculty of the School of Education, University of Southern California in 1929. In 1949, she was married to Ernest W. Teigs, then dean of University College, University of Southern California. With him she was author of the Tiegs-Adams Social Studies Series and of a large number of other educational studies and books in elementary education.

10. Emery Stoops was born in Pratt, Kansas, December 13, 1902. He received his A.B. (1930) at the University of Colorado, and then became teacher-superintendent in the Richfield, Kansas schools. Coming to California, he taught English at Whittier High School and then English and Speech at Beverly Hills High School, and from 1942 to 1943 was principal, University Adult School, Los Angeles. From 1944 to 1953, he was administrative assistant to the Los Angeles County Superintendent of Schools. In 1953, he was appointed to the faculty of the School of Education, where he served many years in the Department of Administration and Supervision. Stoops' published works include more than 60 articles in various periodicals, as well as numerous books, monographs, research studies, and editorials. He held many offices in the Alpha Epsilon Chapter of Phi Delta Kappa, and served as national vice-president of that organization, 1952–53, and president, 1953–54. During his incumbency as president the organization became international in scope. In Stoops' honor the Alpha Epsilon Chapter established in 1964 the Annual Emery Stoops Lecture; and in Waite Phillips Hall the faculty lounge is named in his honor.

11. Wendell Eugene Cannon's entire professional life was devoted to teacher education. A 1928 graduate of the University of Illinois, he obtained from that University his M.A. in 1931 and his Ph.D. in 1948. From 1928 to 1939, he was mathematics teacher and band director in high schools in Illinois; and from 1939 to 1942, assistant director of student teaching, University of Illinois. From 1942 to 1948, he was director of teacher training at Wisconsin State College, Whitewater; and from 1948 to 1966 director of teacher education at the School of Education, University of Southern California. In 1966, he was assigned, at his own request, to the Department of Secondary Education where he coordinated a joint University-Los Angeles City School project, Project APEX, at Dean Melbo's request. At the time of Cannon's retirement, Melbo wrote, in appreciation of his many services to education, and of his selfless dedication to assisting others: "In our field of education, there are a few who stand above the rest in their dedication, and their concern for their colleagues and their students, and their practical expression of the ethics of the profession. You have always been one of those rare persons who was committed more to the giving than to the receiving. This has not gone unnoticed among your students or your friends. As some one said better than I can, a long time ago, 'It is hardly necessary to light a candle to the sun.' "

193

Warters (1972).[12] Among those departing after a number of years of distinguished service with the School of Education were Coss[13] and Teubner.[14]

Added to the faculty in September 1969, as Distinguished Service Professor of Education, was Nila Banton Smith, international authority in the field of reading.[15] On April 23, 1973, the

---

12. Jane Warters served from 1951, with the School of Education as lecturer, adjunct professor, and from 1965 on as visiting professor in the overseas program in Europe. Of her work overseas, Dean Melbo said: "The success of the entire program was in very large part the result of Dr. Warters' personal efforts and interest on the part of students who had the good fortune to be in her classes. The entire School of Education is indebted to her for her distinguished service in Europe." As expert in the field of counseling and guidance, Warters had served, prior to 1951, for more than 18 years with the Miami Senior High School, Miami, Florida, and six years as department chairman in guidance at Lock Haven College, Lock Haven, Pennsylvania. She had received her A.B. (1921) from Shorter College; her A.M. (1926) from Tulane University; and her Ed.D. (1945), Teachers College, Columbia University.

13. Joe Glenn Coss was visiting professor of education, Department of Special Education, from 1966 to 1972; and from March 1968 to September 1971, he served as chairman of that department, winning high praise for his astute management in a position of great responsibility, involving many diverse activities and a large department. Prior to his appointment to the faculty as visiting professor, he had served as superintendent of Downey Unified School District. Coss received his A.B. (1928) from the University of California, Berkeley; and his M.S. in Ed. (1942) and Ed.D. (1960) from the University of Southern California.

14. Long associated with the School of Education as lecturer, Vivien E. L. Teubner was principal of Menlo Avenue School, one of the demonstrating-training schools of the School of Education, and coauthor of a number of primers and readers in the field of reading. In her honor the Vivien E. L. Teubner Seminar Room was named in Waite Phillips Hall.

15. Nila Banton Smith was born in Altona, Michigan. She received her B.A. (1928), University of Chicago; M.A. (1932) and Ph.D. (1936), Columbia University. Her appointments during a long and distinguished career were: teacher and supervisor of reading, Detroit Public Schools, 1928–33; head, Department of Education, Greensboro College, North Carolina, 1934–37; associate professor of education, Indiana University, 1937–39; professor of education, University of Southern California, 1939–49; professor and director of the Reading Institute, New York University, 1949–63; Distinguished Professor, Glassboro State College, New Jersey, 1963–67; and Distinguished Service Professor, San Fernando Valley State College, 1968–69. Perhaps the most prestigious name in the field of reading in the world, Nila Banton Smith was author of innumerable articles and many books in

194

Nila Banton Smith Reading Improvement Laboratory was opened in Waite Phillips Hall. The laboratory was fully equipped with technological devices for the teaching of reading and for the development of curricular materials in that field.

As of 1973, full professors included John W. Stallings, appointed in 1969 in the Department of Administration and Supervision;[16] four promoted from within the faculty: from rank of associate professor to professor: Bloland, John A. Carpenter, O'Neill, and Wilbur; and from adjunct professor to professor, William Allen. The 18 associate professors included eight who held that rank in 1968; seven promoted from within: Dembo, Fox, Hickerson, Ofman, Ransom, Smart, and Robert A. Smith; and three appointed during the period: Robert E. Ferris, Gerald Hasterok, and Frederick G. Knirk. Newly appointed as assistant professors were: Edward H. Berman, F. Roy Carlson, Robert J. Casey, Clive L. Grafton, William L. Harvey, Johanna K. Lemlech, Leon Levitt, Wanda R. Meier, Fred A. Moore, Daniel B. Nowak, Leo Richards, William N. Rueff, Robert B. Rutherford, Audrey J. Schwartz, Bernard Sklar, Eddie H. Williams, and Jerry E. Wulk.

In visiting status were: Professors Paul J. Avery, Lionel De Silva, A. Neil Galuzzo, Jefferson L. Garner, H. Fred Heisner, Homer Hurst, John D. Lawrence, Stuart McComb, Paul V. Robinson, Harry W. Smallenburg, C. R. Von Eschen, and James H. Williams;

that field, as well as frequent lecturer, consultant, and adviser to national and international organizations in reading.

16. Stallings, who was born October 28, 1923, in Oklahoma, received his A.A. from Murray College, Oklahoma; and his B.S. (1948), M.S. (1950), and Ed.D. (1958) degrees from the University of Southern California. With teaching and administrative experience at all levels of education from elementary through university, Stallings had served with the School of Education as adjunct professor since 1961 prior to his appointment to the full-time faculty. In September 1973, Stallings was named interim Dean of the School of Education, a position he filled with great competence and customary modesty. In March 1974, President Hubbard announced that Dr. Stephen J. Knezevich, professor of educational administration at the University of Wisconsin at Madison, and a distinguished educator, had accepted appointment as Dean of the School of Education, effective July 1, 1974.

195

associate professors A. Jean Ayres and George D. Merrill, Jr.; and assistant professors Robert L. Calatrello, Richard D. Hoover, Richard Miller, and Betty A. Walker.

In adjunct status were: Professors Truman N. Case, E. Maylon Drake, Robert H. Fisher, Jerry C. Garlock, Robert C. Gerletti, Chester E. Gilpin, Harry Handler, Richard Koch, Stuart J. Mandell, Leonard L. Murdy, Darcy A. Skaggs; associate professors Vincent E. Alexander, Norman B. Eisen, James E. Gardner, James F. Garvey, Wylda Hammond, Robert D. Leland, Penrod Moss, Elizabeth L. Simpson, Allen Paul Webb; and assistant professors William I. Erickson, Robert L. French, William Hirsch, Donald A. Kirsner, Kathryn L. Lewis, Gerald I. Lubin, John R. McCarthy, Samuel I. Rowe, James R. Rudolph, Alathena Smith, and Ivor J. Thomas.

Among the lecturers were Virginia R. Archer, Richard M. Clowes, Wallace F. Cohen, Vincent Crowell, Verna B. Dauterive, Logan Jordan Fox, Schuyler C. Joyner, Bernard Kirsch, Margaret H. Miller, Mary S. Reed, Siegfried C. Ringwald, Armen Sarafian, Roy Steeves, Starla Warburton, and Alfred H. Williams.

With Adams' retirement in 1969, the School of Education was deprived of its only woman full professor, with the exception of Nila Banton Smith, appointed that year as Distinguished Service Professor; and with the death in 1973 of Lenore C. Smith, its only woman professor in dual appointment. Women on the faculty, as of 1973, totaled 41, or approximately 20 per cent of the faculty. In the spring of 1973, the School of Education of the University of Southern California, together with other elements of the University and many institutions of higher learning across the country, was the subject of federal investigation into the number of women employed and their status on the faculty.[17]

17. According to a study by the U.S. Office of Education, in 1972–73, the percentage of women faculty at four-year colleges was 20.6 per cent, a figure only slightly larger than for 1962–63, which was 19 per cent. Preliminary figures of the Office of Education also indicated that women received average salaries almost $2,500 less than those given their male counterparts. According to the survey, only

Credentials

In 1969, in anticipation of more drastic changes shortly to follow, California institutions of teacher education were permitted to devise programs which, in the considered judgment of the institution, met the requirements of proper professional preparation for credentials under the Fisher Bill. The so-called Approved Programs for elementary and secondary credentials became operative June 13, 1969; and for supervision and administration credentials April 22, 1970. On July 1, 1970, the community college credential became operative in theory, although applications were not ready for processing until September of that year. As of December 31, 1970, the former junior college credential was completely phased out.

In 1970, the expected decisive change in California's credential system came about with the signing into law of the Teacher Preparation and Licensing Act, more familiarly known, after its author, Assemblyman Leo Ryan, as the Ryan Act. This act not only established a new framework for credential requirements in California, but substantially altered the organizational and administrative alignment of the state's educational system. It abolished the State Accreditation Committee and transferred its function to a new commission, the Commission for Teacher Preparation and Licensing. This commission, composed of professionals and laymen appointed by the governor, was charged with promulgation of credential requirements, accreditation of teacher education programs in colleges and universities, the issuance of credentials, adoption or development of examinations, development of standards for evaluating teacher competence and for identifying specialist teachers, and the suspension and revocation of credentials. Under the act's provisions, institutions of teacher preparation might offer subject matter and professional preparation programs which complied with the guidelines to be laid down by the commission.

9.7 per cent of all female faculty had achieved the rank of professor, compared with 25.5 per cent of all males. (*Education U.S.A.,* April 30, 1973)

The Ryan Act was passed with a beginning date of January 1, 1973. Nonapproved standard credentials elementary and secondary were to be phased out July 1, 1974; nonapproved standard supervision and administration credentials were to be phased out September 1, 1974; and the so-called approved programs were to be phased out September 15, 1974. Students who could not fulfill by September 15, 1974, the requirements for a Fisher Credential (issued on the basis of partial fulfillment) would fall under the new provisions to be set up by the Commission for Teacher Preparation and Licensing. The period between the passage of the Ryan Act in 1970, and its operative dates was taken up with the development by that commission of the necessary guidelines.

As has been noted, the credential system in California had been considerably fluctuating since passage of the Fisher Bill in 1961. Much credit must be given to Melbo, Frahm, and the credentialing staff of the School of Education for their time-consuming, taxing, and meticulous efforts to provide counseling and guidance to the many applicants for credentials under the various systems which prevailed during these years. Melbo's policy was expressed in the introductory note to the School of Education's Accreditation Report, prepared in 1972.[18]

> It is recognized that several credential programs are in a state of flux and guidelines for new licensing under the most recent State legislation are forthcoming. However, the University submits its programs as listed herein requesting accreditation for these programs, and indicating its intention to adapt and conform to such guidelines as are developed and found applicable.

Accreditation

The School of Education continued during the 1970s to be accredited by both the National Council for Accreditation of Teacher Education (NCATE) and the State of California and Western Col-

___

18. Accreditation Report, University of Southern California, School of Education (1972), p. v.

lege Association. In 1961, the NCATE had accredited all programs of the School of Education for all degrees through the doctorate for the ten year period, 1960–70. In 1970, therefore, the School was again visited by an NCATE team for purposes of re-accreditation. The NCATE evaluators visited the school March 16–18, 1970. In preparation for the visit, a comprehensive three-volume report had been prepared under Muelder's supervision. Following the visit, the University of Southern California was informed that the NCATE had reaccredited the School of Education for all programs for all degrees through the doctorate until 1980.

Changes in California's credential system inevitably affected also the State's accreditation process. Prior to the visit of the State Accreditation Committee, scheduled for December 2–4, 1970, the State Board of Education had agreed that the document prepared for the NCATE visitation the previous March would serve as the written document and that, unless otherwise indicated, the existing programs would be considered "Approved Programs," as defined by state requirements. Following the visit of the State Accreditation Committee, the School of Education was informed that the State Board of Education had extended the School of Education's accreditation for the academic year 1971–72. Another visit was scheduled for April 1972, at which time it was believed that the Teacher Preparation and Licensing Commission, established under the Ryan Act, would have defined its requirements.

In preparation for the April 1972 visit, a report was prepared by the School of Education which included all programs of the school as well as the new diversified major program.[19] Following the visit, Dr. John R. Hubbard, who in 1970 had succeeded Dr. Topping as president of the University of Southern California, was informed that the California State Board of Education had

19. University of Southern California, School of Education (1972). At the University of Southern California, the program suggested for this credential incorporated parts of both the current B.S. in Education and the A.B. curricula, but followed a more definite pattern than either. In April 1973, the title of the degree Bachelor of Science—Diversified Major was changed to Bachelor of Science—General Studies (*Minutes,* April 5, 1973).

199

acted favorably on the recommendations of the visitation committee and had reaccredited all programs for four years, to June 30, 1976, with the exception of the standard teaching credential with a specialization in early childhood teaching, which was accredited for three years, to June 30, 1975.[20] In November 1972, the State Accreditation Committee administratively approved the four-year baccalaureate degree programs for standard elementary and secondary teaching credential, valid to the date approved for other credentialing programs of the School of Education. Current law authorized the granting of these credentials on an initial basis to September 14, 1974, inclusive.[21]

Degrees

Bachelor of Science. During the 1969–73 period, three types of Bachelor of Science degrees were offered by the School of Education. For those students who could meet standard teaching credential requirements with a specialization in elementary teaching on the basis of partial fulfillment or with all requirements met and the credential granted prior to September 15, 1974, were offered a Bachelor of Science (For Standard Teaching Credential Candidates). In 1972, in conformance with the Teacher Preparation and Licensing Law of 1970, a new type of Bachelor of Science degree was offered. This degree, first designated Bachelor of Science—Diversified Major, was changed in 1973 to Bachelor of Science—General Studies.[22] Students expecting to qualify for a credential to teach in the elementary schools of California after September 17,

20. Letter, Wilson Riles to Dr. John R. Hubbard, dated June 23, 1972.
21. Letter, Carl A. Larson, secretary, State Accreditation Committee to Dr. Irving R. Melbo, dean, School of Education, dated November 10, 1972.
22. Within the 128 units required by the University for a bachelor's degree, 84 must, for the Bachelor of Science—General Studies degree, be in the diversified major area and 24 units in education. Throughout the undergraduate program, the student was enrolled in courses applicable to the major selected. Both lower and upper division courses were included in the four areas of study encompassed by this degree: English-speech; mathematics and physical and life sciences; social sciences; and the humanities and fine arts, including foreign languages.

200

1974, were required to earn this degree or a bachelor's degree in a subject matter field. In addition, in order to meet a demand for supervisors and teachers with vocational specialization, the School of Education had devised in 1968 a degree curriculum leading to the Bachelor of Science in Education—Technical Studies. As has been noted, this degree was established primarily for the benefit of foreign students and, as of 1973, it was confined to the international market. Foreign students electing this program were directed in its pursuit by the Center for International Education.

Master of Science in Education. Although requirements for the degree of Master of Science in Education remained essentially unchanged during the 1968–73 period, three modifications were approved in the basic program leading to the degree under certain specified programs.

In 1969, an M.S. in Ed. program for members of the dentistry profession who held a professional degree (D.D.S. or D.D.Sc.) was approved. Under this program, the minimum requirement for 28 semester hours of acceptable graduate work in education was lowered to 24 semester hours, and the requirement for the Aptitude portion of the Graduate Record Examinations (GRE) was waived. In 1972, this program was expanded to include members of the various health professions (M.D., Pharm.D., etc.).[23]

In 1970, following representations by students in the National Teacher Corps program who desired the M.S. in Ed. degree but objected to taking the Aptitude portion of the GRE for admission to candidacy, the faculty approved the policy that the GRE was to be used as only one possible indication of success in graduate study. Waiver of the examination for members of the Teacher

23. These programs were developed in coordination with the School of Medicine. Under a grant from the U.S. Public Health Service, the School of Medicine was undertaking to train health professions teachers holding medical professional degrees in matters pertaining to the improvement of teaching and learning in health professions schools. The grant provided that Fellows might pursue graduate study in a school of education, if they so desired, including both master's and doctoral degrees.

201

Corps was not, however, approved, should they apply for admission to candidacy.

In 1971, the concept of alternative degree "packages" leading to the M.S. in Ed. received faculty approval. This modification was urged by those who believed that revision of the degree requirements should be considered in order to permit more flexibility for individual students. Departmental autonomy was retained, under the concept, with regard to specification of unit requirements beyond the minimum (28 semester hours of acceptable graduate work), and departments were encouraged to use certificates or advanced master's degrees to indicate special competencies.

Following faculty approval of the concept, the Departments of Teacher Education and Special Education jointly offered and gained approval for a program leading to the M.S. in Ed. degree for college graduates who wished to obtain the standard elementary teaching credential with a specialty in the area of special education. The Department of Teacher Education also offered a "package" program for an M.S. in Ed. in Bilingual Education and a program for certificate in TESOL (Teaching of English to Speakers of Other Languages). The Department of Counselor Education also offered and obtained approval for a program for an M.S. in Counselor Education which required a minimum of 36 semester hours.

Doctoral Program. A number of major changes were made in the doctoral program during the 1969–73 period. In each instance, the changes reflected a growing flexibility in the requirements for this degree.

In 1971, new regulations were adopted on an experimental basis which permitted course work prior to the dissertation to be built around three options: (1) a major field, specialization within that field, and a supplementary field; (2) a major field with two specializations and no supplementary field; and (3) an interdepartmental major with no supplementary field. Selection of either (2) or (3) as an option required the approval, through petition, of the Committee on the Doctoral Program, and was subject

202

to the subsequent ratification of the candidate's committee on studies. In December 1972, the Doctoral Committee recommended to the faculty that the use of two specialties in lieu of a supplementary field be discontinued as of the spring semester of 1973. Experience indicated that of 25 petitions received during the preceding year, 15 had been in the Department of Counselor Education, which strongly favored its continuation. Following faculty discussion, the matter was tabled and referred back to the doctoral committee, where it was decided that, because of the opposition to the recommendation by certain departments, the matter would not be revived.

Effective September 1972, the name of the examinations required for entrance into the doctoral program was changed from Comprehensive Examinations to Admissions Examinations, and the content of the examinations changed from five separate examinations in four specified fields and the student's proposed major field to four separate examinations, two each from specified areas, and a fifth in the student's proposed major field.[24]

In April 1973, the faculty approved the deletion of the requirement that a period of six months must elapse before a student, who had failed the Admissions Examinations, might take them a second time, but required written approval of the student's adviser.[25]

Overseas Programs

Student Teaching in Europe. Beginning in 1966 and continuing thereafter each year, the Department of Teacher Education pro-

---

24. Under the new system, Admissions Examinations consisted of: (1) Choice of two objective examinations from the areas of educational psychology, sociology of education, and philosophy of education; (2) Choice of two objective examinations from the areas of administration, elementary education, secondary education, and higher education; and (3) An essay examination in the student's proposed major field. Students in the major fields of counselor education, instructional technology, international education, or special education might elect to substitute an objective examination in their major field for one of the objective examinations listed in (2) above.

25. *Minutes,* April 5, 1973.

vided for selected students in its teacher preparation program to perform their last semester of directed teaching in certain schools of the United States Dependent Schools in the European Area (USDESEA). An average of six students was placed each year in directed teaching situations overseas. Instructor-coordinator during the early 1970s was Sue Reese Mason.[26] While in Europe, students took courses in curriculum and methods as well as international education. In addition, they participated in various educational meetings and seminars and in planned educational field trips.

M.S. in Ed. Program in Europe. During the 1968–71 period, the School of Education continued to conduct, under contract with the United States Air Force, its M.S. in Ed. program at five centers in Germany (Birkenfeld, Hahn, Ramstein, Rhein Main, and Wiesbaden), one center in Spain (Torrejon), and two centers in Southeastern Europe (Athens, Greece; and Izmir, Turkey). A major factor in the success of the program was the support rendered it by the Commander-in-Chief, United States Air Forces in Europe, General Horace M. Wade. In recognition of General Wade's extraordinary contribution to the program, the University of Southern California in June 1969, conferred upon him the Honorary Degree of Doctor of Laws. The citation, presented by Dean Melbo, read in part:[27]

Now, in further recognition of his outstanding service to his

---

26. Sue Reese Mason was the wife of Joseph A. Mason, Director of the USDESEA. She received her A.B. (1945) at the University of Alabama, and her M.A. (1953) at California State College at Los Angeles. Her professional experience included service as elementary teacher, demonstration teacher, and reading teacher at the 32nd Street Elementary School, a demonstration school of the School of Education, University of Southern California; and experience in the USDESEA system as assistant principal, principal, middle-grades coordinator, and assistant superintendent for central Germany. In 1969, she became overseas coordinator for the student teachers of the School of Education; and in 1969 also entered the first doctoral program of the School of Education in Europe. Taken with incurable illness prior to the first graduation of the students in that program, she was awarded the doctorate just prior to her death in 1972.

27. Fourth Annual Commencement, University of Southern California, European Graduate Program, June 29, 1969.

profession, of the special high calibre of military and diplomatic knowledge he has created and shared, of his far-reaching contributions to personnel of the United States Air Force, and of his exceptional ability in balancing aspects of military, civilian, and governmental interrelationships, the University of Southern California is proud to honor this citizen of the world, Horace M. Wade.

In 1971, under revised policy of the Air Force, the University of Southern California was invited, along with a number of other institutions of higher learning, to bid on a continuation of the USAFE program in Europe. The University, however, took the position that no bid would be made on the single criterion of tuition cost. The USAFE contract therefore was terminated as of August 15, 1971. By policy set by Melbo, all centers of the School of Education were staffed through the summer session in order that as many students as possible might finish their degree. This demonstration of good faith and of concern for student welfare was to have an important influence on the acquisition of later contracts. To Melbo it was simply a matter of his and the School of Education's traditional mode of operation. Said he in 1973:[28]

> Even though we knew the enrollments would be low and the program would operate at a deficit in the last terms under the Air Force contract, I considered it to be absolutely necessary to maintain a full schedule at all locations until the very last day, in order to enable as many students as possible to complete their degree requirements, and thus to maintain the professional integrity of the School of Education. I was determined to show all concerned that we were genuinely committed to our students and that we would do everything we had ever said or implied that we would do. I believe this demonstration of professional integrity and good faith was not lost upon either the military or civilian observers of our performance.

In 1971, thanks to Melbo's initiative, the European program of the School of Education was reinitiated under the sponsorship of the United States Army, which contracted with the University

28. MS comment, 1973.

of Southern California for the M.S. in Ed. program in Europe. As related by Dean Melbo in 1973:

> Early in 1971, believing that our performance record was a good one, and drawing upon a certain reserve of personal contacts, I made a trip to Europe to meet and talk with the U.S. Army education personnel, their education advisers, and key personnel in the command, in order to negotiate a contract whereby the U.S. Army in Europe would become our sponsor for a graduate degree program in Europe. I gave them a frank and honest report of the USAFE situation and found them perhaps better informed than I was. It was at this point that our performance record for good teaching, intense concern for students, and a reputation for administrative integrity stood us in good stead. I left Europe with the feeling and some assurances that our presence in Europe would be continued, and what followed was our Army contract and sponsorship.

> Upon reflection, if I hadn't moved when I did, we would have been out. Since that time, the relationship has been a cordial one and, as Dean of the School of Education, I have "leaned over backwards" to do what was expected of us—and hopefully a little more—to maintain an absolute "quality control" of this and all other overseas programs.

As of 1973, the M.S. in Ed. program in Europe was being offered in Germany, Spain, and Belgium.[29] It was with sincere regret that students, as well as resident faculty, learned of the discontinuation of the program in Greece and Turkey. The remoteness of these areas had added to the program's value to both military and civilians stationed there, and the ancient sites of Greek and Turkish civilizations evoked much interest on the part of resident faculty. Of particular interest because of the University of Southern California's "Trojan" traditions was the site of ancient Troy.[30]

---

29. Sites in Germany included Baumholder, Darmstadt, Frankfurt am Main, Fulda, Hanau, Kaiserslautern, Nurnberg, Schweinfurt, and Wurzburg. In Spain, the program was conducted at Rota; and in Belgium, at Brussels and SHAPE (Supreme Headquarters Allied Powers Europe).

30. In addition to the statue of the Trojan warrior (a modern creation) which

206

USC-Asian Study Program. In 1971, Dean Melbo opened two advanced study centers in the Far East for graduate work in Education. This program, known as the USC-Asian Study Program, was conducted by the School of Education in cooperation with the system of overseas American-sponsored elementary and secondary schools assisted by the United States Department of State. As of 1971–72, the advanced study centers were at the Taipei American School in Taipei, Taiwan (Republic of China), and the International School of Bangkok, Bangkok, Thailand. The first classes in Taipei were offered in January 1971, and in Bangkok in March 1971, with Nelson the first professor assigned. During the next year and one-half, the cycle at these two locations was continued, with full-time faculty members from the School of Education or adjunct professors of comparable rank and stature assigned. Classes were conducted in six-week cycles at each location.

In Taiwan, approximately 50 students, mostly teachers at the Taipei American School, entered the program, pursuing course work leading to the M.S. in Ed. degree. Of these, 37 completed

---

had been erected on campus in 1930, near Founders Hall had been dedicated in 1952 a portion of a column from the ruins of ancient Troy. The column, which was the gift of the Turkish Republic, arrived on campus in 1950, as a result of negotiations of the Acacia fraternity to acquire a stone from Troy. The column, mounted on a pedestal, was dedicated October 29, 1952, the Twenty-ninth Anniversary of the Republic of Turkey. It was presented on behalf of the Turkish Government by Dr. Bedri Gursoy, then a visiting scholar from Ankara University; and was accepted by President Fagg, in the presence of Chancellor von KleinSmid. The column is believed to have formed part of a column in the Temple of Apollo at ancient Troy. Of quartz monzonite porphyry, it was quarried without the use of iron tools some time in all probability before 1200 B.C. Commemorative verses inscribed on plaques at the base of the column include two anonymous verses and a verse from the poet, Byron. The anonymous verses read: "Hector and Paris saw me at Troy/ I suffered the wrath of Agammemnon/ And once, as she passed, golden Helen/ Brushed me with her sleeve" and "From a far place and long ago, and broken/ I have come at last to another Troy/ But still I am, and Troy lives once again." The verse from Byron reads:
Ye parent gods! Who rule the fate of Troy,
   Still dwells the Dardan spirit in the boy;
When minds, like these, in striplings thus we raise,
   Yours in the godlike act, be yours the praise.

207

their work and were graduated May 27, 1972, in ceremonies held at the Taipei American School. Milton C. Kloetzel, Academic Vice-President of the University of Southern California, and Dean Melbo presented the diplomas to the graduates. Arrangements for the ceremony and festivities were made by Herbert R. Miller of the Department of Instructional Technology, who was teaching the last course in the cycle in Taipei. Following the graduation, the University was host to a reception for graduates and their guests in the Maili Lounge of the Military Assistance Advisory Group (MAAG) Annex, Taiwan. A formal dinner on the following evening, held in the Maili Lounge, was attended by a distinguished group of Chinese and American educators and officials, including the American ambassador to the Republic of China, the Honorable Walter P. McConaughy and Mrs. McConaughy; the ambassador of Thailand to the Republic of China; and the Republic of China's Minister of Education.

On May 30, 1972, the first graduation for the Advanced Center in Thailand was held at the International School in Bangkok. The 37 graduates, mostly from the teaching staff of the International School in Bangkok, included 32 who received their M.S. in Ed. degrees and five who received the advanced master's degree. Among the graduates was one Thai, Mrs. Premchitt Sidhisiri, a teacher in the International School of Bangkok. Presiding at the graduation ceremonies were Vice-President Kloetzel and Dean Melbo. At the graduation dinner held in the Dusit Thani Hotel, Bangkok, distinguished guests included Thai Ministry officials, representatives of the United States Embassy and the United States Forces in Thailand, and four USC alumni, three of whom were Thai.[31]

As of the spring of 1973, plans were made for the extension of the USC-Asian Study Program into Okinawa, Korea, and Japan

31. Professor Sampon Verangoon, head, Audio-visual Education Department, Chulalongkorn University; Mr. Pholhakdi Karnehanachri of the International Engineering Company, Thailand; Mr. Raks Durongapidya, general manager, Aik Hong Company; and Mr. Davis J. Pratt, Operations Division, SIU, Cooperating Thai Industries.

208

in cooperation with the United States Forces in these areas, the contract for which was signed in August, 1973.

USC-USDESEA Doctoral Program. On August 20, 1972, an event unprecedented in the history of the University of Southern California took place when ceremonies awarding the doctoral degree were conducted, not at the University campus as had been customary since the first doctoral degree was awarded in 1927, but on an off-campus site, and one which was 7,000 miles from campus in Heidelberg, Germany. Under special arrangements between the School of Education and the United States Dependent Schools in the European Area (USDESEA), and under the sponsorship of the United States Army in Europe, 17 recipients of the Ed.D. from the University of Southern California pursued their doctoral studies for the most part while continuing their duties as educators abroad.

In a brochure describing the highlights of the program's history, Helen Jones, administrative assistant to Dean Melbo, noted with a good deal of understanding as well as understatement: "The efforts needed and the foresight necessary to accomplish the awarding of these doctoral degrees involved many persons."[32] Carpenter of the Center for International Education and an educator formerly associated with the USDESEA program had indicated to Dean Melbo the need for such a graduate program. At his urging, Melbo conferred with Dr. Joseph A. Mason, director of the USDESEA, on the possibility of instituting a doctoral program with main center in Europe.[33] By April 1969,

32. Jones (1972), p. 2.
33. Major provisions of the program included the agreement that all academic and administrative requirements established by the School of Education would be fulfilled; that the program would serve the personnel development needs of qualified overseas American educators, with a minimum number of 30 candidates at the Graduate Center; that substantial library resources would be made available, with a professional educator assigned by USDESEA as coordinator in Germany; that areas of specialization would be initially confined to educational administration, secondary education, and social and philosophical foundations (international education); that residence requirements would include one semester of study on campus; and that overall control of the program would be the responsibility of the

209

preliminary plans had been formulated and were presented by Melbo for faculty approval which was soon forthcoming. The program opened in September 1969, at Karlsruhe, Germany, the location of the office of the director, USDESEA. Students accepted into the program numbered 34 (31 men, three women). All were qualified educators in the USDESEA system.

The basic format for course conduct was established by Nelson, the first professor to be assigned to the program. Under arrangements made by him and continued thenceforth, students met with the professor three consecutive weekends in each eight-week course, thus fulfilling the required number of contact hours. Following completion of the required courses, comprehensive examinations were held for admission to the doctoral program. These were conducted in May 1970, in Germany for 33 persons, of whom 29 were successful. During the summer of 1970, and again in the summer of 1971, members of the group studied on the campus of the University, thus meeting the 12-week residence requirement, as established under the agreed program.

In 1971, all students passed the qualifying examinations for the doctorate and entered upon the dissertation phase. The first dissertation to be completed was that of Sue Reese Mason, which was completed in December 1971. By May 1972, 16 other candidates had completed their dissertations. For these oral examinations were conducted and awarding of doctoral degrees approved. Sue Reese Mason, who had succumbed in the spring of 1972, received her degree prior to her death; the other 16 were awarded degrees in graduation ceremonies held at Heidelberg in the Headquarters, United States Army, Europe on August 20, 1972. Principal speaker at the graduation ceremonies was General Andrew J. Goodpaster, Supreme Allied Commander Europe and Commander-in-Chief, United States Army, Europe. The degrees were conferred by John S. Cantelon, Vice-President of Undergraduate

School of Education working through its established decision-making procedures, with coordination provided by a faculty member with international education experience and one preferably also familiar with USDESEA administrative processes.

CHANGE: 1969–1973

Studies, representing President John R. Hubbard of the University. Dr. Cantelon was assisted by Dean Melbo, representing the School of Education.

In 1971, a second advanced study center for the doctoral program was opened in Darmstadt, Germany; and in 1972, a third center in the United Kingdom. Programs at each center were conducted in accordance with the plan developed for the first pilot program in Karlsruhe, and each center was staffed by regular members of the faculty of the School of Education or by visiting professors of comparable rank and stature. Prime mover and organizer of the entire overseas program of the School of Education was Melbo, whose reputation as an international educator was among the first in the United States.

University-USDESEA Consortium. In late 1971, the United States Department of Defense took the first tentative steps to establish a consortium of universities who were giving or were interested in giving professional education overseas. Through the consortium, the Department of Defense proposed, first to assist the USDESEA in providing systematic inservice, degree-granting professional education of high quality to its staff; and second, the Department of Defense aimed at reducing the proliferation of programs being established abroad by American universities.

At an organizational meeting held in Karlsruhe, Germany, in January 1971, representatives of seven major American universities[34] met to consider the first cooperative effort of its kind between American universities and a single public school system. At the meeting, the University of Southern California, which had indicated its willingness to study the consortium plan, was represented by Dean Melbo. The consortium concept was the subject of later meetings at Lansing, Michigan, and Washington, D.C. One of the items discussed was how to transfer more easily

---

34. Participating universities were: Boston University, Florida State University, Michigan State University, the State University of New York (SUNY), the University of Houston, the University of Oregon, and the University of Southern California.

from one university to another credit earned under one university. Said one member of the USDESEA administrative staff:

> If the universities are able to agree about interchanging credits, then our teachers will be able to return to the States for graduate studies, and take with them all credits they've earned during summers or evenings while they were here. They will be able to fit automatically in a campus somewhere in a variety of geographical areas.

Following a meeting in Washington, D.C., Dean Melbo announced that the University of Southern California had been allocated three summer institutes to be conducted in Europe during 1973. These were: the Early Childhood Institute, to be conducted by Dr. Margaret Smart with 12 designated USDESEA participants; the Institute for Audio-Visual Coordinators, to be conducted by Dr. Herbert Miller for 35 designated participants; and the Institute in Cinematics, to be conducted by Dr. Bernard Kantor, Mona Kantor, and Russell McGregor for 15 USDESEA designated participants. Under the arrangements, USDESEA would pay the tuition for each participant at current established overseas rate of the University of Southern California and, in addition, participants would receive a stipend from the USDESEA as a designated participant in a professional inservice program. The institutes were to be conducted in Europe during the latter part of July and the first weeks of August, 1973.

While the School of Education, under Melbo's direction, was thus expanding its program overseas, on the domestic front it was also meeting the new demands and new challenges with new programs and with innovative approaches to teacher preparation. These programs, which ranged from early childhood education through advanced seminars for superintendents, supplemented and complemented the regular programs which continued to be carried out at the highest professional level. Special programs, initiated and developed by the various departments of the School, are noted below.

212

Administration and Supervision

Leadership Workshop. Since 1957, the University of Southern California's School of Education, in cooperation with the South Coast Section of the California Elementary School Administrators Association (CESAA), had conducted on the University's campus an annual administrative leadership workshop for elementary school administrators. Each workshop brought together a great array of resources to focus attention on an integrated topic of importance to elementary school teaching and administration. Hailing the tenth USC-CESAA workshop, the *California Elementary Administrator* commented:[35]

> During the past decade, the subjects considered in the CESAA-USC workshop consistently have been well ahead of the times, and the topics discussed here first have spread widely throughout the state and other parts of the country. Perhaps no professional activity has achieved greater distinction than these summer workshops, with the joint contribution of faculty and students. CESAA congratulates South Coast Section and the University of Southern California on a decade of leadership.

Adding to the accolade, Dean Melbo said in 1973:[36]

> These Elementary School Administrators Workshops have proved to be an enormously productive and influential professional development program. They were well attended, frequently involving a hundred or more experienced elementary school principals from all over the state. Moreover, the programs were so significant and timely that the topics first presented and discussed at the USC-CESAA summer workshops became the program topics for meetings held elsewhere for the next few years. There was a tremendous "ripple" effect, and their influence is still felt. It would be a good thing to reactivate them.

The chief organizer of the USC-CESAA workshops was Virginia R. Archer, then principal of the Shenandoah Avenue Elementary School, and for many years also training principal and

---

35. *California Elementary Administrator,* 30(3), p. 3.
36. MS comment, May 1973.

lecturer for the School of Education.[37] Assisting her were a number of other elementary school principals, notably, as of 1967, Verna B. Dauterive, principal of Laurel Street School in Los Angeles; Virginia H. Mathews, principal of Kettering Elementary School in Long Beach; and Walter S. Zebrowski, principal of Lunada Bay Elementary School in Palos Verdes Estates.

Capitalizing on the dozen-year experience of the Western educators, the Department of Elementary School Principals of the National Education Association (NEA) held in 1969, for the first time in the Far West, its National Conference and Workshop for Elementary School Principals, in cosponsorship with the California Elementary School Administrators' Association and the School of Education, University of Southern California. The conference-workshop, which was held on the campus of the University of Southern California from July 7 to July 18, 1969, had as its theme, "Leadership Styles for Today's Realities." Under the joint directorship of De Silva of the School of Education and Archer of the CESAA, a stellar faculty was assembled from around the nation. One of the distinguished speakers was the honorable Edith Green, member from Oregon to the House of Representatives and ardent member of the House Committee on Education and Labor. Other speakers, selected for the role they played in school administration, included: Irving R. Melbo as statesman; Dan T. Dawson as articulate "gamesman"; T. M. Stinnet, former assistant executive secretary, NEA, as visionary; J. Graham Sullivan, chief deputy superintendent of Los Angeles city schools and former associate U.S. Commissioner of Education, as

37. From 1957 to 1967, Virginia R. Archer headed the planning committee for the USC-CESAA workshops, and from 1962 to 1969 was chairman of the workshops. Her association with the School of Education was extended when, in 1964, she was appointed to the committee which developed the Mid-Career Program for Elementary Administrators at the School of Education. A member of the first group, she received her certificate of completion of this program in 1967, and the Ed.D. degree in 1973. Her other affiliations with the School of Education included membership on the Board of Directors of EDUCARE, presidency of the Honorary Association of Women of Education (HAWE), and presidency of the Eta Chapter of Delta Kappa Gamma.

214

energizer; Verna B. Dauterive, administrative coordinator for Integration in the Los Angeles City Schools and authority on the history of Negro education, as advocate; and David W. Martin, professor of education and director for the Urban Semester at the University of Southern California, as bridge-builder for the inner city's socio-economic and cultural gap. The role of the speakers was to stimulate thought about various tasks as a school administrator and educational leader. Presentations were designed to provide provocative ideas relevant to issues, trends, and confrontations facing the principal, and divergencies in viewpoint and bases for discussion and discourse were emphasized.

Annual Seminars for Superintendents. In 1970, under Stallings' impetus, the Department of Administration and Supervision inaugurated a series of annual summer seminars for school superintendents. Participants were one or more representatives from an average of 47 districts in southern California. Seminar themes centered on problems faced by superintendents in the '70s, and on ways of approaching these problems. The 1970 seminar on "Strategies for Leadership," was followed by a 1971 seminar stressing accountability, a 1972 seminar on management of conflict, and a 1973 seminar on "Politics of Leadership." The 1973 seminar, which treated of this subject at the Federal, state, and local level included such timely topics as Federal aid to education, revenue sharing, budget cutbacks at the federal level; the political realities of the superintendent and the city, minority group relations, models of power structure in the community setting; and employee organizations. The final sessions, which were held in Sacramento, were devoted to meetings with chairmen of the various State Education Committees of the Senate and Assembly, and with A. Alan Post, legislative analyst. For each seminar in the series distinguished figures in the field of education, administration, or related areas were invited as speakers and discussion leaders.[38]

---

38. Notable among these were: for the 1970 seminar Norman Cousins, editor of *The Saturday Review,* and Gordon Winton, author of the Winton Act; for 1971,

215

Curriculum and Instruction

Early Childhood Education. Appointment by Dean Melbo in 1969, of Margaret E. Smart as assistant professor in the Department of Elementary Education, with responsibility for the development of early childhood education, brought to that program the impetus desired by Dean Melbo. Among the innovations introduced by Smart in 1969 were the enrollment of students in programs leading to the standard teaching credential with specialty in early childhood education, and in programs leading to advanced degrees in that specialty; establishment of a USC School for Early Childhood Education as a clinical facility for the preparation of teachers in early childhood education; and inauguration of an annual conference and of periodic workshops in this specialized field of knowledge.

The school was located from 1969 through the academic year 1972–73, on the downtown campus of Mount St. Mary's College, at 17 Chester Place, the former residence of President von KleinSmid.[39] Carrying forward Melbo's now well-established policy of providing clinical facilities for the School of Education's teacher preparation programs, the school became, under Smart's direction, a laboratory setting for integrating the practical and the theoretical experience of early childhood education and for interweaving the strands of the foundations, curricula, and field experience. Primary funding for the school (approximately 85 per cent of its operating expenses) came from the California State Preschool Compensatory Program.

Robert Townsend, executive and author of *Up the Organization;* Wilson Riles, California State Superintendent of Public Instruction; and Alex Sherriffs, education advisor to Governor Reagan; and for 1972, Rensis Likert, internationally recognized authority in the field of social psychology and author of several books on management; Paul Salmon, executive secretary, American Association of School Administrators; and John Stull, assemblyman and author of the Stull Bill.

39. This residence, the first floor of which was rented from Mount St. Mary's College, had been previously used by the School of Education for the Instructional Materials Center under the Department of Special Education and later for special aspects of teacher preparation under the Department of Teacher Education.

216

As a university-based school, the purposes were to train students qualifying for the standard elementary teaching credential with specialization in early childhood education; to provide field experience and research opportunities for graduate students in this specialization; and to demonstrate "The Model for the Development of Competency in Young Children," an innovative program developed by Smart. This Piaget-oriented program was designed to provide children with functional learning situations in which they might develop personal competency, skills in relating successfully to things and people, reciprocal associations between the real world and symbolic representations, and the use of language as the mediator of ideas. The organizational structure of the model emphasized small groups and individual instruction, with many opportunities for problem-solving and answer-seeking behaviors.

As a community-oriented school, the purposes were to provide a model educational program for three- and four-year-olds whose families, living in the community surrounding the University's campus, were welfare recipients or potentially eligible for financial assistance; to initiate and coordinate parent involvement and educational opportunities; and to coordinate University-based health, dental, and social services for the community families.

In carrying out these facets of its educational mission, the school made use of both parents and the many resources available through existing community and welfare structures. Each teacher made at least two home visits during the year; meetings were planned around the interests and requests of parents; newsletters kept parents informed about various activities of the school. Parents were used as volunteers for field trips, for repairing toys, as aides in classrooms, and, with some training, for home visitation. One of the most important aspects was the school's support of parents in the physical well-being of the children. The University Affiliated Program, a coordinated project of the School of Education and the USC School of Medicine through its affiliated Childrens Hospital, provided annual physical examinations for the children, as well as follow-up care, as required.

217

The success of the school was evidenced in the growth of the children's competency skills. Samples of *verbatim* comments from parents also revealed the extent to which they observed changes in their children:[40]

> I became aware of my child way of learning by what she see on field trips and things in which she plays a part in.

> I have seen the teachers treat the children at the preschool to make each one feel individually important, so I trying to give my child that attitude.

> Before he did not want to talk to no one because he was very shy. Now he learning the language, I can't stop him.

In April 1972, Melbo announced that the University's Board of Trustees had approved his proposal for construction of a new multicultural preschool unit for the USC School of Education. He also announced that a donor, who preferred to remain anonymous, had committed the funds for the building. The school was to be constructed to house 120 three- and four-year-olds, twice the number of children who could be accommodated in the previous facility.

Ground for the new USC School for Early Childhood Education was broken in September 1972, and the building was opened the following year in September 1973. Dedication ceremonies, at which Melbo presided, were held October 3, 1973. The handsome structure, located on 27th Street, near the University and in the complex of various agencies devoted to the service of children, such as the John Tracy Clinic and the Los Angeles Child Guidance Clinic, marked the new interest in this phase of education and the increasing importance given to the formative years of the child. Said Dean Melbo:[41]

> In the new facility, USC will continue its commitment to complex leadership roles in an urban community. The unique composition of the married students' population at the Universi-

---

40. *Project Description,* Department of Curriculum and Instruction (1972), unpublished.
41. EDUCARE *Newsletter,* 12(3), p. 3.

CHANGE: 1969–1973

ty and the nature of the immediate neighborhood offer ideal resources from which to draw children of differing ethnic and social backgrounds.

Adding to the scope of the early childhood program at the School of Education were annual conferences and periodic workshops, centering on significant state and local problems or projects in prekindergarten and primary education.

Center for Excellence in Education. In 1968, Georgiades, who in the 1960s had acquired a national and international reputation in secondary education, established at the School of Education a Center for Excellence in Education. This center, which was a nonprofit organization, had two purposes: to assist through its publications persons, school systems, and teacher preparation institutions in making the modifications and changes which Georgiades considered essential if "excellence in education" was to be more than a political phrase; and to provide Georgiades and his colleagues in the educational enterprise with a forum in which to set forth their theory and the practice of the ideas and innovations advocated by them.

As of May 1973, the center had issued 11 publications, of which five dealt with the "pontoon transitional design" for curriculum change;[42] three discussed the various methods of individualized instruction; and the remaining three had as their subject, respectively, instructional aides, learning packages, and variables to be considered in planning for educational change. Each publication set forth in a preface the philosophy espoused by the center:

> Excellence in education is a theoretical frame of reference and nothing more than a skeleton until it is defined in practice.

42. The pontoon concept was identified by Georgiades as an interrelating two or more subjects under the leadership of teachers from different disciplines in a block of time in which each would ordinarily operate independently. The pontoon might be considered, according to Georgiades, as a higher form of team teaching, incorporating the large group presentations, small discussion groups, and individual study of team teaching, with the added interrelationship of various disciplines in a flexible block of time. Eventually, in some areas, the goal was "total" learning.

219

Ultimately, excellence will be determined by the patterns of adult behavior, affective and cognitive, both the products of the process that we call education. It is meaningless to talk about excellence, to shadow-box with vocabulary, to prepare theoretical constructs until such constructs are pragmatically utilized.

While theory is essential to experimentation and practice, practice and experimentation are equally essential in theory. This interrelationship has too frequently been overlooked. One of the basic objectives of the Center for Excellence in Education is to wed theory and practice, to build a sound theoretical base for practice and in turn to alter theory.

A man of dynamic ideas and one gifted with boundless energy, Georgiades had been associated with the faculty of the School of Education since 1956, when Melbo selected him for appointment.[43] It was during the 1960s that Georgiades rose to national and international fame as a critic of traditionalist methods of instruction. A peripatetic lecturer at the meetings of professional societies, conferences, and schoolmen's groups, his travels took him cross-country yearly and abroad into 10 foreign countries. His associate and colleague at the center after 1972 was Dr. (Brother) Flavian Udinsky.[44]

Georgiades was also associate director of the Model Schools Project, a project in secondary education funded by the Danforth Foundation and sponsored by the National Association of Secondary School Principals (NASSP). This five-year project, directed by J. Lloyd Trump, noted educator and innovator in education, involved some 30 junior and senior high schools nationwide in an experiment aimed at individualizing learning and professionalizing teaching. Georgiades' special contribution to innovative de-

43. Georgiades received his A.B. (1946) from Upland College; his M.A. (1947) from Claremont Graduate School; and his Ed.D. (1957) from the University of California at Los Angeles. In 1964, he was Fulbright scholar and lecturer in Cyprus and Greece.

44. Udinsky, a Christian Brother of the Roman Catholic Church, has served in a number of schools in Alabama, Louisiana, and Missouri prior to his appointment to the faculty of the School of Education in 1972. He received his A.B. (1947) from Springhill College; his M.Ed. from Louisiana State University in 1950; and his Ed.D. from the University of Southern California in 1972.

220

signs incorporated in the Model Schools Project was the pontoon transitional design.

Special Education

Teachers of the Mentally Retarded. During the period from 1967 through 1973, the School of Education greatly increased its emphasis upon the preparation of teachers of the mentally retarded. From 1967 to 1972, a total of 637 students took core courses in the area of mental retardation and 186 teacher candidates did student teaching in this specialty (159 students from 1969 to 1972). In cooperation with the Los Angeles Unified School District and the Los Angeles county schools, a number of special programs were developed by the Department of Special Education for teacher preparation in this specialized area.

In concert with the Special Education Branch of the Los Angeles Unified School District, a program was developed to prepare teachers for classes of the trainable mentally retarded (TMR). Candidates did their student teaching in several of the district's special schools, with training teachers designated by the school principals and the administrative personnel of the Special Education Branch. Another of the programs developed in the area of the mentally retarded was the internship program to train teachers for classes of the educable mentally retarded (EMR) at the secondary level in the district's inner city schools. As of 1972, those trained in this program already constituted 30 per cent of the teachers employed in this category in the Los Angeles Unified School District, and the turnover rate in the schools involved had dropped from 39 per cent in 1969, to 10 per cent in 1971.

Beginning in 1971, a program was instituted which led to the M.S. in Ed. degree with specialty in the area of special education. This program, developed jointly by the Department of Special Education and the Department of Teacher Education, met two needs. First, it met the need for elementary teachers who were trained in areas of special education; and second, it met the desire

221

on the part of a considerable number of college graduates who entered teaching in order eventually to teach in the area of special education. The course work in this program, which was designed to meet these specific and express needs, was related to a directed teaching experience in specified schools of the Los Angeles county school system.

Teachers of the Deaf. The long-standing program of the School of Education in cooperation with the John Tracy Clinic in the preparation of teachers of the deaf and hard of hearing received great impetus in 1971, with the completion that year of the new Speech and Research Center of the John Tracy Clinic. The new building, dedicated September 19, 1971, was described by Lowell, administrator of the clinic, as clearly a milestone in the clinic's history. Designed and constructed in many of its aspects specifically for teacher preparation in this specialized area of the aurally handicapped, the facility provided 10 instructional booths for individual teaching, each booth equipped with technological devices of the latest development to assist in the instruction of the deaf and hard-of-hearing. The new facility also included equipment and facilities for the production of educational film and video tape material to extend the educational program of the clinic. Operational by 1971 were such major improvements as the demonstration home, student teaching area, television studio, media center, parent classroom, educational materials distribution center, and staff offices. By 1973, the automated instruction room and research area were also operational.

University Affiliated Program. In 1970, the School of Education acquired an important addition to its clinical facilities for teacher preparation through the designation that year of Childrens Hospital, Los Angeles, as one of the sites of the federally funded University Affiliated Programs.[45] Selection of Childrens Hospital owed its impetus to Melbo, who perceived in the already existing

45. The University Affiliated Program at Childrens Hospital was one of 19 similar projects throughout the United States. All were funded by the Maternal and Child Health Services of the U.S. Department of Health, Education and Welfare.

relationships between the University of Southern California and Childrens Hospital the basis for such a development.[46]

Dr. Wylda Hammond was appointed director of the University Affiliated Program; coordinator of the orientation block was Magary of the Department of Special Education of the School of Education. Under the program qualified trainees were provided training and clinical practice at Childrens Hospital, its Rehabilitation Center, and in the community. Core training was provided through direct and indirect service, seminars, and lectures. All trainees observed a case selection committee in operation, the various disciplines at work, inter- and intra-agency conferences, and program critiques. Those whose interest and training needs required practicum experience were provided those services under the supervision of their own disciplines.

Programs inaugurated under the auspices of the University Affiliated Programs included an annual conference on "Piaget and the Helping Professions." These one-day conferences, cosponsored by the School of Education, featured addresses and papers by Piagetian scholars. At the 1973 conference, held February 16, C. Edward Meyers presented the major address, entitled, "Can Piaget's Theory Provide a Better Psychometry?" A paper relating Piaget and early childhood education was presented by Margaret E. Smart.

Widely welcomed was the Annual Film Festival on the Ex-

---

46. Childrens Hospital was an affiliated hospital of the University of Southern California's School of Medicine. It served as a major division of the School's Department of Pediatrics, providing both undergraduate pediatric training and postgraduate pediatric training in many subspecialties. All members of the staff of Childrens Hospital were on the faculty of the School of Medicine, and the physician-in-charge of Childrens Hospital was cochairman of the Department of Pediatrics. A close relationship between the School of Medicine and the School of Education in the field of mental retardation had existed since 1964, when, under Melbo's impetus, Dr. Wylda Hammond had been engaged by the University of Southern California to coordinate the planning for an integrated professional training program in mental retardation. The program began in 1965, with the University of Southern California as prime affiliate. Dr. Hammond served in dual appointment as associate professor of pediatrics, School of Medicine, and associate professor of education, School of Education.

223

ceptional Individual, sponsored by the University Affiliated Program in cooperation with the Southern California Region of American Association on Mental Deficiency (Region II). Coordinating the three-year-old program in 1973 were Magary and Molly C. Gorelick, associate professor, California State University at Northridge.

Instructional Materials Center. The Instructional Materials Center, which had been developed as a pilot program in 1964 in cooperation with the U.S. Office of Education, had developed by 1973, into a large operation designated the Regional Instructional Materials Center for Special Education. Located off campus in the Broadway Building at Twelfth and Broadway, Los Angeles, the center functioned as a resource center for various public agencies such as state departments of education; offered consultation services; prepared prepackaged materials; and served as a link into the national network of Instructional Materials Centers. Until June 1971, the center was under the direction of Robert B. McIntyre as principal investigator. At that time, McIntyre returned to full-time duties with the Department of Special Education, and Charles A. Watts assumed direction as principal investigator.

Special Lectures. The annual summer Distinguished Lecture Series in Special Education and Rehabilitation was continued, as was also publication of the lectures in monograph form. In addition, in 1970, the Marcella R. Bonsall Lectureship in special education was established by gift of Joel and Marcella Bonsall.[47] The gift provided for an annual lecture by a leader in the field of psychology and education of the gifted and creative. First Bonsall lecturer was Albert R. Hibbs, of Jet Propulsion Laboratory, and host of many television series and programs related to science and creative exploration.

Research. A graduate research training program in problems of the handicapped was conducted, open only to doctoral candi-

---

47. Marcella Ryser Bonsall (Ed.D., 1952, University of Southern California) was for a number of years adjunct assist professor in special education. She was a teacher of note and consultant in classes for gifted elementary children.

224

dates committed to careers in research. They were assigned to work with research specialists of the Rancho Los Amigos Hospital, with special education staffs of metropolitan school districts, and other professional centers and institutions. The program was conducted with the assistance of Michael, Smith, and Fox of the Department of Educational Psychology. A special research project of some magnitude was conducted from 1969 through 1971. Entitled "Sensory Integrative Processes and Learning Disabilities," the project was carried out at the School of Education under the direction of A. Jean Ayres,[48] as a funded project of the Children's Bureau, Department of Health, Education and Welfare. The investigation was distinguished from most research efforts in learning disabilities by its neurophysiological approach. Four Los Angeles county school districts cooperated in the endeavor, and approximately 60 children received special remedial work in the form of developmental activities planned to activate specific sensory integrative mechanisms. The research project was designed to contribute to teacher education through assisting teachers in the utilization of knowledge of brain functions in their neurophysiological aspects.

Center for International Education

(Social and Philosophical Foundations)

During the 1969–73 period, the Center for International Education continued, on an expanded scale, to assist international students

48. Ayres received her B.S. (1945) and her M.A. (1954) degrees in occupational therapy, and her Ph.D. (1961) in educational psychology at the University of Southern California. She also performed postdoctoral work at the Brain Research Institute, University of California at Los Angeles. Her professional experience included a number of appointments in occupational therapy, working with neurological disorders. From 1955 to 1964, an associate professor of Occupational Therapy with the University of Southern California, she had been appointed in 1966, visiting associate professor in the School of Education. In 1969, she was also consultant to a tri-county (Santa Barbara, San Luis Obispo, and Ventura) ESEA Title III project on perceptual-motor development and training.

225

at the School of Education and to plan, coordinate, and conduct the visits of various foreign scholars and students to the School of Education. In addition, several innovative programs were initiated in the field of international education.

Vietnamese Education Institute. On June 30, 1969, the Center for International Education convened the opening session of a seven-week Vietnamese Education Summer Institute. The institute was conducted under the auspices of the U.S. Agency for International Development (AID) and was directed by Carpenter, with codirectors Myron H. Dembo of the Department of Educational Psychology and Do Ba Khe, former secretary general of education in Vietnam, and in 1969 a doctoral student at the School of Education in the Department of Higher Education.

The participants were 26 Vietnamese students pursuing bachelor's and master's degrees in educational psychology, counseling and guidance, and related fields at 12 American colleges and universities throughout the nation. All had had teaching experience in Vietnam and all were to assume positions related to teacher preparation upon their return to their homeland. The institute was conceived as a means of providing them with a systematic opportunity to know and analyze critical, current needs and developments in Vietnam as they related to educational psychology; and to view their training in the United States in the light of the conditions and situations they would encounter upon their return. This approach required selective coverage of the content of educational psychology and teacher education, with emphasis upon its relation to Vietnamese problems and development.

The five major components of the program were: three days a week for presentations and discussions with American and Vietnamese specialists on selected topics; field visitations directly related, insofar as possible, to the previous day's discussion; group project on a selected problem; weekly evaluations of events of the previous week; and social visits in American environments. Participants earned eight units of credit for successful completion of the course work.

226 An evaluation questionnaire completed by the participants

indicated favorable response, with 96 per cent stating that they would recommend the institute to a good friend who expected to teach in Vietnam. Said one participant:[49]

This seven-week seminar, well planned, dealt with topics quite relevant to Vietnam situation. Besides field trips and visitations which supported classroom lectures, the idea of small group work and discussion and team approach was introduced, shared and applied by participants. It is most desirable to have similar seminar organized every summer so that Vietnamese participants have the opportunity to meet together, and on the basis of real problems in Vietnam discuss realistically how they will apply their study in the U.S. for the benefit of their fatherland.

African Studies Program. One of the more innovative attempts to reduce prejudice, ignorance, and provincialism in the school systems of America was the African Studies Personnel and Curriculum Development Program for Elementary and Secondary School Personnel. This project was funded by the U.S. Office of Education through a grant to a consortium formed between the University of Southern California and the University of California at Los Angeles. The period of the grant was from June 15, 1970 through January 31, 1971.

As expressed by its program sponsors, the *raison d'etre* for the African Studies Program was to introduce, however modestly, the realities of contemporary Africa into the American classroom. It was widely recognized that, although the political and economic life of Africa had changed dramatically since World War II, most Americans still clung to the clichés of colonial Africa. These stereotypes reflected a cultural bias which was being perpetuated in the school systems of the United States. Specific objectives of the project were, therefore, to train a cadre of teacher-leaders in grades from kindergarten through high school in the area of African studies; to develop and acquire instructional materials utilizing the conceptual social studies teaching strategies; to effect more

---

49. University of Southern California, School of Education, Center for International Relations (1969), p. 81.

positive and more accurate understanding on the part of American students about Africa and Africans; to promote a greater awareness and sensitivity to the need to study Africa at the elementary and secondary level; and to initiate permanent collegial relationships between African and American teachers.

The program which was developed provided a six-week visit to Africa as field experience, preceded by a formalized conceptual inquiry into social science teaching strategies and followed by a structured evaluation. Within the consortium, the University of California at Los Angeles provided through its African Studies Center the general academic component, and the University of Southern California provided through its Center for International Education the conceptual-inquiry teaching strategies. Codirectors of the program were T. O. Ranger, professor of African History at UCLA, and John A. Carpenter, director of the Center for International Education at USC. Field director was Edward Berman, associate director of the Center for International Education. Arrangements for the visit to Africa were coordinated by a number of persons associated with institutions of higher learning in Africa which were part of the group's itinerary, or by officials of the U.S. Department of State who were stationed in those locales.

Two participants were selected from each of 12 school districts in Los Angeles, San Bernardino, Orange, and Riverside counties. The 24 selectees, 17 women and seven men, represented each level within the elementary and secondary schools. Following the conceptual-inquiry portion of the program, the group departed from Los Angeles July 12, 1970, and returned August 24, 1970. The visit in Africa included four days in Senegal; three weeks in Kumasi, Ghana; five days at the University College, Cape Coast, Ghana; and one week in Nigeria. The one-month residency in Ghana emphasized academic work; other portions provided an intimate view of Ghanian, Sengelian, and Nigerian life.

On their return, participants readily agreed that their knowledge of numerous facets of life in West Africa had been greatly expanded by their experience, and most felt that their positive

228

attitudes would be transferred to the presentation of classroom material. To assist in this phase of the project, meetings were held in the fall of 1970 and assistance given in the preparation of curriculum materials. The project was part of an ongoing five-year program, during which local districts would exchange curriculum materials under arrangements made by the county offices of the four districts involved and with the assistance of the University consortium.

India Institutes. During the summer of 1972, and again in 1973, the Center for International Education, in conjunction with the U.S. Office of Education, conducted an eight-week intercultural study institute in India. The basic goals of these programs were to generate an understanding of Indian culture and to communicate that awareness to others for mutual growth and enrichment. More specifically defined, the program centered on personnel and curriculum development programs on India for elementary and secondary school personnel, kindergarten through high school. Developed along lines similar to the African Studies Program, participants were given an opportunity to experience during their eight weeks in India the Indian culture directly and through informal processes. To enhance the benefits of these experiences, participants were introduced through formal sessions extending over a period of several weeks of one-day meetings to the conceptual-inquiry methodology, and were later assisted in the preparation of curricular materials and evaluative procedures.

Both institutes were undertaken with Melbo as principal investigator, and were directed, under Melbo's guidance, by Vasisht K. Malhotra, assistant director for Asian Programs in the Center for International Education. Others associated with the institutes were Robin J. McKeown, in 1972 as project associate director for curriculum development and in 1973 as curriculum specialist; and W. Paul Fischer, in 1973 project associate director for curriculum development. Arrangements in India were made by the staff of the Educational Resources Center, a branch of the State University of New York (SUNY) in New Delhi.

Each institute comprised 24 participants selected from the

229

teachers in the elementary and secondary schools of Los Angeles, Orange, Riverside, and San Bernardino counties. In 1972, two participants were included from the U.S. Dependent Schools in the European Area. The field experience, which formed the core of the institute, included group activities in which seminars were conducted by foremost scholars and specialists on varied aspects of Indian culture and visits to cities, villages, homes, and places of cultural significance; team activities under the guidance of Indian resource persons; and free time in which to explore Indian life, either in teams or as individuals. Evaluation sessions were conducted periodically to seek the participants' views about the program and, whenever possible, to modify the program according to suggestions made by the participants.

Although it was difficult to assess immediately whether the basic goals of institutes had been achieved in generating a better understanding of Indian culture and thereby breaking down some of the stereotyped attitudes of the participating teachers and through them, of their students, the institute staff was optimistic in the eventual impact of the program:[50]

It can be categorically stated that not only the knowledge of participants about the various aspects of Indian culture was greatly enhanced but through this experience they gained in such intangibles as tolerance, maturity, and understanding. As some of the participants put it, "Unbelievable! I will never be the same and that is good." "Never had I learned so much in such a short period." "The trip provided all that books and films cannot." That these experiences and attitudes would be transmitted to the children in the classroom is fairly certain.

American Civilization/Language Institute. Beginning in 1970, an annual American Civilization/Language Institute was conducted at the University of Southern California as part of a two-month program for foreign educators. The program was sponsored jointly by participating nations' ministries of education and the U.S. Department of State. Administrative agency for the program was

50. University of Southern California, School of Education, Center for International Education (1972), p. 29.

230

the U.S. Office of Education. The four and one-half week program at the University of Southern California was organized to provide knowledge of, and experience in, American civilization; and to introduce recent developments in the fields of linguistics and the teaching of English as a foreign language. The institutes of 1972 and 1973 were directed by Grafton and sponsored by the Center for International Education, which provided administrative and logistical support.

Teacher Education

The thrust of the '60s in the School of Education's teacher preparation programs had been directed toward meeting the needs of districts facing chronic teacher shortages. The challenge of the '70s was the development of teacher preparation programs to meet a diverse school population, of whom many were speakers of a language other than English and still more were the unwilling victims of adverse physical, psychological, and socio-economic circumstances. Melbo's strategy in meeting the new requirements was the planned and directed capitalization on the diversity and strengths of the teacher candidates, and on the experience gained from many decades of teacher preparation. Advances in technology, social theory, and educational psychology were used and modified, as necessary or appropriate. Particularly valuable were the experiences gained in some of the newer developments at the University of Southern California, such as the Teacher Corps (both Rural-Migrant and Urban), the University's Urban semester, and certain paraprofessional programs undertaken within the professional schools. Principal facets of the teacher preparation programs for the '70s were increased emphasis on classroom competence and the evolution of creative cooperative relationships with school districts.

In attempting to meet the new needs, there were the inevitable constraints of quality, time, and money. Quality of the prospective teacher's experience remained the prime concern. Beyond the minimum requirements set by the state for certification, the

231

School of Education sought to maintain a high standard for pre-service performance and preparation. Time, an increased constraint since the length of preservice training had been reduced, was compensated by rigorous selection of candidates, redesign of course content, and increased personal supervision of the candidate. Funds, always a constraint and one of increasing concern in the '70s, were used with maximum effectiveness. In addition, through cooperative planning with school districts, the School of Education was able to offer to candidates district-paid teacher assistantships at a salary seven-eighths that of a beginning teacher, paid while the candidate was completing the requirements for a teaching credential.[51]

Operating within these constraints and seeking to develop programs consistent with the School of Education's objectives and responsive to the new needs of a rapidly growing and changing society, Melbo, with the outstanding cooperation and support of Wilson, developed teacher education programs which were able to attract, select, and evaluate qualified individuals from diverse cultural backgrounds to prepare for teaching in urban and suburban schools; meet both the varying needs and skills of teacher candidates and cooperating school districts; provide financial assistance to prospective teacher candidates and professional assistance to cooperating school district; and provide continuing education and leadership to the profession and the community.

---

51. The three programs in which students might be employed in cooperating public schools while completing the requirements for the credential were: *Teacher Assistantship,* which entailed salary for one year, with professional and academic studies of the basic programs in a sequence oriented to the gradual developmental field experiences of teacher assistantship and directed teaching; *Honors Internship,* in which the student participated as a student teacher and salaried teacher assistant in a school district during the first semester, with related university course work scheduled in the late afternoon or evening; and in which, during the second semester, the candidate might continue with directed teaching and assistantship work or be employed by the school district as a full time intern teacher; and *Teacher Internship,* in which outstanding candidates might complete course work covering curriculum and methods and directed teaching during the first semester, followed by two semesters as a salaried intern teacher, and one summer in which the candidate completed the units of work for credential requirements.

232

Teacher Learning Centers. In 1968, a new dimension to teacher preparation and to inservice renewal was initiated through the development by Wilson of the concept of the Teacher Learning Center. The basic purpose of the Teacher Learning Center was, as Wilson pointed out, a way of releasing and developing individuals' potentials for teaching:

> The teaching process is a resultant of numerous intrapersonal and interpersonal processes. Personal differences are apparent in any given group of learners; this wide variety of differences is evident in learning styles, teaching styles, paces of achieving and levels of accomplishment. At a time when psychological and sociological research emphasizes the importance of recognizing and developing individual differences, we are cognizant of day to day schooling of children in classrooms where all are treated alike and year after year training of teachers in situations where all are expected to memorize uncritically and imitate passively. A failure to make use of information at hand appears to be a stumbling block to educational progress. In order to maintain and refine our democratic way of life, we must depend on educating each individual to his highest possible level of achievement. John Gardner has reminded us that the basic American commitment is to the liberation of the human spirit, the release of human potential, and the enhancement of individual dignity. We have a responsibility to encourage variabilities within children and teachers by individualizing learning opportunities for both. USC Teacher Learning Centers serve as models of learning atmosphere where pupils and educators are involved in individualized instructional programs.

Basically a classroom with provisions for cooperative teaching activities, Teacher Learning Centers were established, in cooperation with the Los Angeles Unified School District, in five of the School of Education's cooperating schools for teacher training. In these schools the Teacher Learning Centers served not only the school in which they were established but also nearby schools. Basically a classroom for cooperative teaching activities, the Teacher Learning Centers were centers for inquiry into the nature of the learning process in pupils and in teachers. The program was

233

one of teacher development: of preservice laboratory experience for student teachers, and of inservice education for training teachers and staff teachers. The center also served as a communication structure for all persons from the Los Angeles Unified School District and from the University of Southern California who were involved in teacher education, enabling them to plan and work in the context of the school. Carrying out in essence Melbo's strong conviction that every type of teacher preparation can and must be supplemented by clinical experience, the Teacher Learning Centers provided the laboratory setting for effective teacher preparation and self-renewal as intimately related to the operating school system. In summarizing his approach to the Teacher Learning Center, Melbo said:[52]

> The Teacher Learning Centers operated in a classroom provided by the cooperating training school. The School of Education provided equipment, materials, and supplies, and a budget for additional help to staff the centers. The "hardware" and "software" provided represented a substantial investment of funds and made possible the most sophisticated processes of individualized and personalized instruction. The centers thus served pupils and classrooms directly, and enabled teachers in the training school (and those from other nearby schools who wished to observe) to have firsthand experiences with the best of the modern media and methods for learning. Principals in the schools having these centers also were able to use them in the orientation of parent-aides and other paraprofessionals employed by the schools. Both Wilson and I regarded these Teacher Learning Centers as a vital part of a teacher education program, and as a genuine joint venture between the University and the cooperating school district.

As of 1973, the School of Education had established Teacher Learning Centers in five elementary schools of the Los Angeles city school system.[53] Under the school principals and with the assistance of coordinators both from the cooperating school and

---

52. MS comment, May, 1973.
53. Wilbur Avenue School (Virginia R. Archer, principal); Menlo Avenue School (Frederick D. Jones, principal); Los Feliz School (Edith P. Dury, principal);

the University, the centers functioned as preservice student teaching laboratories and a location for inservice seminars, demonstration areas, and, when approved through district channels and by the administrator, for investigations and experimental studies conducted in the center or with nearby schools. Programs for pupil personnel with special needs included English as a Second Language (ESL), corrective reading, and enrichment for the capable learner.

In effect, the Teacher Learning Center concept was a key to the "strategy of innovation," providing a means of overcoming the tendency of American education to resist change, through the demonstration of model ways to make operational what had been discovered in educational research. "When we talk about change," said Dean Melbo on one occasion, "we have to do it with planning and direction, with some model of the future before us."[54] The Teacher Learning Centers provided that model, as well as the opportunity to evaluate pragmatically various types of teaching and learning styles, with full recognition of individual differences in the teaching-learning cycle. Through the involvement of university scholars, preschool, elementary, and secondary educators, pupils, and community leaders, the centers provided a complete circuit of experience that gave each individual a learning opportunity and, at the same time, an opportunity to contribute to the learning of others.

Training ABE Teachers. An important project of 1970–71 was the national model Institute for Training Adult Basic Education (ABE) Teachers. The institute was a one-year federally funded project, conducted by Levitt, under the supervision of Wilson.[55] The project participants were 30 persons who entered the program

Vermont Avenue School (Charles H. Palmer, principal); and Denker Avenue School (Meno Phillips, principal).

54. Melbo, I. R. "Educational and Cultural Needs for Fresno County," *EDICT Symposium,* April 28, 1967.

55. The institute was funded by the Division of Adult and Vocational Programs, Bureau of Adult, Vocational, and Technical Education, U.S. Office of Education, under Title II of the Adult Education Act of 1966.

235

for training as professional ABE teachers, with emphasis on teaching English as a Second Language. Innovative in concept and approach, the program utilized a team structure in modular modifications of existing course structure. It included modules of field experiences, directed teaching, paid experience in adult school teaching, and other innovative methods and experiences in a competency-based program.

While the giant Adult Education Division of the Los Angeles Unified School District was the prime cooperating agency for the program, school districts in Whittier, Compton, and Burbank also participated. A supportive factor of great importance was the close cooperation developed between the project directors and the Bureau of Adult Education of the California State Department of Education. In addition to subscription by the bureau of partial funding via a contractual arrangement with the Los Angeles schools, the bureau later contracted with the University of Southern California to fund an inservice training course for a group of working full-time ABE teachers. Particularly helpful in these arrangements and in consultation was Roy Steeves, assistant chief, Bureau of Adult Education, State Department of Education, with office in Los Angeles.

In 1971, in response to the request of a group of local adult education administrators that the School of Education offer a doctoral sequence emphasizing adult education, such a program was initiated through the good offices of Dean Melbo, in cooperation with the associate dean, Graduate Studies, and the Departments of Higher Education and that of Administration and Supervision. Thus the project achieved one of the expressed goals of the Adult Education Act of 1966, under which it was funded, namely, the initiation, or expansion, in major universities of programs to prepare professional personnel for adult education and for research in the field.[56]

---

56. University of Southern California, School of Education, Department of Teacher Education (1970), pp. 142–43.

Teacher Corps

Teacher Corps: Urban. By 1971, "Teacher Corps: Urban" had completed six cycles of interns to meet the needs of students in inner city schools. In that year, the University of Southern California unit was selected by the U.S. Office of Education as the first Teacher Corps unit in the United States to develop a correctional education sequence. This sequence had as its objective the preparation of teachers to meet the educational needs of delinquent-prone, highly mobile troubled youth. The program, which began with Cycle VII (1972–74), was developed under a U.S. government contract as a joint training effort between the University of Southern California and participating school districts of Compton, El Monte, and Los Angeles county special schools in juvenile correctional institutions. The need for a program of this type, and the choice of Los Angeles for a pilot project of this nature, were underscored by the fact that some 20,000 youths were processed yearly through the Los Angeles County Juvenile Hall. The program was one to which the "Teacher Corps: Urban" Associate Director, Annette Gromfin, brought both academic and professional expertise.

Working within the framework of teacher education programs at the School of Education, the program design for the correctional education sequence drew upon the fields of special education, sociological and psychological foundations of education, and secondary education. It aimed at interrelating educational and social strategies to meet the needs of rejected youth who are faced with previous academic failure, psychological disorganization, and dysfunctional socialization processes. As a competency-based program with a self-paced, personalized modular curriculum, the program was organized around four major profiles which examined the environment of troubled youth and the strategies necessary to intervene. These profiles were: inner city troubled youth, learning environment, community, and the juvenile justice system.

Among the innovations developed in the program were "por-

237

tal learning centers," an adaptation of the Teacher Learning Center concept. Under the portal learning center concept, participating schools provided sites for the development of learning centers in which curricula and methods appropriate to troubled youth could be initiated. Each "Teacher Corps: Urban" team was responsible for developing a learning center adapted to the needs of its school site. The center also served for inservice training of personnel for developing alternative classroom strategies. Another innovation was cross-institutional planning, which aimed at helping to provide educational continuity for youth with highly fractionated educational patterns.

Teacher Corps: Rural-Migrant. From 1968 through 1971, "Teacher Corps: Rural-Migrant" continued to be a joint program of the University of Southern California and school districts in Tulare County. Under this program, four Teacher Corps cycles (II through V) were trained. A 1971 program assessment by the General Accounting Office of the Comptroller of the United States concluded that the program had strengthened the educational opportunities available to children in the schools where corpsmen were stationed; that school officials and teachers generally believed that the interns were well prepared for teaching and communicated well with the children; that some believed that the individual instruction and classes taught in Spanish were especially beneficial in improving the children's educational achievements; and that the program had been successful in broadening the University's teaching program.[57]

With Cycle VII (1971–73), the locale of "Teacher Corps: Rural-Migrant" was transferred to Ventura County, California. There, in cooperation with five school districts (six schools), a training program was undertaken which moved by design toward the development of competency-based performance criteria and community-based education that utilized previously untapped human resources. In Ventura County, as in Tulare, a large population of Spanish-speaking farm workers was emerging on the

238

57. The Comptroller General of the United States (1971).

fringes of the local communities, but with little involvement in the life of the rural society. Children were monolingual, usually in some form of Spanish, with few opportunities to encounter bilingual or bicultural teachers and counselors. From the very beginning, the "Teacher Corps: Rural-Migrant" program in Ventura County was programmed to involve the schools and community in the selection, training, and performance of the interns.

One of the principal differences from the program in Tulare County was that team leaders were selected from each of the cooperating school districts and, whenever possible, from the schools which served as Teacher Corps training sites. A link was therefore formed of a firm nature between the Teacher Corps program and the cooperating school. Interview committees to select the interns were composed of the superintendent or his representative of the district, a member of the board of education, a principal, a member of the target community, and a representative of the University of Southern California. Following an exhaustive selection process, including personal interviews, a summer live-in experience in a secluded area of Ventura County was conducted for the team leaders and the interns, during which districts and communities involved made their final selection of the interns they desired for their own districts.

The program developed was one of progressive work-study, with "Teacher Corps: Rural-Migrant" staff working cooperatively with the trainees to develop guidelines and to establish evaluation procedures for the seven teaching strategies upon which the program was based. These seven strategies were: facilitating human relations, mediating learning, diagnosing and prescribing, building curriculum, researching, utilizing human resources, and bilingual teaching. Within these strategies, program characteristics included self-paced learning, alternative learner options, regenerative devices, modularized and mediated components, and emphasis on developing self-actualized learners. Other innovative components were High Intensity Language Training (HILT), TESOL, development of learning centers for bilingual education, community education projects, and inservice educational assistance to school staffs working with the corpsmen.

239

In 1971, the "Teacher Corps: Rural-Migrant" was invited as one of 12 Teacher Corps units to participate in the production of "Teacher Protocols," which were defined as teacher-pupil interaction when the pupil was a preadolescent Spanish speaker. The situations identified for which the protocols were to be developed were withdrawal, rationalization, competition, negative responses, and cooperative endeavor.

Projects undertaken in the "Teacher Corps: Rural-Migrant" program represented a high degree of innovation, creative research, and concern for the human dimension in the teaching-learning process. Much of the creativity of the program stemmed from the creative talent and energetic leadership of the program's associate director, Patricia Heffernan Cabrera. Notable among the projects of the "Teacher Corps: Rural-Migrant" were the Seville Dental Clinic, a joint project with the University of Southern California's School of Dentistry; bilingual Mexican-American history curriculum, a dictionary of *pochismo,* the Spanish-English dialect of the local rural area; a visual literacy sensory experiencing project; cross-age tutoring; photography workshop for adults; and a consumer education project. The many faces of the Teacher Corps formed the subject of a booklet illustrating through photographs and captions teacher-pupil interaction in the learning process. As perceived by the children, learning was represented by such catch phrases as:[58] "Pancakes and chemistry—and eating them, too; Two's and three's in English and in Spanish; Being eye-level with the teacher; Painting seashells with the teacher—eyeball to eyeball; Having the teaching all to yourself." The teacher, proclaimed the booklet was "A man who looks like my father, my uncle, my *padrino,* and who is MY TEACHER."

Teacher Corps—VISTA. In 1964, under the Economic Opportunity Act, a "domestic Peace Corps" had been established. From 1969 through 1971, a VISTA program was conducted under the

---

58. University of Southern California, School of Education, "Teacher Corps: Rural-Migrant" (1971).

supervision of "Teacher Corps: Rural-Migrant" staff members. This program, designated Teacher Corps-VISTA, offered a special training program to young men and women which led to the Bachelor of Science degree in TESOL and to the California teaching credential with specialization in adult basic education and early childhood education. Participants in the Teacher Corps-VISTA program were Mexican-American and other Spanish-speaking undergraduates who had the desire, awareness, and sensitivity requisite to the VISTA purposes, and who had satisfactorily completed 70 units of college work and met entrance requirements for the University of Southern California, but who could not complete their third and fourth years of college because of limited finances.

As developed by the staff of "Teacher Corps: Rural-Migrant," the University of Southern California provided the necessary course work for a comprehensive background in language teaching, and, as with the "Teacher Corps: Rural-Migrant," the University staff brought the required course work to interns living and working in Tulare County. Under the program, 27 VISTA interns were assigned to Richgrove, Tulare City, and Earlimart school districts in Tulare County. There they organized day nurseries for working mothers, evening adult basic education classes in English as a Second Language, and recreational and other experience-expanding activities for the rural migrant population.

Education Library

Collectively, over the years, the School of Education had made a significant contribution through its alumni, students, and faculty to the advancement of American education. No one was more aware than Dean Melbo of the importance of a superior professional library in the maintenance of high standards of scholarship, and no one contributed more than he in time, effort, and dedicated support.

241

Prior to 1968, the Education Library was mainly housed in rooms set aside for it in Doheny Library. In the spring of that year, when the School of Education moved into the newly constructed Waite Phillips Hall of Education, the Education Library acquired a building of its own. Located diagonally across from Waite Phillips Hall was a former Los Angeles City Branch Library. This building had been acquired from the city of Los Angeles in 1967, and had been completely remodeled at a cost of $261,555 under a plan which provided 10,561 gross square feet for the library holdings. From 1968 through 1973, the Education Library and its collection became prime targets for a concentrated drive on Melbo's part to bring both the physical environment and the library collection to a level which could properly support the School of Education, its highly trained and dedicated faculty, and its outstanding student body. "I thought," said Melbo in 1973, "it most important to have a library which was itself a *first-class* resource, in support of a *first-class* professional school operation."[59]

Melbo's attack was three-pronged: first and fundamental to all improvement was the acquisition of funds for the purchase of new and additional materials and for the improvement of the library's appearance and functions; second was the directed study by the faculty's Library Committee, representing all departments of the School of Education, in cooperation with the University Librarian, of the Education Library's needs and the formulation of a developmental program; and third was the encouragement of gifts to the Library either in the form of special collections or additions to the collections already in existence.

During the 1968–73 period, Dean Melbo was instrumental in obtaining more than $300,000 in special gifts for the Education Library, the largest of which, a gift which came about through the efforts of Dr. Earl V. Pullias of the Department of Higher Education, was one of $60,000 from the James Irvine Foundation. This grant, which was received in 1969, was used for library holdings

59. MS comment, May 1973.

and library services. Also in 1969, at Melbo's recommendation, EDUCARE allocated an annual gift of $20,000, to be used for improvement of the physical facilities of the Education Library and for the acquisition of modern media in order to expand its services. The Library Committee was working during the same five-year period on the developmental plans for the Education Library. Under the successive chairmanship of Naslund, Miller, and Robert A. Smith, the long-range issues of equipment in the form of microfilm or microfiche readers; identification of books and periodicals which should be purchased; policies on departmental collections, their cataloging, and storage; inter-library agreements; and noncredit courses to acquaint students with the use of the library were discussed. Melbo himself took a prime interest in the furtherance of the special collections of the library, fostering through his personal contacts this altruistic expression of memorials to both the living and dead. Supporting all these endeavors was the dedicated service of Mrs. Harvey and her staff, to whom the expansion of the library and its resources was both a matter of professional concern and personal pride.

Fortified with the necessary funds, remarkable improvements were made in the physical appearance and holdings of the Education Library during the years following its movement to the renovated quarters. Among the most important were the acquisition of new furniture, installation of wall-to-wall carpeting for the first floor reading room, and installation of attractive panels for the special collections. With funds from EDUCARE, the physical appearance of the Library and the comfort of its users were matched by a noteworthy expansion of its resource capability. Among the materials involving media other than the printed page were the acquisition of the complete ERIC (Educational Research Information Center) microfiche collection and microfilms of doctoral dissertations from major universities throughout the country. Microfiche readers and reader-printers, as well as microfilm reader-printers, were also installed with EDUCARE funds. As Dean Melbo noted, "EDUCARE's generous support has made all

243

the difference in the world in the library's appearance, holdings, and service to students."[60]

To the special collections which had been presented in previous years to the Education Library now were added other important collections. In 1969, Dr. Theodore Hsi-En Chen, professor of Asiatic Studies and of Education, presented to the library the famed Chen Collection on Asian and Oriental Educational Materials, the finest collection in the United States and perhaps in the world of materials on Asian education. In 1970, Betty Finn presented the James D. Finn Collection, containing some 1400 items on a variety of subjects from the library of her late husband, with particular emphasis on Finn's own field of instructional technology. For the Chen Collection an addition to the library was constructed on the second floor, and for the Finn Collection which was catalogued and shelved according to subject content, a special bookplate with his portrait was designed. Prior to his death, Louis P. Thorpe had presented to the library a number of rare books related to educational psychology. For these a special shelf was used although, at his request, no bookplate was designed. More recently, Donald E. Wilson presented to the Education Library his personal collection of old American textbooks. This collection, known as the Donald E. Wilson Old Textbook Collection, consisted of more than 300 volumes used in elementary schools in the nineteenth century and a speller published as early as 1773.[61]

---

60. EDUCARE *Newsletter,* 11(1), p. 2.

61. The Wilson Collection, presented in 1972, represented one of the most unusual and valuable collections of its kind. Included was a complete set of the original McGuffey Eclectic Readers; several editions of Noah Webster's "Blue Back Spellers," once rated second only to the Bible in volume of sales and general use; and a child's history of America, which claimed that the Speedwell, not the Mayflower, brought the first Pilgrim settlers to the New World. The collection offered a dramatic profile of elementary education in the United States during much of the nineteenth century. Wilson began gathering the books in 1947, while initiating a study of the development of educational curricula. "I wanted the original books," he said, "because only from them could I learn of their content and also of the recommendations for how much material should be taught." (EDUCARE *Newsletter,* 11(2), p. 3) The collection's identifying bookplate contains a reproduction of one of his favorite illustrations from an old book, representing an elderly schoolmaster at work, while children doze and play in the doorway

244

As result of Melbo's outstanding success in library improvement, by 1973 the Education Library was generally recognized, in terms of its holdings, as the best in the entire Western region for its specialized collection, and as among the best in the country. By that time, however, it was also in desperate need of new and larger accommodations. One of the time-consuming tasks of Mrs. Harvey and her staff was the "selection out" process, whereby unused books were removed from the stacks for secondary storage. Recognizing that this situation was one which would increase in complexity, particularly with the greatly accelerated production of educational materials, Melbo initiated plans for a new structure. In 1972, architectural drawings were presented to the faculty and the University Library Committee for consideration. The plans called for a learning resources center, involving approximately 66,000 square feet of space on six levels. The plans met the concurrence of the University Librarian, who saw the proposed center as an opportunity to develop a nationally significant model of a university branch library which would provide not only printed matter but the learning resources inherent in the newer technological media. Construction of the new facility was made an item of highest priority in Melbo's plans for the School of Education, 1973–76.

While awaiting final decision on construction of the new facility, the Education Library continued to render outstanding service to its rapidly growing clientele. A 1972 report indicated that library usage had increased during the 1967–72 period by more than 78 per cent, with an increase in 1972 of 13 per cent in total circulation above that of 1971. "We are here to serve," said Mrs. Harvey, "and we are very grateful to Dean Melbo for all he has done for the Education Library. Without his support, none of what we now have could have existed at all."

which invites to the great outdoors. Said Wilson, "Coming from five generations of teachers, I can identify with that old man," and added whimsically, "I don't recall from what book I took that picture, but I keep it framed on the wall of my office, and when things become 'too much,' I get inspiration from looking at it." (Personal interview, May 1973)

Awards

In addition to the intrinsic reward represented in the knowledge of a task well done, outstanding students of the School of Education had for many years received more tangible recognition. The awards program of the School of Education began in 1947, when Dean Hull obtained from the honorary societies of Phi Delta Kappa and Pi Lambda Theta, awards for outstanding scholarship, in order that the School of Education might be represented on the University's commencement program. By 1951, a portion of the meeting of the Education Alumni Association at commencement time was devoted to the presentation of a small number of awards. Beginning in the fall of 1951, at the instigation of Melbo, who was then a member of the faculty in the Department of Administration and Supervision, a committee of the Education Alumni Association under the chairmanship of Stoops, worked with representatives of the School of Education and others in developing the idea of the Honors Convocation, to be held annually at commencement time and to be devoted to the presentation of awards to students of the School of Education. The Honors Convocation, which proved to be a most successful innovation, continued as an annual occasion.

In 1954, Melbo appointed a special committee on awards, to review the current status and make recommendations. The committee reported that, in general, three types of awards were presented at the Honors Convocation: Education Alumni Association Awards, awards of special organizations such as Pi Lambda Theta and Phi Delta Kappa, and service citations of student organizations such as the California Student Teachers Association and the Education Council. As of 1954, awards were considered almost exclusively undergraduate awards in that the first criterion of eligibility was completion of a credential in June of the current year. Participating honoraries named their own recipients under their own criteria, within general guide lines issued by the Education Alumni Association. Under the policy current in 1954, no person received two awards, exclusive of the service citation, and

246

the number was not to be over 10 per cent of the eligible group. The committee noted, however, that the current awards program did not provide adequately for recognition of graduate work and field performance. Since these were important functions of the School of Education, it was felt that additional awards should be planned to fill this gap.[62]

With the firm support of the faculty, students, alumni, and many organizations in the educational world, awards presented to students, both graduate and undergraduate, of the School of Education, received enormous impetus under Dean Melbo's leadership. Among the awards presented annually were those of the California Congress of Parents and Teachers, which offered, beginning in 1958, a number of elementary teacher education scholarships and secondary teacher education scholarships to students preparing for the California teaching credentials; EDUCARE Awards in the form of a fellowship and a scholarship, as well as a tuition scholarship; the Susan M. Dorsey Scholarship award presented by the Honorary Association for Women in Education; the Sophia T. Salvin Scholarship award presented by the California Association for Neurologically Handicapped Children, Los Angeles Chapter; the Robert Irving Fatt Fund award; and the Una B. Cameron Fund award. In addition honor awards were presented for directed teaching, basic program; honors internships, teaching assistantships, specialized programs such as early childhood education, library science, "Teacher Corps: Urban"; "Teacher Corps: Rural-Migrant"; and Teaching English to Speakers of Other Languages. In accordance with the 1954 recommendations of the Special Awards Committee, outstanding doctoral research was recognized through the presentation of awards to the two doctoral candidates who had submitted the most outstanding dissertations of the current year among all the departments of the School of Education. By 1973, the Honors Convocation, a formal event held in the Town and Gown Foyer on the University campus, featuring an outstanding speaker, and attended by friends and family of the

62. "Report of the Special Committee on Awards," *Agenda,* October 4, 1954.

247

awardees, as well as by cooperating school representatives and supervising teachers, had become an event of much importance. Widely recognized and highly appreciated by both those awarded and those awarding the honors, it was a tribute to Dean Melbo's conviction that *the prime mission of a professional school is to help students to achieve their goals.*

Awards that brought national recognition to the University of Southern California were those presented annually by the American Association of School Administrators to graduate students for outstanding achievement in educational administration. The high level of professionalism of the School of Education and its Department of Administration and Supervision was evidenced by the fact that from 1956 through 1973, 15 graduate students at the School of Education were recipients of the AASA Awards, notably the Shankland Award. Among the recipients were Maxwell L. Rafferty, first USC recipient (1956); E. Maylon Drake (1960); Robert E. Ferris (1964); Lane E. Teaney (1971), who was also the 1600th successful doctoral candidate of the School of Education whose diploma was signed by Dean Melbo; and John L. Nelson (1972), son of Professor and Mrs. D. Lloyd Nelson. (Appendix H contains a list of the AASA Award winners who, at the time of the award, were successful school administrators and graduate students at the School of Education.)

In 1972, Dean Melbo noted with justified pride: "As the record shows, many more students from the USC School of Education have received the Shankland Award than have those from any other institution. This is a tribute to both our students and the School."[63] With equal pride, in 1973, at the University's annual commencement exercises, Dean Melbo presented to Daniel L. Towler the diploma signifying award of the degree of Doctor of Education. Towler's work at the School of Education had been performed in the Department of Higher Education, with Professor Pullias as chairman of his doctoral committee. During the last years of his work, also, he had been awarded, through Dean

248

63. EDUCARE *Newsletter,* 11(2), p. 2.

Melbo's support, an EDUCARE scholarship. As an ex-Ram star, Christian minister, and religious adviser to college students, "Deacon Dan" was the subject, at the time of his graduation, of a feature story in the *Los Angeles Times.* Quoting him, the article stated:[64]

> Dan Towler thinks as he once ran—fast and hard. Yet, it took this football star and humanitarian more than three years to earn his doctorate degree, a job tougher than running into professional linemen. . . .
>
> "I believe the reason not many minority people sought doctor's degrees is that they didn't think that they had this opportunity, and maybe they didn't. Also, they didn't know what would be expected of them. I didn't."
>
> Towler became an EDUCARE scholar with the support of Dean Irving Melbo. . . . "The Rams didn't help me get my grades. I had to stay up and study. Maybe it helped me get the scholarship. I don't know. But I do think that anyone who goes after the opportunity, and gets it, can earn the degree if he really wants to work and discipline his life."

A catalyst in the lives of many students like Dan Towler, and a "significant other" in the careers of thousands more, Dean Melbo once said about his role as leader: "It means doing little things and . . . tasks that no one will know about except our Heavenly Father, and for which no human praise or credit will ever be given."[65] Those who admired Dean Melbo and who knew of the many quiet, thoughtful acts he had performed to smooth countless thorny paths were happy that, in the instance of "Deacon Dan," his support had been given earthly recognition.

Societies

Educational Graduate Organization (EGO). EGO, the Educational Graduate Organization, was established in the spring of 1968, as

64. *Los Angeles Times,* June 6, 1973.
65. Melbo, I. R. "Commencement Address," Summer Commencement Exercise, Brigham Young University, August 16, 1957.

a forum for the expression of ideas on the part of graduate students in the School of Education and for activities planning. A steering committee, composed of two representatives from each department of the School, coordinated the activities of the society.

Beginning with the academic year, 1969–70, members of EGO served on all faculty committees of the School, with the exception of the Committee on Salary, Promotion, and Tenure. EGO members were also cordially invited to participate in departmental meetings, and designated representatives attended general faculty meetings as participatory observers.

The purpose of EGO was not only a forum for graduate students' ideas but the establishment of communication channels between faculty and the graduate students. Said Frances Peavey, first president of EGO, at a faculty meeting in May 1969:[66]

> Our primary purpose is to establish some kind of communication with the faculty through organizational representation. We have appointed different students to be concerned about certain committees. We expect students to attend some meetings of the faculty committees, and we are pleased at the cooperation that you have extended to us. We are hoping over the summer to have a subcommittee work on a faculty evaluation and course content project. Another concern we have is inter-departmental rivalry and lack of cooperation, and we are concerned about it.

The following fall, in November 1969, representatives of EGO reported to the faculty that a questionnaire pertaining to the doctoral program had been prepared by the graduate students in cooperation with the Doctoral Committee. Results of the questionnaire, which was submitted to graduate students attending classes in the School of Education, indicated that "on the average, students did not think poorly of communications between the School of Education and themselves." The results also indicated that students felt they could freely see their instructors and advisors, when they so desired. Strong feelings, however, were ex-

250

66. *Minutes,* May 12, 1969.

pressed concerning the need for a School of Education newsletter. The need was filled in part by publication in 1969–70 of *The Educator,* a "house organ," published with funds provided by EDUCARE. In 1972, a newssheet published by EGO itself, titled *QUIDNUNC?* became a sounding device for ideas and for conveying information of interest to graduate students of the School of Education.

During the years of its existence, EGO also scheduled various workshops and conferences. Informal assistance for students about to take the admissions and qualifying examinations was arranged by EGO, including a discussion session led by Fox of the Department of Educational Psychology. More formal workshops sponsored by EGO included a high-participation workshop arranged in May 1973, on "Your Personal Power in a Bureaucracy," led by James Ross Warren, management consultant.

Education Alumni Association. Since its founding in 1947, the Education Alumni Association continued to play an important part in the support of the School of Education. The first association to contribute funds toward the construction of a new building for the School of Education, a foremost donor of the Waite Phillips Hall of Education, the Education Alumni also fostered a spirit of comradeship and goodwill through its annual "Steak Bakes," at which Dean Melbo customarily presided as chief "steaksman." "No organization," said Dean Melbo, "more courageously carries out the principles for which the School of Education stands and none has more faithfully supported our purposes."

Honorary Association for Women in Education (HAWE). On May 10, 1968, an organization known as the Honorary Association for Women in Education (HAWE) was organized at the School of Education to take the place of the former USC chapter of Pi Lambda Theta. The purposes of HAWE were to stimulate professional growth among women educators, foster leadership in education, stimulate creativity in education, keep members abreast of current educational research, recognize the problems of education in current society, and advance the work of the School

251

of Education. Membership was by invitation to women in education, based on academic standing, professional attainments, and
personal qualifications. Leader in HAWE's establishment was
Virginia R. Archer, who also served as president, 1971–72. Other
prominent members were Frances Boyer, Verna B. Dauterive, Dor-
othy Washington, and Mary Alice Zalesny. Faculty adviser was
Clive L. Grafton of the Department of Higher Education. In addition to holding dinner meetings with speakers of distinction,
HAWE made annual awards to outstanding women students of
the School of Education. These included awards for outstanding
student service and the Susan Miller Dorsey award for proven
leadership of women in education.[67] The Susan Miller Dorsey
Fund was set aside by the members of HAWE for use in the
establishment of a chair of education.

Phi Delta Kappa. The USC Chapter of Phi Delta Kappa (formerly the Alpha Epsilon Chapter) continued its outstanding support of the School of Education. In 1972, at the Golden Jubliee of
the chapter, the society published a compilation of the annual
Emery Stoops lectures which had been presented since the
inauguration of the series in 1964. Distinguished speakers who
were named to deliver the annual Emery Stoops lecture were Dr.
Frederick Mayer, John F. O'Toole Jr., Dr. John Dunworth, Dr.
Maynard Bemis, Dr. Max Rafferty, Dr. Leonard L. Murdy, Senator George Murphy, Dr. E. Maylon Drake, Dr. Lowell Rose, Dr.
Leland Newcomer. Senator Murphy's address centered on his personal appreciation of education as a "dropout":[68]

So here I am tonight—a dropout—amidst a room filled with
scholars and I feel inadequate to the occasion. I wasn't a dropout
by design or desire—I like to think I was a victim of circumstances. That is partially true. I answered a question one day

67. Susan Miller Dorsey was the first and, to date, the only woman superintendent of Los Angeles city schools. Appointed in 1919, she served until 1929. One
of California's most outstanding educators, Mrs. Dorsey was elected in 1933
Honorary President of the National Education Association. She died February 5,
1946. In her memory is named the Susan M. Dorsey High School in Los Angeles.
68. Alpha Epsilon Chapter, Phi Delta Kappa (1972). The quotation is from the
7th Emery Stoops Lecture (1970) by Senator Murphy.

252

honestly. The Dean of Students at Yale University said to me, "Murphy, did you come here to play football or to study?" And I told him the truth, and I told him why. And he said, "Well, you've got the wrong attitude," and he put me on probation, so I couldn't play football, so I couldn't stay in college. And the older I get, the more I think back on the fact of the responsibility that rests with all of you. The responsibility not only for expertise in your line, your particular endeavor, but in the knowledge of human engineering, the knowledge of the association of human beings which after all, I think, has to supercede all of the other important things from which this complex society of ours is made. So I left, and I met a girl—she wanted to be a dancer and I was afraid she would be lonesome if she went off by herself so I went with her. And I don't know anybody whose life I would trade for mine. It's been remarkable. It's been exciting. I work harder now than I did ever before. I have to be able to appear to be an expert in practically every facet of our society and problems. I assure you I'm not.

I have been interested in Education because I realize the importance, maybe because I have never finished mine. I have a greater appreciation than some of you who have been so successful and who have gone so far. And I am particularly honored tonight to be here to join with "Stoop's Troups." I think that the record this man has made is most remarkable and I wish we could hear more about this sort of achievement, this sort of dedication and service, and less about some of the unfortunate problems that beset us ...

Developmental Priorities

In 1958, the late Merritt M. Thompson had closed his chronicle of the School of Education with a look at the future as seen through the eyes of Dean Melbo. In 1973, Dean Melbo himself, with his steady eye on the future, prepared a statement of developmental priorities which he foresaw for the School of Education in the immediate future, 1973–1976.

The three large projects he foresaw were the construction of the Learning Resources Center, for which the architectural plans

253

had been drawn; construction of the USC School for Early Childhood Education, and improved facilities for the Educational Placement Office. Melbo himself had the pleasure of presiding at the dedication of the USC School for Early Childhood Education in October 1973.

Off campus, Melbo foresaw the need for continuation of a number of the services of the School of Education. It would be necessary, he thought, to continue to house certain programs and activities at the Broadway Building or another location in Los Angeles. Cooperative arrangements with the National Charity League would continue to house programs of the reading center in the NCL-USC Reading Center on Hollywood Boulevard. Other cooperative arrangements which he anticipated would continue were those with the John Tracy Clinic and other training facilities in the greater metropolitan area. These relationships he considered indispensable to the maintenance of the professional stature of the School of Education.

In response to the impact of demographic factors on the schools and to the developing patterns of public and private education, the dean foresaw the requirement to continue the rapid expansion of certain existing programs. One of the most important of these would be early childhood education. With the anticipated legislation providing state funding for programs in public schools designed for three- and four-year-old children, an increased effort to recruit and prepare well-qualified teachers and other personnel in the field of early childhood would be necessary. Appointment of additional faculty and clinical staff in the specialization would be required.

Demographic data pertaining to Los Angeles and its environs pointed to the need for expansion of existing arrangements for cooperative contractual agreements with school districts in order to assure employment to those who entered teacher preparation in the face of a shrinking job market. This development would require from the administration and faculty of the School of Education an extension of field contacts and relationships. The demographic data also pointed clearly to an increased enrollment in Los

254

Angeles and adjacent communities of children from low socioeconomic backgrounds. The nature of this enrollment would require an expansion of programs and faculty for preparing specialized teachers in the areas of the educationally handicapped and of specialists in the teaching of English as a Second Language. Analysis of the trends of public education also made it clear that adult education enrollments would increase in the area of vocational and technical curricula. This development would require an expansion of adult education teacher preparation and adult education administrators. He advocated that, in the light of current trends in education, the existing program for the Bachelor of Science—Technical Studies be expanded to the domestic market as a means of preparing specialists in technical and vocational education.

At the doctoral level, Dean Melbo foresaw an excellent opportunity to develop a high degree of specialization in child growth and development, to include an intense emphasis on learning strategies and methods that would increase the productivity of the teaching-learning situation and reduce the number of failures to achieve basic skills of literacy. Such a program, for which a base existed in the joint activities of the School of Education and the School of Medicine's Department of Pediatrics, would provide a new type of specialist for whom there would be great demand and ready employment.

In teacher preparation, Melbo foresaw the opportunity to design a program for the preparation of master teachers who could function within any large school as directors of learning for a complex of from 150 to 200 children. These master teachers would direct the process of individual diagnosis of learning capabilities, of existing school and non-school achievements, and would prescribe an individualized learning program, to be followed by a periodic evaluation of learning accomplishments. Assisted by appropriate aides, these master teachers offered, said Dean Melbo, the best prospect of a breakthrough which would permit the effective individualization and personalization of instruction, thus moving away from the obsolete class-grade organization;

255

and would increase the productivity of the teaching force as related to teacher-pupil ratios and costs per pupil in current expense. Development of this concept into operational status could be, said Dean Melbo, the most significant single educational accomplishment of the twentieth century.

The School of Education, with its great background of providing administrators and educational leaders, must continue and expand its concern for the preparation of school administrators who would enter the field in various leadership roles. It was a well-established fact, he noted, that alumni of the School of Education in such positions were vital factors in meeting the competition from other less expensive and less demanding programs in the field of education. Specifically, it would be necessary to develop certain new specializations, such as school-community-public relations, the educational ombudsman, and the personnel administrator with special skills in grievance and negotiation procedures. Perhaps most significant would be, he foresaw, the development of a kind of preparation for *educational statesmanship* which would pave the way for a position as commissioner of education, who would be appointed to give leadership, direction, and coordination to the pluralisms of educational activities, public and private.

Activities of the School of Education in conducting advanced study centers throughout the state of California and abroad would continue, he foresaw. With continued emphasis on high-quality instruction from selected faculty and with diligent attention to the special needs of the clientele of such programs, it was reasonable to expect that they would continue to be productive, not only in enrollments, but as part of the national and international commitment of a major professional school.

On the matter of personal interest in the student, the dean pointed to the remarkable record of the School of Education since its establishment. This traditional emphasis had been continued under this incumbency as dean. Among the best "recruiters" for the School of Education, he frequently noted, were those faculty members in other institutions who tended to regard students as

256

an "annoyance" and barrier to their own personal writing and research activities. "In a true professional school," he reminded his faculty, "the faculty must develop and maintain a personal interest in each and every student." With this philosophy and, at the same time, more difficult economic conditions, it would be increasingly important for the School of Education to obtain sources of student aid to be applied to the recruitment of students and to the support of graduate students through fellowships and research assistantships. While these matters were of concern to the total faculty, he noted that it should be the special concern of a position in the School of Education at the level of associate dean, responsible for research and development, including the generation of an increased support base for the student population.

As a professional school, the School of Education must be concerned with the continued development of its present competency-based curricula and with the exercise of a personalized and individualized program of service and instruction to its students which would, in effect, guarantee success. With forceful words he warned:

> It is the personal interest of the faculty in our students that attracts and holds enrollments. This interest must be a career commitment. The School cannot afford under any condition to have a body of unemployed or unemployable graduates.

With similar urgency he warned against both extremes of innovation and extremes of conservatism in educational programs:

> The School cannot afford the bad judgment of attempting to match its program to the headlines of the day. It must give continuing attention to the significant trends which determine the direction of future educational enterprise at all levels. It must attempt to be slightly ahead, perhaps by three to five years, of these evolving trends so that it does not have to be in a position of attempting to play catch-up with the profession. This is a part of our established leadership commitment to the field.

Given continued autonomy on the part of its faculty to design and develop programs pertinent to its professional field, and

257

freedom to engage in reasonable ventures, Melbo was confident that the School of Education would continue to prosper and to maintain its role as one of the major and most productive divisions of the University.

Post-Retirement Honors

Following Dean Melbo's retirement, EDUCARE and the various professional societies of the School of Education, including the USC Chapter of Phi Delta Kappa, Education Alumni, HAWE, and the Society of Delta Epsilon, established within the School of Education the Irving R. Melbo Chair. The establishment of this, the first endowed chair in the School of Education, was announced at a dinner held in Dr. Melbo's honor May 16, 1974 under the aegis of the contributing societies. Dr. Melbo, as Dean Emeritus, was appointed as first incumbent of the chair, to be held for the academic year 1974–1975.

Also following Dean Melbo's retirement, the faculty of the School of Education, in appreciation of his distinguished service, honored him by affixing to the wall of the foyer of Waite Phillips Hall a bronze plaque, matching in size and composition that which had been affixed in honor of the donor, Waite Phillips. Dean Melbo's words, inscribed on the plaque, signalized his ambition for the School of Education and his ultimate confidence in man's efforts to better himself and the world. The words, composed by the dean himself, read:

Our goal is to develop standards to which others will aspire in the field of education; the future is a world limited only by ourselves.

Envoi

This book has traced the history of the School of Education from 1953 to 1973. (For a chronology of the School of Education from its earliest beginnings to 1973, see Appendix I.) As higher education is molded and influenced in all ages by a variety of historical forces, so the School of Education, during those two decades from

258

1953 to 1973, was molded and influenced by forces on the national, state, and local scene with which it was inextricably bound.

With firm purpose and determination to accomplish what he had visualized, Dean Melbo guided the School of Education of the University of Southern California through 20 years of extraordinary change. It was the greatness of Irving R. Melbo that, while looking back with pride, his eyes were constantly fixed on the future. With inner security and unshakeable confidence, he saw beyond the ebb and flow of events the movement toward a great Golden Age for public education—a Golden Age in which the mighty potential of public education would at last be realized. It was the hope and the determination of this one man who made those years for the School of Education "The Melbo Years."

259

JOHN R. HUBBARD

President, USC (1970-   ).

DELTA EPSILON LECTURERS (1969-73)

Upper left: Howardine G. Hoffman (1969); **upper right:** W. Earl Brown (1970); **lower left:** Armen Sarafian (1973); **lower right:** Leonard L. Murdy (1972).

IN
MEMORIAM

James D. Finn (1915-1969)

Daniel T. Dawson (1914-1972)

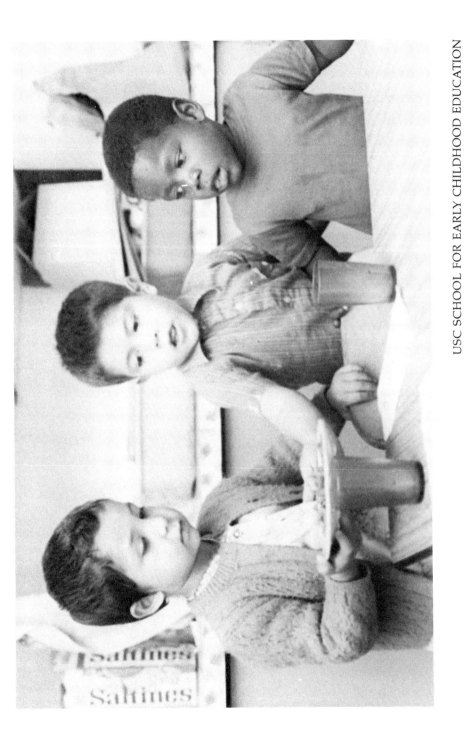

USC SCHOOL FOR EARLY CHILDHOOD EDUCATION

Nursery school children preparing food, USC School for Early Childhood Education (1973).

USC SCHOOL FOR EARLY CHILDHOOD EDUCATION

Playground area adjacent to classroom (1973).

INTERNATIONAL RELATIONS

Upper photo: Dean Melbo **(center)** and John A. Carpenter **(far left)** visit classroom, Saudi Arabia, 1969.

Lower photo: African Panel, 1967. **Left to right:** Alemayehew (Ethiopia), John A. Carpenter, Sidibe (Mali), Chisanu (Malawi), Kalambatore (Malawi), Abele (Congo).

HONORS OVERSEAS

Upper photo: Dean Melbo **(right)** accepts from General Horace M. Wade, CINCUSAFE (left), the Air Force Exceptional Service Award, with medal. Wiesbaden, Germany, August 1968.

Lower photo: General Horace M. Wade, CINCUSAFE, receives USC honorary degree, Wiesbaden, Germany, June 1969. **Left to right:** Dean Melbo; General Wade; Dr. Herold A. Sherman, Executive Director, Safety and Systems Management, USC.

GRADUATIONS, OVERSEAS MASTER'S PROGRAM
IN EUROPE AND ASIA MINOR.

Upper photo: Faculty members at graduation reception, Efes Hotel, Izmir, Turkey, June
1969. **Left to right:** Mrs. Wagner, Professors Elmer E. Wagner, Jane Warters, D. Lloyd
Nelson, Mrs. Nelson.

Lower photo: Commencement dignitaries, Athens, Greece, May 1971. **Left to right:** Stuart
. McComb, faculty marshal; Dean Melbo; Colonel Teague Harris, USAF, Athens Airport
Base Commander; Wallace R. Muelder, Associate Dean, School of Education.

STUDENTS, OVERSEAS MASTER'S PROGRAM
IN EUROPE AND ASIA MINOR.

Upper photo: Students at Parthenon, Athens, Greece, 1968. **Left to right:** Lynn Dorris, Aphrodite Allsebrook, James Yeros, Clinton J. Noid, Joseph Martin, Billie McKenzie, Peter Moustakes.

Lower photo: Student, Donna Cooper, on camel, Izmir, Turkey (1968).

GRADUATION, HEIDELBERG, GERMANY, AUGUST 20, 1972

General Andrew J. Goodpaster, USA, SACEUR (Ph.D., Princeton University, 1950) leads graduation procession. Following are General Frederic E. Davison, USA, CINCUSAREUR, Dean Melbo, and, to far right, D. Lloyd Nelson. **Inset:** Sue Reese Mason, member of the graduating class, whose untimely death some months prior to graduation precluded her from participation in the ceremony.

Upper photo: Dean Melbo presents diploma to graduate, Taipei, Taiwan, May 27, 1972.

Lower photo: Graduating class, Bangkok, Thailand, May 30, 1972.

ACADEMIC HONORS

Upper photo: William J. Johnston, president, EDUCARE, **(right)** presents award to EDUCARE Scholar Daniel L. ("Deacon Dan") Towler **(left)**. Honors Convocation, 1972.

Lower photo: Dean Melbo **(left)** with Lane E. Teaney **(right)**, the 1600th successful doctoral candidate whose diploma was signed by Dean Melbo. (Photograph, January 1973).

HONORARY DEGREES AWARDED, USC COMMENCEMENT, JUNE 1970

Dean Melbo with recipients of honorary degrees. **Left to right:** Dean Melbo, Professor Emeritus Louis P. Thorpe, Jack P. Crowther, former Superintendent, Los Angeles City Schools; Sidney W. Brosman, Chancellor, California Community College System.

LOS ANGELES AREA SUPERINTENDENTS

Left: William J. Johnston (B.A., '49, M.S. in Ed., '51, USC; Ed.D., '65, UCLA) Superintendent, Los Angeles Unified School District (1970-   ).

Right: Richard M. Clowes (A.B., '38, M.S. in Ed., '51, Ed.D., '60, USC) Superintendent, Los Angeles County School System.

EDUCARE PRESIDENTS (1960-1968)

Upper photo: Left to right: Isaac McClelland (1966-67); C. C. Trillingham (1960-62); Schuyler C. Joyner (1962-63); C. C. Carpenter (1965-66); W. Earl Brown (1963-64); Jack P. Crowther (1964-65). EDUCARE Dinner, April 15, 1966.

Lower photo: Left to right: Richard H. Lawrence (1968-69); E. Maylon Drake (1967-68). EDUCARE Dinner, May 17, 1968.

EDUCARE
PRESIDENTS
(1969-1972)

Left to right: Dean Melbo, Wayne
Butterbaugh (1969-70), Donald
Shroyer (1970-71). EDUCARE Black-
Tie Dinner, April 17, 1970.

Left to right: Dean Melbo, Leonard L.
Murdy (1971-72). EDUCARE Black-Tie
Dinner, April 17, 1970.

EDUCARE PRESIDENTS (1972-1975)

Upper left: William J. Johnston (1972-73); **upper right:** Frank W. Kittinger (1973-74); **lower left:** Verna B. Dauterive (1974-75); **lower right:** Richard B. Horne, President-Elect (1974-75).

FRIENDSHIPS RENEWED AT EDUCARE DINNERS

Upper photo: Two former superintendents, Los Angeles City Schools. **Left to right:** Ellis A. Jarvis, Jack P. Crowther. EDUCARE Dinner, April 17, 1970.

Lower photo: Left to right: Robert E. Cralle, former Director, Educational Placement Office; John C. Whinnery, former Superintendent, Montebello City Schools; Mrs. Trillingham; C. C. Trillingham, former Superintendent, Los Angeles City Schools. EDUCARE Dinner, April 18, 1969.

ALBERT S. RAUBENHEIMER

Professor Emeritus and former Educational Vice-President, USC. EDUCARE Dinner, April 18, 1969.

1969 EDUCATION ALUMNI ANNUAL STEAK BAKE

Upper photo: Dean Melbo and Professor Charles M. Brown on the serving line.

Lower photo: Professor and Mrs. Lionel De Silva on the receiving line.

Selected Bibliography

Books and Pamphlets

Alpha Epsilon Chapter, Phi Delta Kappa. *PDK-USC: Our golden jubilee threshold to the future: Dr. Emery Stoops Lecture Series, 1964-1972.* Los Angeles, 1972.

Cloud, Roy W. *Education in California: Leaders, organizations, and accomplishments of the first hundred years.* Stanford: Stanford University Press, 1952.

El Rodeo. Annual of the University of Southern California, 1899–

Gardner, John. *No easy victories.* New York: Harper & Row, 1968.

Henley, W. Ballentine, and Neelley, Arthur E., eds. *Cardinal and gold.* Los Angeles: General Alumni Association, University of Southern California, 1939.

Hill, Herbert W., ed. *Proceedings of the Twenty-Fifth Anniversary Celebration of the Inauguration of Graduate Studies, The University of Southern California, 1910-1935.* Los Angeles: University of Southern California Press, 1936.

_____. *The semicentennial celebration of the founding of the University of Southern California.* Los Angeles: University of Southern California Press, 1936.

Hunt, Rockwell D. *The first half-century.* Los Angeles: University of Southern California Press, 1930.

Jones, Helen M. *In recognition of an accomplishment: Heidelberg, Germany, August 20, 1972.* Los Angeles: School of Education, University of Southern California, 1972.

Lefever, D. Welty. *Bibliography of publications and achievements of D. Welty Lefever upon his retirement after forty years of service to*

261

the University of Southern California. Los Angeles: School of Education, University of Southern California, 1966.

Melbo, Irving R. *The restoration of confidence in public education.* Twelfth Annual Grady Gammage Memorial Lecture. College of Education, Arizona State University, February 6, 1972.

Meyers, C. Edward; Cannon, Wendell, E.; Lefever, D. Welty. *The recruitment and training of teacher interns: A report of the Southern California Teacher Education Project, 1954-59.* Los Angeles: School of Education, University of Southern California, 1960.

Servin, Manuel P., and Wilson, Iris Higbie. *Southern California and its University: A history of USC, 1880-1964.* Los Angeles: The Ward Ritchie Press, 1969.

Topping, Norman H. *Inaugural address.* Los Angeles, 1958.

University of Southern California. *USC aspects.* Los Angeles, 1971.

———. *USC review.* Los Angeles, 1971.

———. *Waite Phillips Hall of Education Dedication, May 17, 1968.* Los Angeles, 1968.

University of Southern California, School of Education. *Distinguished Lecture Series in Special Education and Rehabilitation.* Los Angeles, 1962, 1966–

———. *Education Monographs.* Los Angeles, 1933–

University of Southern California, School of Education, "Teacher Corps: Rural-Migrant." *First papers on migrancy and rural poverty: An introduction to the education of Mexican-Americans in rural areas.* 3 pamphlets. Los Angeles, 1967–68.

University of Southern California, School of Education, Teacher Corps: Rural-Migrant Cycle IV and Teacher Corps: VISTA. *The many faces of Teacher Corps: An overview of two years of teaching/learning activities.* Los Angeles, 1971.

Articles

Bell, David E. The university's contribution to the developing nations. *Higher Education,* 1964, 6(4), 5–8.

Finn, James D. A walk on the altered side. *Phi Delta Kappan,* 1962, 44(1), 29–34.

Gaw, Allison. A sketch of the development of graduate work in the University of Southern California, 1910-1935. *Development of graduate education in USC.* Los Angeles: University of Southern California, 1935.

262

Gay, Leslie F., Jr. The founding of the University of Southern California. *Historical Society of Southern California Quarterly,* 1909, **8,** 37–50.

Healy, Ezra A. A personal appreciation of Doctor Stowell, *USC Alumni Magazine,* 1921, **3**(1), 10.

Hunt, Rockwell D. Dr. Hoose as colleague. *USC Alumni Magazine,* 1921 **3**(1), 8–9.

Knoles, Tully C. James Harmon Hoose, A.M., Ph.D., LL.D. *Historical Society of Southern California Quarterly,* 1915–16, **10,** 75–79.

_____. James Harmon Hoose, A.M., Ph.D., LL.D. *USC Alumni Magazine,* Special Number, June 1917: 23–26.

Melbo, Irving R., and Martin, David W. Building morale in teachers of the deprived. *The educationally retarded and disadvantaged. Sixty-sixth Yearbook of the National Society for the Study of Education, Part I,* pp. 328–349. Chicago: National Society for the Study of Education: 1967.

_____. The superintendent of the seventies. *The California Administrator,* 1970, **25**(1), 20–23.

_____. Teachers for metropolis. *Great ideas of education,* edited by Frederick Mayer, **3,** 200–209. New Haven: College and University Press, 1966.

_____. Tribute to Sophia. *Sixth Annual Distinguished Lectures in Special Education and Rehabilitation,* Summer 1967, pp. v–vi.

_____. What can school board members do to answer criticisms of public education? *American School Board Journal,* 1951, **122**(5), 27–28, 86.

Pearse, Benjamin H. Volunteers to America. *American Education,* 1968, **4**(7), 22–25.

Simpson, Roy E. The development of new credential requirements. *California Schools,* 1962, **33,** 265–288.

_____. A new credential structure for California. *California Schools,* 1960, **31,** 161–171.

_____. Reactions to the Report of the Committee on the Revision of the Credential Structure in California. *California Schools,* 1958, **29,** 525–535.

Reports and Bulletins

American Council on Education. *Education for development: Report of the survey team on education in Malawi.* Washington, D.C., 1964.

263

Comptroller General of the United States. *Report to the Congress: Assessment of the Teacher Corps Program at the University of Southern California and participating schools in Tulare County serving rural-migrant children.* Washington, D.C.: U.S. General Accounting Office, 1971.

University of Southern California. *Bulletin.* Published semi-monthly. "School of Education Announcement" issued biennially as part of the *Bulletin* since 1918.

――――. *Final Report: Polytechnic project, University of Malawi.* Los Angeles, 1970.

――――. *Report of the President: The University and its family, October 1964-October 1969.* Los Angeles, 1969.

――――. *Report of the President: University in transition, October 1958-October 1961.* Los Angeles, 1961.

――――. *Report of the President: University on the move, October 1961-October 1964.* Los Angeles, 1964.

――――. *Report of the survey: Soche Hill College, Malawi.* Los Angeles, 1966.

――――. *Report of the survey: University of Teheran.* Los Angeles, 1958.

――――. *The University and the future.* Los Angeles, 1961.

University of Southern California, School of Education. *Final report: Specialist-Teacher Program.* Los Angeles, 1965.

――――. *First annual report: Specialist-Teacher Program.* Los Angeles, 1960.

――――. *Reaccreditation report to the California State Board of Education.* Los Angeles, 1972.

――――. *A reaccreditation report to the California State Board of Education and the National Council for Accreditation of Teacher Education.* Los Angeles, 1961.

――――. *A reaccreditation report to the National Council for Accreditation of Teacher Education.* 3 vols. Los Angeles, 1970.

――――. *Report of the University of Southern California for the Joint Accreditation Committee, California State Board of Education and Western College Association.* Los Angeles, 1956.

――――. *WE: An experiment in international understanding.* Los Angeles, 1955.

University of Southern California, School of Education, Center for International Education. *African studies personnel and curriculum development program for elementary and secondary school teachers.* Los Angeles, 1971.

――――. *American Civilization/Language Institute.* Los Angeles, 1972.

264

_____. *An evaluation of the Volunteers to America training program.* Los Angeles, 1968.

_____. *International Teachers Development Project: Italian School Administrators Project.* Los Angeles, 1969.

_____. *Personnel and curriculum development program on India for elementary and secondary school personnel, K-12.* Los Angeles, 1972.

_____. *Vietnamese Education Institute: The psychological foundations of teacher education in Vietnam.* Los Angeles, 1969.

University of Southern California, School of Education, Teacher Education. *Institute for training adult basic education teachers.* Los Angeles, 1970.

_____. *Teacher education process through Teacher Learning Centers.* Los Angeles, 1972.

University of Southern California, School of Education, "Teacher Corps: Rural-Migrant." *A creative bilingual/bicultural teacher training program to meet the critical needs of Mexican-American children and others in rural communities: Final report, Cycle II.* Los Angeles, 1969.

Wilson, Donald E. *Report to the United States Department on the Contemporary Pedagogue Program.* Los Angeles, 1972.

Newsletters, Newspapers, Magazines

Alumni Magazine, University of Southern California, 1917–1923.
Alumni News, University of Southern California, 1923–1924.
Alumni Review, University of Southern California, 1925–
California Elementary Administrator, 1968, **30**(3), 3.
EDUCARE *Newsletter,* University of Southern CAlifornia, April 1961–
Education, U.S.A., National School Public Relations Association, April 30, 1973.
Faculty News, University of Southern California, September 1948–
Illustrated News, University of Southern California Alumni, 1924–1925.
Los Angeles Times, October 5, 1953–June 30, 1973.
Specialist-Teacher Program Newsletter, University of Southern California, School of Education, 1960–1964.
Stars and Stripes, European Edition, November 18, 1968.
Time, March 14, 1960.

265

Trojan. University of Southern California. September 16, 1915–
May 1918; February 21, 1919– . Also known intermittently
as the *Daily Trojan, Summer Trojan,* and *Daily Southern Californian* (1912–1915).
Trojan Bell, Education Alumni, University of Southern California.

Manuscripts, Dissertations, Theses

Brown, Jane W. *An analysis of selected data pertaining to Master's
degrees in Education at the University of Southern California.*
(Master's thesis: University of Southern California) 1961.
Bundy, Stuart McLeod. *Prediction of success in the doctoral program
of the School of Education of the University of Southern California.* (Doctoral dissertation: University of Southern California) 1968.
Calvert, Spencer E. *A follow-up study of the doctoral graduates in
Education at the University of Southern California.* (Doctoral
dissertation, University of Southern California) 1947.
Cannon, Wendell E. *On the state of disunion.* Address presented at
California Council on the Education of Teachers, Santa Bar-
bara, April 2, 1964.
Gates, Samuel E. *A history of the University of Southern California,
1900-1928.* (Master's thesis: University of Southern Cali-
fornia) 1929.
Gay, Leslie F., Jr. *History of the University of Southern California.*
(Master's thesis: University of Southern California) 1910.
Hungerford, Curtiss Randall. *A study in administrative leadership:
Rufus B. von KleinSmid and the University of Southern California,
1921-1935.* (Doctoral dissertation: University of Southern
California) 1967.
Levitt, Leon. *A history to 1953 of the School of Education of the
University of Southern California.* (Doctoral dissertation: Uni-
versity of Southern California) 1970.
Melbo, Irving R. *Board-superintendent relationships.* Address
presented at Clinic for New School Board Members, Univer-
sity of Southern California, July 20, 1963.
———. *Commencement address.* Address presented to graduates,
Brigham Young University, Summer Commencement Exer-
cise, August 16, 1957.
———. "Education in '70 one of change, controversy." *Los Angeles
Times,* January 10, 1971.

266

_____. *The education of metropolitan man.* Address presented at Phi Delta Kappa Symposium, July 2, 1964.

_____. *The need for educational statesmanship.* Address presented at University of Hawaii, July 5, 1956.

_____. *Wanted—educational statesmen.* Address presented at Administration Conference, University of Southern California, July 9, 1954.

Thompson, Merritt M. *Highlights in the history of the School of Education of the University of Southern California.* Address at Golden Jubilee banquet of the School of Education, University of Southern California, October 16, 1958.

_____. Untitled chronicle of events in history of the School of Education, University of Southern California, n.d.

Walker, Margarette Wible. *An analysis of the doctoral program in Education at the University of Southern California.* (Doctoral dissertation: University of Southern California) 1953.

Minutes and Agenda

Agenda. Faculty meetings, School of Education, University of Southern California, October 5, 1953–

Minutes. Faculty meetings, School of Education, University of Southern California, September 19, 1923–

267

Appendices

APPENDIX A

CREDENTIALS ISSUED ON RECOMMENDATION OF THE
UNIVERSITY OF SOUTHERN CALIFORNIA
1953–1972

CREDENTIAL	1953	1954	1955	1956	1957	1958	1959	1960	1961	1962	1963	REMARKS
Kindergarten-Primary	84	66	84	92	96	92	92	93	57	62	33	
General Elementary	206	168	211	270	302	306	299	254	258	300	279	
General Secondary	127	110	154	158	156	161	208	224	213	245	211	
Junior College	3	4	4	12	18	23	41	29	28	23	5	
Special Secondary												
Art	6	5	10	1	14	9	9	13	8	10	14	
Business Education	8	3	5	9	13	16	11	17	18	14	9	
Music Education	23	10	11	25	18	20	22	24	18	17	12	
Physical Education				5	8	19	10	9	19	13	16	
Librarianship	6	4	13	10	10	17	15	13	10	12	9	
Exceptional Children												
Deaf & Hard of hearing					5	1	3	3	4	8	6	
Speech Correction/Lip Reading	12	5	7	9	7	6	3	1	3	3	4	
Mentally Retarded	2	2	1	1	4	2		4	4	3	2	
General Pupil Personnel	16	16	24	30	47	21	30	49	64	88	74	
Supervision	8	17	6	16	24	38	25	14	4	9	11	All types
Elementary School Admin.	86	99	121	110	110	101	77	93	87	84	90	
Secondary School Admin.	46	74	61	93	75	56	70	61	48	64	57	
General Administration	40	30	32	47	48	37	42	40	46	45	60	
TOTAL	673	623	744	888	955	925	957	941	898	1000	911	

Kindergarten-Primary	25	11	159	92	9	32			
General Elementary	317	323	201	116	10	19			
General Secondary	248	241							See below (1)
Special Secondary									
Art	9	6	5						
Business Education	8	4	6						
Music Education	31	25	11						
Physical Education	16	6	4						
Librarianship	11	29	12						
Exceptional Children									
Deaf & Hard of hearing	10	17	9						
Speech Correction	5								
Mentally Retarded	5	4							
General Pupil Personnel	76	96	121	38	15	38			
Supervision	27	22	22						
Elementary School Admin.	77	103	165	73	9	16			
Secondary School Admin.	72	77	152	66	9	9			
General Administration	57	62	173	110	13	25			
Standard Elementary		2	38	120	107	147	200	183	213
Interns				50	79	45	34	23	12
Standard Secondary		6	140	280	148	171	238	226	182
Interns				57	88	53	23	6	8
Standard Designated Svc		3	18	25	53	60	52		
Counseling								23	14
Psychometry								3	4
Psychology								22	26
Early Childhood								7	7
Orthopedically Handicapped								1	
Standard Librarianship	11	29	12	3	5	6			
Standard Supervision			19	19	37	29	41	30	43
Interns						14	4	7	8
Standard Administration			1		3	5	6	2	4
Interns						1		1	1
TOTAL	998	1042	1274	1061	597	672	602	535	522

(1) As of June 1968, Librarianship issued as a minor on Standard Elementary of Secondary Credentials.

APPENDIX B

DOCTORAL DEGREES AWARDED
SCHOOL OF EDUCATION
UNIVERSITY OF SOUTHERN CALIFORNIA
1927–1973

Year	Ph.D.	Ed. D.	Total	Year	Ph.D.	Ed.D.	Total
1927	1	—	1	1951	8	23	31
1928	3	—	3	1952	4	29	33
1929	—	—	—	1953	12	26	38
1930	2	—	2	1954	7	27	34
1931	5	2	7	1955	7	44	51
1932	—	5	5	1956	10	53	63
1933	4	10	14	1957	9	26	35
1934	2	7	9	1958	14	50	64
1935	—	—	—	1959	6	51	57
1936	2	2	4	1960	7	54	61
1937	3	6	9	1961	6	51	57
1938	3	5	8	1962	5	55	60
1939	2	10	12	1963	8	48	56
1940	2	8	10	1964	8	54	62
1941	5	10	15	1965	15	58	73
1942	5	6	11	1966	18	58	76
1943	2	11	13	1967	20	67	87
1944	1	7	8	1968	27	81	108
1945	—	3	3	1969	18	68	86
1946	—	3	3	1970	43	92	135
1947	2	10	12	1971	55	99	154
1948	8	17	25	1972	39	122	161
1949	6	22	28	1973	57	139	196
1950	5	28	33	Total	466	1547	2013

APPENDIX C

DELTA EPSILON LECTURESHIPS

The Society of Delta Epsilon and the faculty of the School of Education jointly select each year one eminently successful doctoral graduate of the School of Education, University of Southern California, to lecture in the field of the graduate's professional specialization. The Delta Epsilon lecturers from 1954, the year in which the lectureship was established, through 1973, are listed below in the position they held at the time of their appointment.

1954 Harry M. Howell, Ed.D., Associate Superintendent, Los Angeles City Schools
1955 Stuart F. McComb, Ed.D., Superintendent, Pasadena City Schools
1956 Paul Fisher, Ed.D., Principal, Washington High School, Los Angeles
1957 Charles C. Carpenter, Ed.D., Assistant Superintendent, Los Angeles County Schools
1958 H. Fred Heisner, Ed.D., Superintendent, Redlands City Schools
1959 Harry Smallenburg, Ed.D., Director, Division of Research and Guidance, Los Angeles County Schools
1960 Jessie Graham, Ph.D., Supervisor of Business Education (retired), Los Angeles City Schools
1961 W. Norman Wampler, Ph.D., Superintendent, Bellflower Unified School District
1962 C. C. Trillingham, Ed.D., Superintendent, Los Angeles County Schools
1963 Schuyler C. Joyner, Ed.D., Business Manager, Los Angeles City Schools
1964 Herman J. Sheffield, Ed.D., President, San Bernardino Valley College
1965 John C. Whinnery, Ed.D., Superintendent, Montebello City Schools
1966 J. H. Hull, Ed.D., Superintendent, Torrance Unified School District

1967 Gunnar L. Wahlquist, Ph.D., Assistant Superintendent, Instruction, El Monte Union High School District

1968 Theron Freese, Ed.D., Associate Professor of Education, Wisconsin State University, Oshkosh

1969 Howardine G. Hoffman, Ed.D., Assistant Superintendent, Los Angeles County Schools

1970 William Earl Brown, Ed.D., Superintendent, South Bay Union High School District

1971 Truman N. Case, Ed.D., Principal, Northridge Junior High School, Los Angeles City Schools

1972 Leonard L. Murdy, Ed.D., Superintendent, Fullerton Union High School District

1973 Armen Sarafian, Ph.D., President, Pasadena City College and Superintendent of Pasadena Area Community College District

274

APPENDIX D

EDUCATIONAL SURVEYS FOR PUBLIC SCHOOL SYSTEMS
IRVING R. MELBO, DIRECTOR
1947–1972

General

Alameda School District, 1956
Antelope Valley Joint Union High School District, 1956
Arcadia City School District, 1947
Artesia School District, 1949
Barstow Union and Barstow Union High School District, 1961
Bear Valley Unified School District, 1962
Bellflower School District, 1949
Bonita Union High, La Verne City Elementary, La Verne Heights Elementary, San Dimas Elementary, School Districts, 1955
Castaic Union, Newhall, Saugus Union, Sulphur Springs Union, William S. Hart High, School Districts, 1966
Centinela Valley Union High School District, 1955
Coachella, Desert Center, Indio, Mecca, Oasis Joint, Thermal Union, Coachella Valley Joint Union High, School Districts, 1962
Colton Joint Unified School District, 1968
Excelsior Union High School District, 1949
Huntington Beach Union High School District, 1958
La Canada Elementary School District, 1952
Laguna Beach Unified School District, 1961
Lancaster School District, 1956
Lawndale Unified School District, 1953
Lennox Elementary School District, 1951
Mesa (Arizona) Public Schools, 1955
Monrovia City School District, 1951
Morongo School District, 1957
Norwalk Elementary School District, 1950
Oxnard Union High School District, 1949
Palm Springs Unified School District, 1964
Palo Verde Valley Unified School District, 1953
Palos Verdes Unified School District, 1956

275

Paramount Elementary School District, 1950
Phoenix (Arizona) Union High Schools and Phoenix College System, 1954
Pomona Unified School District, 1957
Rosemead School District, 1968
San Gabriel Elementary School District, 1949
San Luis Obispo City Schools, 1959
Santa Paula Union High School District, 1954
South Pasadena City Elementary School District, 1952
South Pasadena Unified School District, 1952-53
South San Francisco Unified School District, 1967
Taft City School District, 1960
Ventura City Elementary Schools, 1959
Victor Valley Union High School District, 1957
Westside Union High School District, 1956
Whittier Area Public Schools, 1948
Whittier Union High School District, 1959
Yuma (Arizona) Union High School District, 1950

Special

Administration
Ventura Union High School District, 1948
Administration, Organization, and Certified Salary Programs
Fullerton High School District, 1968
Administration, Organization, and Functions
West Covina School District, 1958
Administration, Organization, and Personnel Factors
Placentia Unified School District, 1968
Analysis of Financial Status
Monrovia-Duarte High School District, 1956
Business Management and Financial Status
Cerritos Junior College District, 1959
District Growth and Community College
Palo Verde Valley Unified School District, 1964
Educational Program
Calexico Public Schools, 1958
Cypress School District, 1964
Educational Specifications
Elsinore Union High School, 1965
San Jacinto Unified School District, 1965

Factors in District Organization
  Alhambra City High, Garvey, San Gabriel, School Districts, 1965
  Baldwin Park, Charter Oak, Covina, West Covina, Covina Union High, School Districts, 1958
  Centinela Valley Union High School District, 1960
  Santa Paula Elementary, Briggs, Mupu, Santa Clara, Santa Paula Union High, School Districts, 1959
  Sierra Madre City School District, 1960
  Topanga School District, 1960
Factors in Future District Organization
  Citrus Junior College District, 1965
Factors in Future District Planning
  Anaheim City, Centralia, Cyprus, Los Alamitos, Savanna, and Anaheim Union, School Districts, 1962
  Antelope Valley Joint Union High School District, 1956
  Costa Mesa Union, Newport Beach City, Newport Harbor Union High, School Districts, 1962
  El Monte, Mountain View, Rosemead, Valle Linda, and El Monte Union High, School Districts, 1963
  Excelsior Union High School District, 1964
  Fountain Valley, Huntington Beach City, Ocean View, Seal Beach, Huntington Beach Union High, School Districts, 1963
  South Bay Union High School District, 1963
Factors in Future Educational Planning
  Cupertino Union, Sunnyvale City, Fremont Union High, School Districts, 1961
Financial Status and School Plant Needs
  Glendale Unified School District
Future District Organization
  Las Virgenes Union School District
Future School Housing and District Organization
  Placentia Unified, Yorba Linda Elementary, School Districts, 1962
Future School Plant Needs
  Antioch Unified School District, 1969
  Ventura Union High School District, 1961
Legal and Financial Problems Involved in Unification
  Inglewood City Schools District, 1952
Organization and Functions of District Administrative Staff
  San Luis Obispo City Schools, 1963

Organization, Finance, and Personnel
   Orange Unified School District, 1966
Personnel and Finance
   Calexico Elementary School District and Calexico Union High
       School District, 1952
Population Growth, Housing, Finance, and District Organization
   Excelsior Union High School District, 1953
Population and School Plants
   South Pasadena Unified School District
School District Organization
   Whittier Union High School Area (East Whittier Elementary,
       Little Lake Elementary, Los Nietos Elementary, Ranchito
       Elementary, Rivera Elementary, South Whittier Elemen-
       tary, Whittier City Elementary, and Whittier Union High,
       School Districts), 1955
School Housing
   Calexico Public Schools, 1961
   Duarte Elementary School District, 1948
   El Segundo Unified School District, 1948
   Glendale Union High School, Washington School District No. 6,
       Glendale School District, No. 40 (Maricopa County, Arizo-
       na), 1950
   Hermosa Beach City Elementary School District, 1949
   Orange Elementary School District, 1949
   Ventura Union High School District, 1950
   Wiseburn School District, 1958
School Housing and District Finance
   Whittier Union High School District, 1959
School Housing and District Organization
   Arcadia City School District, 1950
   Coneja, Santa Rosa, Timber, School Districts, 1950
School Plant Needs
   Pasadena Unified School District, 1963
   Santa Paula Union High School District, 1957

278

APPENDIX E

FACULTY OF THE SCHOOL OF EDUCATION
UNIVERSITY OF SOUTHERN CALIFORNIA
1953–1973

Rank	Year										
	1953	1954	1956	1958	1960	1962	1964	1966	1968	1970	1972
Dean Emeritus	1	1	1	1							
Professor Emeritus	1	2	2	3	4	4	4	7	6	9	7
Dist. Svc. Professor										1	1
Professor	10/9*	15/7	16/8	20/9	18/10	22/9	25/10	26/7	28/3	30	30/1
Associate Professor	8/5	7/4	8/7	3/6	7/6	6/6	6/3	11/2	15/4	13/3	18/3
Assistant Professor	2/3		1/4	5/3	2/5	2/5	6/4	11/2	14/2	24/2	24/2
Instructor-Coordinator	8	8	9	6	6	7	8	10/1	9/1	8	8/1
Instructor									1	2	
Coordinator						1				3	
Visiting Professor		1	3	1		1			4	7	6
Visiting Assc. Professor						2	3	4	1	5	2
Visiting Asst. Professor					2	5	6	7	2	2	2
Adjunct Professor					6	6	8	10	9	10	11
Adjunct Assc. Professor					1		3	14	7	7	10
Adjunct Asst. Professor					4	4	4	3	8	8	10

Figures before slash indicate those assigned to School of Education only; figures following slash indicate dual appointment.

279

Year

Rank	1953	1954	1956	1958	1960	1962	1964	1966	1968	1970	1972
Clinical Professor								2	1		
Clinical Assc. Professor									1		
Clinical Asst. Professor									1		1
Clinical Instructor								1	12	12	9
Lecturer	22/5	20	21	27	17/1	11/1	18/1	24/1	26/1	60	57
Research Associate										3	3
Teacher Corps									2	3	3
Total	52/16	54/15	59/19	66/15	67/23	81/20	91/18	129/14	147/11	207/5	202/7
Grand Total	68	69	78	81	90	101	109	143	158	212	209

APPENDIX F

EDUCARE

PAST PRESIDENTS

1960–62 Dr. C. C. Trillingham

1962–63 Dr. Schuyler C. Joyner

1963–64 Dr. W. Earl Brown

1964–65 Dr. Jack P. Crowther

1965–66 Dr. C. C. Carpenter

1966–67 Mr. Isaac H. McClelland

1967–68 Dr. E. Maylon Drake

1968–69 Mr. Richard H. Lawrence

1969–70 Dr. Wayne L. Butterbaugh

1970–71 Dr. Donald Shroyer

1971–72 Dr. Leonard L. Murdy

1972–73 Dr. William J. Johnston

1973–74 Dr. Frank Kittinger

BLACK TIE DINNER SPEAKERS

1961 Dr. Sterling M. McMurrin, United States Commissioner of Education

1962 Dr. Benjamin C. Willis, Superintendent of Schools, Chicago, and President of the American Association of School Administrators

1963 The Honorable Wayne L. Morse, United States Senator from Oregon

1964 The Honorable Terry Sanford, Governor, State of North Carolina

1965 Dr. Harold A. Benjamin, Distinguished EDUCARE Visiting Professor, School of Education, University of Southern California

1966 Dr. Leon T. Minear, Superintendent of Public Education, State of Oregon

1967 Dr. Robert Havighurst, Emeritus Professor of Education, University of Chicago

1968 The Honorable Alphonzo Bell, Member, U.S. House of Rep-

281

resentatives from the 38th Congressional District, California

1969 Mr. Peter Schrag, Editor of *Change* and Associate Editor of *Saturday Review*

1970 The Honorable Houston I. Flournoy, Controller, State of California

1971 Carl M. Franklin, Vice-President, Finance, University of Southern California

EDUCARE SCHOLARS

1962–63 David B. Whitcomb	1969–72 Daniel T. Towler
1963–64 Judilynn Foster	1970–72 Nicholas Gianulis
1964–66 J. Russell Lindquist	1971–73 Joseph Compese
1966–67 Muriel Lombrozo	1972–73 Richard Knapp
1967–68 Estelle Lit	1973–74 Michael Locke Botsford
1968–69 Mabel F. Priestley	1973–74 Margaret Anne Najarian
1969–70 Emmell J. Beech	1973–74 Charles David Steinle

1973–74 William Broderick

EDUCARE FELLOWS

1962–64 Dale C. Carlson	1968–70 Shirley Mydland
1964–66 Albert H. Miyasato	1970–71 Jack Watkins
1966–68 Jack Dale Burke	1972–73 James M. Jenkins

DISTINGUISHED VISITING PROFESSOR

1964–65 Dr. Harold R. W. Benjamin

EDUCARE PROFESSOR

282

1968–71 Dr. John A. Carpenter

APPENDIX G

MEMORIALS AND HONORS

Over the years, the School of Education of the University of Southern California has been the recipient of generous gifts from friends, alumni, faculty, and students or former students. A number of these donations have been made in the name of a particular person, either *honoris causa* or *in memoriam.* These gifts have been designated as contributing to funds to furnish a room in Waite Phillips Hall, as scholarships, or as special collections in the Education Library. Rooms in Waite Phillips Hall so furnished are marked by a memorial bronze plaque; special collections are donated by an individualized book plate.

WAITE PHILLIPS HALL OF EDUCATION

Room	Honoree	Donor
Foyer	Waite Phillips, bronze plaque to	School of Education
Foyer	Irving R. Melbo, bronze plaque to	Faculty, School of Education
Foyer	Education Alumni, bronze plaque to	School of Education
Foyer	EDUCARE, bronze plaque to	School of Education
B-49	Vivian E. L. Teubner Room	Vivian E. L. Teubner
104	Frank L. Kendall Memorial Seminar	Violet C. Kendall
200	Ida E. & Gilbert A. Cowan Memorial Seminar	John Allan & Mary Helen Smith
203	W. Earl Brown Model Classroom	W. Earl Brown & friends
204	Reuben D. Law Seminar	Reuben D. Law
301	Student Seminar	Education Alumni
302	Sophia Tichnor Salvin Memorial Seminar	Friends
303	C. C. Trillingham Suite	Friends
303-A	Delta Epsilon Office	USC Chapter, Delta Epsilon
303-B	Education Alumni Office	USC Education Alumni
303-C	Honorary Association of Women in Education	HAWE
303-D	Hugh Chock Memorial- Phi Delta Kappa Office	Friends
303-E	EDUCARE Office	EDUCARE
303-F	Student California Teacher Association Office	USC Chapter, SCTA

283

Room	Honoree	Donor
400	Louis P. Thorpe Seminar	Louis P. Thorpe & friends
401	Nila Banton Smith Reading Improvement Laboratory	Nila Banton Smith & friends
403	Evelyn Frieden Memorial Center	Friends
403-B	Lucelia M. Moore-Boris V. Morkovin Memorial Room	Friends
404	D. Welty Lefever Measurement Laboratory	D. Welty Lefever & friends
500	Counselor Education Reading Room[1]	William F. & Madge Johnson
503D	The Elmer E. Wagner Office	School of Education
600	Libby & Joseph Zahradka Seminar	Libby & Joseph Zahradka
700	Leonard Calvert Memorial Seminar	Friends
701	Elementary Education Offices	Robert A. Naslund & friends
701 B	The Raymond C. Perry Office	School of Education
704	Higher Education Reading Room[2]	Earl V. Pullias, family, & friends
800	James D. Finn Instructional Technology Memorial Seminar	Friends
803	Graduate Study Room	EDUCARE
804	Theodore Hsi-En and Wen-Hui Chen Room	Theodore H. E. & Wen-Hui Chen & friends
900	Ardella B. Tibby Memorial Seminar	Friends
901	Schuyler C. Joyner Educational Administrative Laboratory	Friends
_____	D. Lloyd Nelson Model Board Room	Friends
902	Educational Administration Offices in memory of Osman R. Hull	Friends
903	Institute for Administrative Research	Virco Manufacturing Corporation
904	Educational Administration Offices	Roy Adamson, E. W. Beaubier, Cymbre Ferguson, and W. Tracy Gaffey
904B	The Edward H. LaFranchi Office	School of Education
905	R. Bruce Walter Seminar	Friends
1000	Donald Anthony DeSantis Seminar	Donald A. DeSantis
1005	Grace M. Drier Memorial Seminar	Friends
1101	Office of the Dean	United Desk Company
1101-B	Irving R. Melbo Conference Room	Board of Directors, EDUCARE
1102	Emery Stoops Faculty Seminar	Emery & Maude Stoops
_____	Courtyard Pool and Fountain	Half-Century Club

284

1. In honor of Joan Johnson Michael.
2. In memory of John Malcolm Pullias.

APPENDIX G

MEMORIAL FUNDS

The C. C. Carpenter Memorial Scholarship Fund
The Jean Burton Clark Fund (for books in higher education)
The Dan T. Dawson Memorial Fund (for establishment of a school administration textbook collection)
The James D. Finn Memorial Fund
The Ethel D. Keenan Memorial Scholarship Loan Fund
The Leonard H. Langer Memorial Fund
The Clara Duer Marble Memorial Fund (for books in higher education)
The Ruth Russell Shelby Scholarship Fund (early childhood education)
The John Allan Smith Memorial Fund
The Chester A. Taft Student Loan Fund (for teachers of the handicapped)
The Louis A. Tallman Memorial Loan Fund
The Vivien E. L. Teubner Student Aid Fund
The Merritt M. Thompson Student Aid Fund
The Louis P. Thorpe Scholarship Fund
The Dan T. Dawson Memorial Fund (for textbooks in educational administration)

SPECIAL COLLECTIONS[1]

The Theodore H. E. Chen Collection of books and other pertinent materials in the field of East Asian education and culture.
The Jean Burton Clark Browsing Shelf for books in higher education.
The James D. Finn Memorial Collection, concentrated in the field of instructional technology.
The William B. Michael Collection.

---

1. All collections are housed in the Education Library, with the exception of the Clara Duer Miller Shelf which is housed in the seminar room for Higher Education.

285

The Clara Duer Miller Memorial Reading Shelf, in higher education.

The Claude L. Reeves Memorial Instructional Materials Collection.

The John A. Sexson Memorial Collection.

The Stowell Research Library, in recognition of Thomas Blanchard Stowell.

The Louis P. Thorpe Collection, in early books on psychology.

The Donald E. Wilson Collection of early American school textbooks.

286

APPENDIX H

AASA AWARDS

From 1956 through 1973, 15 graduate students in education at the School of Education, University of Southern California, were recipients of honorary scholarships from the American Association of School Administrators. These awards, notably the Shankland Award, Finis Engleman Award, and Forrest E. Connor Scholarship, were presented for distinguished achievement in the field of school administration. Recipients of the award, with the year of presentation and the position held by the recipient at the time of award, are given below.

1956 Maxwell L. Rafferty, Jr., Superintendent of Schools, Needles, California
1959 Fred W. Bewley, Schools Organization Advisor, Los Angeles County Schools
1960 E. Maylon Drake, Superintendent, Alhambra City Schools
1961 Walter J. Ziegler, Superintendent, San Gabriel Schools
1962 Edmund R. Harrington, Superintendent, Redondo Beach City Schools
1964 Robert E. Ferris, Superintendent, Hemet Unified School District
1965 Gordon Harrison, Superintendent, Perris School District
1966 Glenn H. Grant, Placement Office, University of Southern California
1966 Clarence T. Bowman, Superintendent, San Jacinto School District
1967 Erwin N. Jones, Superintendent, Covina Valley Unified School District
1969 Walter F. Hauss, Superintendent, Newhall Elementary School District
1970 Tom Van Groningen, Superintendent, Porterville Elementary School District
1971 Lane B. Teaney, Superintendent, Valle Lindo School District
1972 John L. Nelson, Associate Superintendent, Business, Arcadia Unified School District
1973 Stuart E. Gothold, Superintendent, South Whittier Schools

287

APPENDIX I

CHRONOLOGY
SCHOOL OF EDUCATION
UNIVERSITY OF SOUTHERN CALIFORNIA
1876–1974

YEAR	*EVENT*
1876	Los Angeles Academy founded September 11, 1876 by Southern California Conference of the Methodist Episcopal Church.
1880	University of Southern California founded, incorporating the Academy as its preparatory school. First president was Marion McKinley Bovard.
1884	First class graduated, with A.B. degrees conferred on three students, one of whom was George Finley Bovard, later fourth President of the University (1903–1921), and the man for whom the George Finley Bovard Administration Building was named.
1884	Cornerstone for the building to be known as "Old College" was laid September 20, 1884 (site of present Founders Hall).
1896	Department of Pedagogy organized in College of Liberal Arts, and placed in the charge of Dr. James Harmon Hoose.
1909	Department of Education organized in the College of Liberal Arts and placed in the charge of Dr. Thomas Blanchard Stowell.
1911	USC granted right by California State Department of Education to confer the high school teacher certificate.
1911	Los Angeles Academy renamed University High School.
1917	Teachers Appointment Registry established under University.
1917	USC granted right by California State Department of Education to issue Special Certificates (Manual and Fine Arts Type, Technical Arts Type, Physical Culture Type, and Miscellaneous Type).
1918	School of Education established, with Thomas Blanchard Stowell Dean (1918–1919).

288

1918	Teacher Appointment Registry placed under School of Education.
1918	University High School placed under general control of School of Education, with Dean of School also the principal of the University High School.
1919	Dr. Lester Burton Rogers named Dean of School of Education, a position he held until 1945, when he retired as Dean Emeritus.
1920	Student teaching in Los Angeles schools at the elementary level inaugurated on informal basis.
1921	School of Education administrative offices moved from "Old College" to newly constructed George Finley Bovard Administration Building. Space occupied by the School of Education (south wing, third floor of Bovard) named the Thomas Blanchard Stowell Hall of Education.
1922	Dr. Rufus von KleinSmid inaugurated as President, USC, a position he held until 1947, when he retired as President and was named Chancellor. Dr. von Klein-Smid remained Chancellor until his death, 1964.
1922	Alpha Epsilon Chapter of Phi Delta Kappa established, June 1922, with 22 charter members, among them Merritt Moore Thompson (1884–1970), Professor of Education 1921–1952.
1923	Teachers Appointment Registry placed under University, with Edith Weir Appointment Secretary.
1923	Bachelor of Science in Education (B.S. in Ed.) degree established.
1924	Doctor of Philosophy (Ph.D.) established under jurisdiction of The Graduate School.
1924	Pi Lambda Theta chapter established at USC, June 1924.
1927	First Ph.D. degree awarded at USC, to D. Welty Lefever, in Education.
1928	Doctor of Education (Ed.D.) degree established at USC under jurisdiction of the School of Education.
1928	University High School closed, September 1928.
1928	Student teaching in Los Angeles city schools extended to the secondary level.
1931	First Ed.D. degrees awarded to George H. Bell and Verne R. Ross.
1933	First issue of *Education Monographs* published.

289

1933	Master of Science in Education (M.S. in Ed.) degree established to replace former M.A. in Education.
1937	Doctoral Club formed at USC, composed of those who had taken doctoral degrees in Education at USC.
1939	Master of Education (M.E.) degree established at USC under jurisdiction of the School of Education as an advanced master's degree in addition to the M.S. in Ed.
1943	University Council on Teacher Education established at USC.
1945	Dean Rogers retired as Dean Emeritus.
1945–46	School of Education headed by Administrative Committee composed of Professors Osman R. Hull, D. Welty Lefever, and Irving R. Melbo.
1946	Dr. Osman R. Hull appointed Dean of School of Education.
1947	Education Alumni Association established March 12, 1947.
1947	Society of Delta Epsilon established May 14, 1947, to replace Doctoral Club.
1948	School of Education organized by departments. Original departments were: Teacher Training (preservice); Audio Visual Education; Elementary Education; Secondary, Higher, and Adult Education; History and Philosophy of Education; Educational Administration and Supervision; Educational Psychology, Counseling, and Measurements; Business Education; Physical Education; Music Education.
1953	Dr. Irving R. Melbo appointed Dean, School of Education, *vice* Dr. Hull who returned to teaching at his own request by reason of health.
1953	First of 18 annual Future Teacher Conferences sponsored at USC by Alpha Epsilon Chapter, Phi Delta Kappa.
1954	First grant ($270,000) from Ford Foundation's Fund for Advancement of Education, used to inaugurate USC Southern California Teacher Intern Program.
1954	Delta Epsilon Lectureship established.
1954	USC and John Tracy Clinic combine resources for training of teachers of the deaf and hard of hearing, particularly those of preschool and elementary age.
1954	First annual Doctoral Breakfast on Commencement Day.

290

1954	Veterans Counseling Center established.
1955	Campaign launched by Education Alumni Association for fund for new Education Center.
1955	First of series of International Teacher Programs inaugurated at School of Education, under auspices of U. S. Office of Education and U. S. Department of State.
1955	On-campus Reading Center established.
1956	First of 15 Shankland Memorial Scholarships awarded to USC graduate students in educational administration.
1956	Advanced Study Centers program inaugurated, later to develop into program throughout California and in Nevada and overseas.
1957	First of 11 annual leadership conferences for elementary school teachers, cosponsored by School of Education and South Coast Section of California Elementary School Administrators Association (CESAA).
1958–59	Golden Jubilee Year of USC School of Education.
1959	First of series of NDEA counseling institutes.
1959	Educational Placement Office established within School of Education, to replace Bureau of Teacher Placement under University.
1959	Second grant ($660,000) from Ford Foundation, used to inaugurate Specialist High School Teacher Project.
1959	Adjunct ranks established for School of Education part-time faculty.
1960	Provisional plans laid for EDUCARE.
1961	EDUCARE formally launched, with Charter Dinner April 28, 1961, for 150 Charter members.
1961	First of annual conference hospitality hours, sponsored by Education Alumni Association.
1961	First U. S. Office of Education grant ($10,000) for development of special education, with emphasis on mental retardation.
1961	School of Education accredited by National Council for the Accreditation of Teacher Education (NCATE) for all programs through the doctorate until 1970.
1962	First of series of annual Distinguished Lectures in Special Education, with addresses published, 1962 and 1967– .
1962	Department of Exceptional Children established (renamed in 1966 Department of Special Education).
1963	First graduate program in education conducted overseas,

291

at Wiesbaden, Germany, at request of U. S. Air Force and U. S. Dependent Schools in the European Area (US-DESEA).

1963   School of Education Library designated one of the depository sites for California state curriculum materials.

1963–69   Malawi Polytechnic Project conducted in Malawi, Africa, by School of Education, under grant of U. S. Agency for International Development (AID).

1964   EDUCARE Distinguished Professorship established, with Dr. Harold R. W. Benjamin first incumbent (1963–64).

1964   Construction of new building for School of Education assured through bequest to USC for this purpose by the philanthropist and financier, the late Waite Phillips.

1964   Instructional Materials Center for Special Education established.

1964   Center for Intercultural Studies (later renamed Center for International Education) established.

1964   National Charity League and School of Education combine resources to establish the NCL-USC Reading Center, on Hollywood Boulevard, Los Angeles.

1965   Mid-Career Advanced Development Program inaugurated for practicing professionals.

1965   Master of Science in Education program inaugurated in Europe under sponsorship of U. S. Air Force and US-DESEA. Later extended from Germany to include Spain, Greece, Turkey.

1965   First seminar conducted in Far East, held at Tokyo, Japan in cooperation with U. S. Air Force and Pacific Area Dependent Schools.

1966   First program for teacher training in ESL (English as a Second Language) and TESOL (Teachers of English to Speakers of Other Languages).

1966   Formation of SWRL (Southwest Regional Education Laboratory).

1966   USC selected as one of 84 university training sites for the National Teacher Corps.

1966   Mid-City Secondary Education Project (Project APEX) inaugurated as joint venture of Los Angeles city schools, USC, and the School of Education, with funds from Title III, Elementary and Secondary Education Act (ESEA).

292

1967	First year of grant awards for Educational Media Institutes.
1967	First overseas graduation in Master of Science in Education program, held in Wiesbaden, Germany.
1967	Teacher Corps program at USC divided into: "Teacher Corps: Urban" and "Teacher Corps: Rural-Migrant."
1967	First NDEA grant for Institute of Early Childhood Education.
1968	Dedication of Waite Phillips Hall of Education, May 17, 1968.
1968	Establishment of Education Library in separate building near Waite Phillips Hall, and inauguration of program of renovation and expansion.
1968	Teacher Learning Centers inaugurated in cooperation with Los Angeles Unified School District.
1968	Department of Higher Education established.
1968	NDEA-sponsored insitutes in African studies and Asian studies, held respectively in Ghana, Africa, and Taiwan.
1968	Honorary Association of Women in Education (HAWE) established at USC School of Education.
1968	EGO (Educational Graduate Organization) established.
1969	National conference and workshop for elementary school principals held at USC under joint sponsorship of National Education Association (NEA), CESAA, and School of Education.
1969	Overseas doctoral program inaugurated in Europe in cooperation with USDESEA.
1969	USC Preschool established in former residence of President von KleinSmid, located on downtown campus of Mount St. Mary College.
1970	Annual seminars for school superintendents inaugurated.
1970	School of Education reaccredited by NCATE for all programs through the doctorate until 1980.
1970	University Affiliated Program initiated, in cooperation with Childrens Hospital and USC School of Medicine, and under sponsorship of Department of Health, Education and Welfare.
1970	Institute for Training Adult Basic Education (ABE) Teachers held, under federal sponsorship.
1970	African Studies Program conducted, funded by U. S. Office of Education.

293

1970	First of annual American Civilization/Language Institutes.
1971	Sponsorship of overseas program transferred from U. S. Air Force to U. S. Army in Europe, with readjustment of centers and expansion in Germany, Belgium, and at SHAPE.
1971	USC-Asian program of studies leading to M.S. in Ed. and M.E. degrees inaugurated.
1972	First of two India Institutes conducted at Delhi, under auspices of U. S. Office of Education.
1972	First doctoral (Ed.D.) degrees conferred at overseas commencement, held in Heidelberg, Germany.
1972	Fiftieth Anniversary, USC Chapter, Phi Delta Kappa.
1973	Nila Banton Smith Reading Laboratory established in Waite Phillips Hall.
1973	On retirement of Dean Melbo from office of dean, Dr. John W. Stallings named Interim Dean, September 1973.
1973	USC School for Early Childhood Education dedicated October 3, 1973.
1974	The Irving R. Melbo Chair established as the first endowed chair in the School of Education. Dean Melbo named first incumbent (1974–75).
1974	Dr. Stephen J. Knezevich named Dean of School of Education, to assume office July 1, 1974.

294

INDEX OF NAMES

296

297

298

299

Perry, R. H. 122, n. 65.
Persellin, L. E. 114.
Peter, L. J. 89; 134; 135; 135, n. 89.
Phillips, E. W. 180.
Phillips, G. E. 180.
Phillips, W. 176-177; 258; 292.
Pocock, S. M. 187, n. 1.
Post, A. A. 215.
Pullias, E. V. 35; 71, n. 55; 109; 109,
    n. 45; 112, n. 53; 154; 177, n. 162;
    180; 242; 248.
Pullias, J. M. 112, n. 53.

R

Rafferty, M. W. 98; 98, n. 30; 248;
    252; 287.
Rand, M. J. 129, n. 78; 166, n. 142.
Ranger, T. O. 228.
Ransom, G. A. 89; 105; 107; 108; 195.
Raubenheimer, A. S. 7; 7, n.8; 109.
Reed, M. S. 91; 106; 196.
Reeves, C. L. 66, n. 50; 68.
Reeves, E. 49.
Reining, H. 71, n. 55.
Richards, L. 195.
Riles, W. 216, n. 38.
Ringwald, S. C. 196.
Robinson, P. V. 36; 90; 195.
Rogers, L. B. 7; 7, n. 9; 8, n. 10; 9;
    10; 11; 13, n. 17; 29; 30; 31; 55, n.
    33; 66, n. 47; 166, n. 143; 289; 290.
Rose, L. 252.
Rose, R. 31
Ross, V. R. 16; 289.
Rowe, S. J. 38; 90; 105; 139; 196.
Rucker, D. 116.
Rudloff, J. F. 89; 136, n. 92.
Rudolph, J. R. 114; 196.
Rueff, W. N. 195.
Rush, R. E. 9; 12.
Rutherford, R. B. 195.
Ryan, L. 197.

S

Sadler, J. 172; 172, n. 153.
Salmon, P. 216, n. 38.

Salvin, S. T. 38; 87; 89, n. 16; 90; 131;
    132; 132, n. 86; 132, n. 87.
Sanford, T. 281.
Sarafian, A. 196; 274.
Schrader, D. 89; 103; 104.
Schrag, P. 282.
Schulte, M. A. 8.
Schwartz, A. J. 195.
Sexson, J. A. 65; 66, n. 48; 67.
Sexson, M. 65; 68.
Sheffield, H. J. 35; 273.
Sheriffs, A. 216, n. 38.
Shroyer, D. 281.
Sidhisiri, P. 208.
Silvers, J. 83, n. 9.
Simpson, E. L. 196.
Simpson, R. E. 45; 96; 97; 98.
Skaggs, D. A. 100, n. 40; 196.
Sklar, B. 126; 126, n. 71; 195.
Smallenburg, H. W. 38; 90; 98; 103;
    195; 273.
Smart, M. E. 105; 106; 106, n. 43; 195;
    212; 216; 223.
Smith, A. 90; 135, n. 92; 196.
Smith, J. A. 90; 187, n. 1; 191, n. 6.
Smith, L. C. 9; 122, n. 65; 192; 192, n.
    8; 196.
Smith, N. B. 194; 194, n. 15; 196; 294.
Smith, R. A. 90; 121; 195; 225; 243.
Smith, W. P. 41.
Spain, F. L. 9.
Stallings, J. W. 21; 90; 100; 100, n. 40;
    195; 195, n. 16; 215; 294.
Steeves, R. 196; 236.
Steinbaugh, J. K. 53, n. 31.
Stinnet, T. M. 214.
Stone, E. D. 178.
Stoner, M. C. 90; 136, n. 92; 190; 191,
    n. 3.
Stoops, E. 9; 22; 22, n. 26; 35; 61; 70;
    100; 102; 126, n. 73; 155; 193; 193,
    n. 10; 246.
Stowell, M. B. 6, n. 5; 66, n. 47.
Stowell, T. B. 5; 5, n. 5; 66, n. 47; 288.
Strayer, G. D. 69.
Strevey, T. E. 53, n. 31; 71, n. 55.

300

301

SUBJECT INDEX

303

305